W9-CNA-125

Praise for
Seven Sisters and a Brother

"In this fascinating group narrative, the organizers of Swarthmore College's 1969 eight-day sit-in join voices to tell the story of how 'Seven Sisters and a Brother' used peaceful protest to effect change. Looking back on the events of fifty years ago, the authors have combined their stories as a 'choral memoir' of the Takeover which forced their college to respond to the demands of Swarthmore's Afro-American Students Society. As well as a history of their activism, this account includes the authors' own autobiographies, providing compelling portraits of the lives of the young people who risked their futures to make a difference."

—**Henry Louis Gates, Jr.,** Alphonse Fletcher University Professor, Harvard University, author of *Stony the Road: White Supremacy and the Rise of Jim Crow*

"*Seven Sisters and a Brother* illuminates the institutional failures of an elite liberal arts college in the 1960s and the work of a dedicated group of Black students to change the culture and policies of their school. Theirs is a story of the power of collective action, the value of shared identity, and the thrill of progress. Framed by a national culture of activism during the time, their account beautifully reflects the changes brought by the Civil Rights Movement and Black activism across the country.

This memoir captures the struggle to bring Black history, Black experiences, and Black lives to the forefront of the academy. It will serve as an important guide for today's students, faculty, administrators, and all others in the world of higher education."

—Donna Shalala, US Congresswoman (D-FL 27th District), former President of the University of Miami, former President of Hunter College, and former US Secretary of Health and Human Services

"Over eight days, eight students sparked change that defined their lives, changed an institution and fueled a movement that continues today. At this contentious time in our nation's history, we can take lessons from the humanity and tenacity of these change makers, and inspiration from their courage and commitment to principle."

—Alberto Ibargüen, President and CEO of the John S. and James L. Knight Foundation and former publisher of *The Miami Herald* and *El Nuevo Herald*

"Anyone who cares about the course of higher education in America should read this book. It tells the important and moving story of how Seven Sisters and a Brother changed the course of history and herstory at Swarthmore College and contributed to bringing a greater presence of Black people and Black Studies to the academy."

—Dr. Johnnetta Cole, President Emerita at Spelman College and Bennett College, former Director of the Smithsonian National Museum of African Art

"*Seven Sisters and a Brother* is a riveting 'choral memoir' that provides a compelling account of the 1969 Takeover of the Admissions Office at Swarthmore College. The authors deftly interweave the story of the movement at Swarthmore that led to profound changes—including the creation of the Black Studies curriculum and concentration and a sustained increase in the numbers of black students and faculty—with their own diverse, often moving, personal accounts.

Although the book focuses on Swarthmore, it will be of great interest to anyone wishing to learn more about broader questions involving student activism, higher education, and movements for social change."

—**Valerie A. Smith,** PhD, President of Swarthmore College, and scholar of African-American literature

"Swarthmore College's small number of Black students, like those on other predominantly white campuses, didn't just seethe in anger and despair after Dr. Martin Luther King Jr.'s assassination—they acted, demanding more Black students, Black Studies programs and hiring of Black faculty. *Seven Sisters and a Brother* tells the story of their courageously managed eight-day sit-in in 1969, activism that enacted positive change and made Swarthmore a better learning environment for everyone who has experienced the institution since."

—**Dr. Mary Frances Berry,** historian and Geraldine R. Segal Professor of American Social Thought and a professor of history at the University of Pennsylvania, former Chairwoman of the United States Commission on Civil Rights

"A powerful, well-written book that challenges the status quo at one of the nation's most prestigious liberal arts colleges. Their demand for recognition of their identity, respect for their culture and history, and their need to connect their studies to their aspirations and talents, is compelling. *Seven Sisters and a Brother* proves the power of conviction can win against overwhelming odds."

—**Ramona Hoage Edelin,** PhD, former President and CEO of the National Urban Coalition, educator and Executive Director of the District of Columbia Association of Chartered Public Schools

"A timely and compelling book chronicling the odyssey of a small group of determined African American students as they endured, confronted, and overcame the painful reality of institutional racism within a well-meaning northern liberal arts college during the 1960s. It's a 'must read' as America is forced to contemplate overcoming the belief in a hierarchy of human value and its institutional legacies; and a reminder that colleges and universities must play pivotal roles in helping our nation jettison racism."

—**Dr. Gail C. Christopher,** former Vice President and senior advisor at the W. K. Kellogg Foundation and one of the nation's leading change-makers on racism and racial healing

"On February 1, 1960, four North Carolina A&T University freshmen began a sit-in at Woolworth's whites only lunch counter in Greensboro, North Carolina. It triggered a wave of student activism that captured a student energy that moved the nation politically. In eight different stories, *Seven Sisters and a Brother* gives illuminating testimony to what it was like being 'young, gifted, and black' in the 1960s. Their stories and bios capture the major themes—black power, student activism, black culture, black achievement, and collective action—that were still so prominent almost ten years after the 1960 sit-ins and continue to resonate today."

—Ed Pitt, 1960 Co-Chair, Student Executive Committee for Justice (SECJ), North Carolina A&T University—Bennett College

SEVEN SISTERS AND A BROTHER

SEVEN SISTERS AND A BROTHER

Friendship, Resistance, and Untold Truths behind Black Student Activism in the 1960s

Marilyn Allman Maye, Harold S. Buchanan, Jannette O. Domingo, Joyce Frisby Baynes, Marilyn Holifield, Myra E. Rose, Bridget Van Gronigen Warren, Aundrea White Kelley

BOOKS & BOOKS PRESS

Books & Books Press

CORAL GABLES

Published by Books & Books Press, an imprint of Mango Publishing, a division of Mango Media Inc.

Cover Design: Morgane Leoni

Cover Photo Courtesy of Marilyn Holifield

Layout Design: Jermaine Lau

For permission requests, please contact the publisher at:

Books & Books Press
Mango Publishing Group
2850 Douglas Road, 2nd Floor
Coral Gables, FL 33134 USA
info@mango.bz

For special orders, quantity sales, course adoptions and corporate sales, please email the publisher at sales@mango.bz. For trade and wholesale sales, please contact Ingram Publisher Services at customer.service@ingramcontent.com or +1.800.509.4887.

Seven Sisters and a Brother: Friendship, Resistance, and Untold Truths Behind Black Student Activism in the 1960s

Library of Congress Cataloging
ISBN: (p) 978-1-64250-160-5 (e) 978-1-64250-161-2

BISAC: HIS056000—HISTORY / African American

LCCN: 2019948615

Printed in the United States of America

Please note some names have been changed to protect the privacy of individuals.

To our parents, whose love, sacrifice, hard work, and determination sustained us through college and who proved to us every day that Black Moms and Black Dads Matter!

To the College's black custodial staff—our true in *loco parentis* at Swarthmore—who supported us, fed us, watched over us, encouraged us, and kept us safe.

To the SASS members and other black students who participated in the Takeover and all the supporters who took up our cause.

Table of Contents

Introduction

We all met between 1965 and 1966 as undergraduates at the highly selective Swarthmore College in the suburbs of Philadelphia, Pennsylvania. It was a time when elite colleges were just beginning to enroll significant numbers of blacks, several being first-generation college students.

We were seven young women and one young man from diverse families and backgrounds. We developed enduring friendships tightly intertwined with activism through the Swarthmore Afro-American Students Society (SASS) which we organized with like-minded black students on campus.

We didn't know that our bond would take on almost mythical proportions and remain in the minds of generations of black students. The legends that emerged did not include our real names, and few knew anything about us as individuals, our motivations, our hometowns, or our stories. Little changed until 2009, on the fortieth anniversary of SASS, when the current black students at Swarthmore invited us to tell them about the founding of the organization.

They had not known about us as Joyce and Marilyn A., who became mathematics majors; Jannette, a political science/ international relations major; Marilyn H., an economics major; Bridget and Myra, biology and chemistry majors, respectively; and Aundrea, a sociology and anthropology major. One of the revelations in this telling of our stories is that they didn't know Harold, another mathematics major, was also an integral part of our group.

They had not heard how we drew on our family and spiritual roots and reached out to the black adults from nearby communities for strength and, ultimately, for rescue. They only knew that we called for black contributions to be represented in classrooms, campus culture, student life, and college faculty and administration, and that, eventually, we took over a major campus space to ensure those demands were taken seriously. That Takeover brought all academic activity to a halt to focus on our demands until a completely unexpected tragedy ended our action abruptly.

Some of the students at the fortieth anniversary event had heard that the period between 1967 and 1970 saw black student protests on hundreds of campuses. Indeed, some of their parents had been involved in these protests, but they had no way of knowing how much the actions at the College we attended were inspired by or looked like what happened elsewhere.

When we gathered at the College all those decades later to share what happened, the rapport that we had developed as undergraduates was still evident among us. We had the mutual trust to tackle and achieve the formidable task of recapturing our stories, some of them shrouded in inaccurate reporting and many others discarded over decades, buried under the dust of history.

After the anniversary reunion, the two Marilyns and Joyce returned home and began to carve out time to capture their memories; however, opportunities to do so always seemed elusive, and not being professional historians or writers, we despaired that we didn't have the resources to do the stories justice. Marilyn A. contacted black faculty to see if there was a current history major who might tackle the task as a research project.

Five years later, with the support of the College's then-President Rebecca Chopp and Dr. Allison Dorsey, a history professor and then-chair of the Black Studies Program, the College mobilized resources to offer a one-time course entitled

"Black Liberation 1969." For their rigorous historical research into the events surrounding "the Crisis," students reached out to us and our contemporaries for photographs, artifacts, and interviews, and digitized the materials for permanent online access.

President Chopp's support of that research and her formal invitation to return to campus deeply moved us. We had lived to see Swarthmore College acknowledge that what we had done had been a gift to the institution, exactly as we had conceived our actions to be, despite all the negative press to the contrary at the time.

> As the College honors its 150th anniversary, or sesquicentennial, we seek to examine our history critically and with self-reflection...
>
> ...to specifically examine events at Swarthmore in 1969 that led to the creation of the Black Cultural Center, the formation of Black Studies at Swarthmore, and ultimately, to a much more vibrant, diverse, and inclusive campus environment.
>
> ...your involvement at this pivotal juncture in the College's history is a critical part... Your story has not been documented formally, even though it is important to anyone who truly wants to understand how the Civil Rights Movement was reflected on Swarthmore's campus. Your activism paved the way for generations of students who now enjoy the fruits of your labor and who...continue to carry your torch...
>
> Because your story is so important to our understanding of Swarthmore's history, I write to invite you...to come to campus Garnet Homecoming and Family Weekend...

> [Your story will be] stored in McCabe Library, so that your [legacies] are forever a part of Swarthmore's narrative...
>
> I hope you will consider this invitation and the powerful impact your presence would have for our students and all of us here at the College.[1]

In the 2014 sesquicentennial anniversary celebration, a chapter of the book published for the occasion, *Crisis and Change,* begins with this statement:

> Institutions can seldom identify a specific moment when they changed direction, but it's arguable that the Swarthmore College we see today—rigorous, creative, accessible, diverse, and committed to civic and social responsibility—issued from the eight-day crisis that rocked the institution in January 1969.[2]

Seeing the College acknowledge that the "eight-day crisis" was central to "the College we see today"—and knowing that the eight of us were at the heart of it—were key catalysts for us getting more serious to record our memories of it. We knew that we had a story to tell, and we had seen prior attempts by others that focused on the "Crisis" as it impacted the College, but did not adequately explore our motivations and actions.

In individual and group dialogue with the young researchers, we made it clear that Quaker values were, implicitly or explicitly, a key factor in choosing Swarthmore for our education. Academic rigor was another key factor. We were not afraid of a challenge. We had not, however, expected that head-on confrontation with the College administration would be the major challenge that it proved to be. Unbeknownst to us, the College was considerably reluctant to accept many of us. Some institutional leaders had expressed concern that we would not and perhaps could not perform up to their standards. Through our actions during the development of SASS, we challenged the administration as equals. In the end, we demonstrated not only that students of color could be the equals of white students, but that we even had something to teach "the adults."

The strong interest of the current generation of students in understanding how and why we were able to do what we did made it clear that we needed to spend time getting back in touch with our youthful selves and reconnecting with the history we had created. When and how to do this? Marilyn H. suggested we meet in Panama, so Bridget could join us, as that was where she lived at the time. So, the next summer, after the sesquicentennial, we met in Panama, with several spouses, and began to document our experiences. The dynamics among us and the drive within us were the same as they were fifty years prior.

As we swapped life stories under cool breezes in tropical Panama City, we were stunned at the many commonalities in our backgrounds that we had not recognized before. Over a three-year period, we embarked on writing our individual and collective memories, and it became clearer why we bonded into an extended family on campus, and how activism in our individual lives since college continues and extends what we did there. The good news is that what we discovered is not specific to our era, but is accessible to any generation. We believe our narratives will answer questions the current college generation, and even our peers, have asked us, and will inspire and empower them and others.

As we unearthed memories during those Panama conversations, we arranged many versions of our common college experiences into piles and sorted them into themes. The most dramatic entries told about the January 1969 Takeover, but we became convinced that the Takeover happened only because of the metamorphoses in our individual lives. So, we interspersed the chronology among narratives of family, first encounters with the College, and lives changed as a result.

Writing a choral memoir matches the way we have always worked together: collaborating in analyzing our situation, planning solutions together, communicating in combined voices, and avoiding highlighting a single leader. This, then, is our shared story. The story of Seven Sisters and a Brother.

THE TAKEOVER

Day Zero

DAY ZERO
Boiling Point

It was shortly before midnight on Wednesday, January 8, 1969, the third day of classes after students had returned to campus from the 1968 winter holiday break. We were seniors and juniors at Swarthmore College in Swarthmore, Pennsylvania, eleven miles southwest of Philadelphia. In those days, fall semester didn't end before the holidays. Classes resumed for two more weeks of instruction before we had to study for exams and turn in final papers and projects.

Even twenty-four hours before the planned action, most of those who would participate did not know the details of what would occur, not even who would be designated as spokespersons.

Only a handful of members of the Swarthmore Afro-American Students Society (SASS) were in on the planning. Since Marilyn A., Jannette, and Harold lived in New York, Marilyn A.'s house in Harlem was designated as the venue to work out details between Christmas and the New Year. Traveling from her home in Boston, Aundrea, the secretary of SASS, joined the three New Yorkers. We represented three of the group known informally as the Seven Sisters, along with Harold, the one brother among the original planners. Harold had visited the admissions office numerous times in the weeks before the holiday break to examine the doors and windows and develop a plan for securing them. He had managed to get floor plans of the office space, and the four of us huddled around them, spread across the Allmans' dining room table, and plotted strategy. If this visit over Christmas week with its intense conversations seemed a little strange to Reverend and Mrs. Allman, they gave no indication beyond their puzzled expressions. It would make sense to them two weeks later, when they received a call from the College stating that their daughter was a ringleader of the group of black students who had occupied the admissions office.

Aundrea, as usual, was recording our decisions in her notebooks. Each of the collaborators had left the Harlem planning session with a list of items to purchase for the action that was beginning to appear inevitable. Now, after classes each day that week, we sisters were checking in at each other's dorm rooms, to make sure we had everything we would need.

> Don't forget to bring Vaseline for your ashy legs.

We might have been preparing for a winter hike in the woods around campus for all anyone could tell.

> Yes, and extra bars of soap and rolls of toilet paper.

Laughing and joking about everything, as we often did, no one observing us would have realized that we were organizing something that might be dangerous or result in our expulsion from college.

> Put cans of sardines and crackers in your bags.

> I hate the smell of sardines. Disgusting.

> No problem, I've got them. I know how to make a great meal with them.

That would probably have been Aundrea. Her father was a military man. She had lived in Asia and Europe and, having been a Camp Fire Girl herself, seemed to know all about survival and making do in difficult situations.

> We'll need flashlights.

That would have been Harold, the practical one, the only brother present in those dormitory planning sessions. He was always a valued addition to our group of seven women because he practiced collaborative leadership as we did and could be trusted to do exactly what he said. We knew we could count on him to show up with the chains, padlocks, and other hardware on his list.

Together, we wrote and practiced saying the words we would use to begin our action. We decided we would rely on others outside our inner circle to be the primary SASS spokespersons to the administration, so we could focus on writing our positions and managing operations.

Don Mizell would be one of the spokespersons. In a 2014 video documentary, he recalls hearing a frantic knock on his dorm room door at midnight, to which he responded reluctantly. Several females from our black student organization, he says, summoned him to a meeting across campus that he was not expecting and didn't know anything about.

Don was not the only one hustled out of bed that Wednesday night to come to Bond Hall's lower level for an emergency gathering of SASS members. The sisters were not among the young ladies who called him. We were already at the surprise briefing getting ready to take and answer questions as various late arrivals, young men and young women, joined, bleary-eyed. The looks on some faces queried:

> Did something happen today that we didn't hear about at dinner?

Others had that knowing look, full of excitement. They had realized since before the break that we might have to back up our demands with more than words if the College administration did not respond with real solutions. Fifteen of us had already met with the faculty and administration on Monday morning, the first day back, to see if the administration had made any progress on our demands while we were away. People on campus in the *Phoenix*, the campus newspaper, and in open letters that were circulated as flyers, referred to these meetings as "negotiations," and everyone on both sides knew that negotiations might break down. These black students were bracing themselves to know what we would plan to do if our demands were not met soon. Maybe this was the time they would find out.

Each of us who were in on the plan took turns carefully introducing it to the group.

> Listen up, everyone. You all remember when SASS members walked out in October and refused to cooperate further with the College Admissions Policy Committee until our four demands were met. Well, our first demand was that the Committee's report be taken out of "General Reserve" in the library and replaced by a new report that SASS would help the Committee rewrite and that would be "suitable for public perusal." Every day that the original report remains open for everyone in the College to read is a day too many.
>
> And every day that the Admissions Committee fails to add their resources to our outreach activities to recruit more Black students for the fall is a day we lose potential applicants to other colleges.
>
> The same is true for recruiting black faculty. Their lack of commitment means other colleges get to hire the best candidates.
>
> So, why are we here in the middle of the night? If you agree that the time for talk without action is over, we invite you to stay tonight for further instructions.

The offending report was the last straw after two years of activism focused on increasing black enrollment in the elite college and on recognizing the contributions of African Americans in academic study. An Admissions Committee set up by the College administration had spent the summer of 1968 preparing a study of all of the "Negro students" who had enrolled in the recent past to justify the slow pace of recruiting more of us. They had violated our privacy by publishing so many details about our families and high school preparation that, although names were not published, the small size of the College and the miniscule black population made it easy to match the data to specific students. When we got wind of the report being made available to the entire college in the campus library, SASS immediately demanded that the report be removed and revised to take out the inappropriate data. The administration took the high-handed position that they would not respond to demands and saw no need to withdraw or revise the report.

Even those black students who were not given to activism were angered by being treated with such insensitivity. Debates in the campus newspaper and a vote of support by the majority white Student Council notwithstanding, the Dean of Admissions had continued to refuse to remove the report. The editorial board of the newspaper and certain other campus constituencies backed the Dean. Things had come to a boiling point.

The midnight meeting at the end of what we would count as Day Zero was seared in the memory of Mike H., a freshman at the time. He recalled it forty years later when he recorded for the *Black Liberation 1969 Archive*:

> ...the leaders came to us and said, "If you cannot go all the way, leave now." They did not define what that meant, "all the way." So, most of the black students

> stayed. There were some who did, in fact, leave... although those students who did not stay wrote a letter to the Phoenix stating that they were in support of what we were doing even though they were not in the building.

Even those who stayed behind when a few others left were not provided with the complete plan. Instead, we told them they would need to prepare backpacks with their books for studying and their most important personal effects in case it took all day and maybe longer to make our point. They should meet after lunch outside the dining hall the next day, where specifics would be given.

We explained that we felt strongly about the need to hold back details until the last minute. And, they trusted us. During more than two years, we had built a strong reputation for being very organized and for following through on commitments. This time seemed bigger and riskier than any previous project. Would we really be able to pull off a major protest that required this kind of secrecy?

When the meeting ended, we dispersed quietly into the starry cold to not draw attention as we fanned out in different directions to our rooms. Some probably had more work to prepare for Thursday morning classes. Everyone had to think about what they would bring the next afternoon.

It was difficult, but we knew instinctively that we'd be better off if we could each get a few hours of sleep. We had a strong sense that the next day would change all of our lives forever.

Children of the Sixties

JANNETTE O. DOMINGO

The Turbulent '60s

We came of age in the turbulent decade of the 1960s. From Florida, Virginia, New York, Massachusetts, and the Caribbean, we saw the protests, the beatings, the deaths. We were in elementary school when the black community of Montgomery, Alabama, boycotted segregated public buses and when Emmett Till was murdered in Mississippi. We were in junior high school when Freedom Riders risked their lives to challenge segregated bus travel in the South. By the time we got to high school, NAACP leader Medgar Evers had been assassinated in Mississippi; four girls, close to us in age, were killed in the bombing of a black church in Birmingham, Alabama; and Bull Connor's storm troopers unleashed fire hoses and police dogs on ordinary people peacefully protesting segregation in Alabama. In the summer of 1963, we were uplifted by the vision of countless people marching onto the mall in Washington, DC to hear Martin Luther King, Jr. affirm the dream of a non-racist America. Two years later he would be on the front line as state troopers savagely beat civil rights marchers on the Edmund Pettus Bridge in Selma, Alabama.

In the midst of all this, Myra Rose was growing up in Virginia where they still celebrated Richmond's glory days as the capital of the Confederacy. Despite the ostracism by white students, her teachers' attempts to ignore her intelligence, and a guidance counselor's efforts to steer her into trade school despite the advanced placement courses she had taken, Myra persevered at a newly integrated high school. Being the oldest sibling in a strong and nurturing close-knit family headed by college-educated parents, and her father's encouragement of her love of writing and debate meant more to Myra than anything she faced at school.

Farther south in Tallahassee, Florida, Marilyn Holifield faced a more aggressively hate-filled environment in her newly integrated high school. White students vilified her daily and called her "nigger." But the child who loved growing roses with her father was well aware of her family's legacy of resistance. Her grandfather had stood up to racist terrorism in Mississippi, and her father had been able to make his way from the Mississippi countryside to college at Tuskegee Institute in Alabama and ultimately to Tallahassee. Her mother had ventured into the South from Boston to practice nursing. Their strength and dignity became her own.

The rest of our group of eight attended high school up north in Massachusetts and New York where de facto segregation and institutional racism collided with the Civil Rights Movement. Aundrea White lived in Boston, a city known for its rabid ethnocentrism, segregation, and racism. Nevertheless, it was a city that was an important destination for southern black migrants like Aundrea's parents as well as Caribbean immigrants like Marilyn H.'s maternal grandparents, who emigrated to Boston from Barbados and Suriname. There was no way Aundrea's father would go back to the indignities he and her mother had suffered growing up in Mississippi. When he retired from the army, the family settled in Boston. Aundrea was an "army brat" who had lived in many different places. She never fully embraced the Boston accent or internalized a Boston-centered view of the world. The one constant was her loving and open-armed family which always incorporated newfound relatives and friends.

Joyce Frisby grew up less than one hundred miles away from Boston in Springfield, Massachusetts. Her parents had left Baltimore, Maryland with ambition and junior high and senior high school educations in search of fewer racially motivated economic limitations. They settled in an integrated neighborhood where class differences were more apparent to a self-conscious Joyce than racial differences. Despite her father's resourcefulness, the family struggled financially, and Joyce would never lose the habits of frugality that she developed in those days. Joyce was the eldest daughter, second eldest of her siblings, and ever the responsible one.

Bridget Van Gronigen, Jannette O. Domingo, and Marilyn Allman lived in New York City and Harold Buchanan lived on Long Island, in the exurbs of the city. Jannette and Marilyn A. were children of working-class Caribbean immigrants. Bridget and her family had recently immigrated to the United States from the former colony British Guiana (now Guyana). Having grown up in British Guiana through her early teens, Bridget's lilting Guyanese accent distinguished her from first generation Caribbean Americans. As a newcomer to the US, she was reserved and formal, negotiating a foreign education system and learning the implications of being black in America. Like those who migrated from the South, for Caribbean immigrants and their children, the promise of better education and health and higher incomes outweighed concerns of being victimized by racism.

Marilyn A. was the youngest child of immigrant parents whose religious and cultural values were reflected in her becoming an exceptionally articulate student. As a scholarship student in a prestigious private school, Marilyn bypassed the New York City public high schools. Her upbringing in the church was evident in the purposefulness and sense of mission that made her a leader. She was elected student government president and head of several clubs—even at a white upper-class girls' high school. Jannette also bypassed the regular public schools, spending six years in one of the city's most selective junior/senior public high schools for girls. She was a popular student, elected captain of the cheerleaders and chairperson—or producer—of the Senior Show, the annual musical revue that was the climax of senior class activities. But few of her friendships extended beyond school hours when she and her white peers returned to sharply different neighborhoods. Her church friends and family filled her social life, and African music and dance, as well as her father's science fiction books, expanded her world. While neither the private school nor the selective examination high school environment was overtly racist, microaggressions communicated clearly that accomplished black students like Marilyn A. and Jannette were considered exceptions to stereotypes internalized by their classmates, teachers, and school administrators.

Meanwhile, Harold and his family had fled New York City for a small black community out past the city limits on Long Island. He was one of a few blacks in school, but he had genuine friendships with white classmates who shared his interest in music. He grew up in a close-knit and outgoing family in which his parents were great role models. They shared tasks and responsibilities without being strictly defined or limited by stereotypical gender roles, an approach to life that would later serve Harold well as the Brother among the Seven Sisters at Swarthmore.

The Northern "struggle for Negro rights"[3] to equal employment, education, and housing opportunities provided the backdrop to our high school years in New York and Massachusetts. Thousands of students boycotted public schools in Aundrea's Boston in 1963 and in Bridget, Jannette, and Marilyn A.'s New York City in 1964. That same year, in New York City, protests of police brutality morphed into the six-day long "Harlem Riot." Violent protests also erupted in response to police brutality and other festering injustices in Philadelphia in 1964, Watts in 1965, and Newark in 1967. On April 4, 1968, we were Swarthmore students, meeting with our counterparts at Haverford College, when we learned that Martin Luther King, Jr. had been assassinated. In the days that followed, anger, grief, and pent up frustration erupted in riots in Chicago, Washington, DC, Baltimore, and more than one hundred other cities across the country.

College Students Take the Lead

When Joyce enrolled at Swarthmore in 1964; Harold, Marilyn A., and Marilyn H. in 1965; and Aundrea, Bridget, Jannette, and Myra in 1966, college students had become the cutting edge of the Civil Rights Movement as the Congress for Racial Equality (CORE) and then the Student Nonviolent Coordinating Committee (SNCC) rose to national prominence. In the early 1960s, college students' non-violent confrontations with segregation and the violent responses to their lunch counter sit-ins, wade-ins at segregated pools, and pray-ins at whites-only churches drew greater national attention to the Civil Rights Movement. CORE's Freedom Rides in 1961 and the Selma to Montgomery March in 1965, in which SNCC played a major role, were highly publicized events exposing the depths of American racism and arousing widespread outrage. SNCC's grassroots voter registration campaign in the 1964 Mississippi Freedom Summer Project and the murder of three of its young volunteers—twenty-one-year-old local organizer James Chaney and two white men from New York City, twenty-year-old Andrew Goodman, and twenty-four-year-old Michael Schwerner—starkly highlighted the commitment of young people to the civil rights struggle.

International conflicts increasingly shaped college students' political perspectives and expanded the scope of our activism to include anti-war, anti-colonialism, and anti-apartheid protests. Opposition to the Vietnam War, in particular, overshadowed the presidency of Lyndon Johnson, forcing him not to seek reelection in 1968. Many of us participated in anti-war demonstrations on campus. Most of the troops were our contemporaries. Because young black men were disproportionately represented among the draftees, we all knew someone—a relative, friend, or acquaintance—who had been killed or maimed or lived in fear of being sent to Vietnam to fight and possibly die in this unpopular war.

Even as the Vietnam War dragged on throughout the 1960s, many African and Caribbean nations won their independence. Their victories generated pride for the African Diaspora and reasons to celebrate. But the ongoing struggles against intransigent regimes in Southern Africa, especially apartheid South Africa and Namibia, known then as South West Africa, resonated with our own African American experience. The 1960 Sharpeville Massacre in South Africa was recent history. As on many other campuses, student activists at Swarthmore commemorated the massacre and called for the College to divest itself of investments in South Africa. As students from South Africa and Namibia became part of our lives, Africa and African liberation movements became much more than just an idealized abstraction.

With anti-war and anti-apartheid activism, the Civil Rights Movement, riots in major cities, and increasing militancy, by the time we arrived at Swarthmore, protests had become commonplace on college campuses across the country. No one in our group knew about Swarthmore's reputation as an activist campus when we applied, but once there, we took advantage of the fertile environment to expand our own political consciousness. In the fall of 1966, some of us were among the Swarthmore students who attended a conference at Columbia University on the role of black students on white college campuses. James Farmer, former director of CORE, was the keynote speaker. He called for a change in direction, emphasizing black empowerment and the right to make our own choices and build our own institutions rather than the push for integration that had been the hallmark of the Civil Rights Movement.[4] Like Stokely Carmichael, the new chairman of SNCC, Farmer called for "Black Power." The conference presenters urged the formation of black student organizations at elite white colleges like Swarthmore. This was a message our group was certainly ready to hear. We were already active on campus and would soon formalize a student organization, the Swarthmore Afro-American Students Society (SASS). We would later learn much from Philadelphia community leaders like Walter Palmer and William Crawford who were very supportive of our role as students, but who also admonished us to remember where we came from and to use our education to help others.

No one in our group ever debated whether to get involved in "the struggle." The only question was what type of involvement we should pursue. Over countless meals in the College dining hall and late-night dorm and study room sessions, we debated the merits of Dr. King's philosophy of non-violence versus the militant rhetoric of Malcolm X. The venerable NAACP had largely taken itself out of the competition after denouncing Black Power as reverse racism and condemning black college students' demands for black cultural centers and black dorms as self-segregation. At the other end of the spectrum, Black Muslims and the Black Panther Party (BPP) focused on black institutions. We heard Louis Farrakhan and the young boxer Muhammad Ali, charismatic spokesmen for the Nation of Islam, speak at Swarthmore and nearby Lincoln University, respectively. The Nation of Islam offered an impressive model of discipline and community development, but their misogyny and rejection of Christianity limited their appeal. The BPP threatened violence with "an eye for an eye" rhetoric that could end in proponents being jailed or killed. Ultimately, the SASS approach to activism ended up being most like the principled non-violence of Dr. King and the consensus-seeking brought to SNCC by veteran civil rights activist Ella Baker. Baker critiqued "leader-oriented" institutions and movements and argued for participatory democracy and grassroots organizing. The leadership philosophy she described was much like the approach our group adopted at Swarthmore.

> You didn't see me on television, you didn't see news stories about me. The kind of role that I tried to play was to pick up pieces or put together pieces out of which I hoped organization might come. My theory is, strong people don't need strong leaders.[5]

Baker insisted that leaders should never become more important than the movement they were leading.

Prioritizing the Struggle

Within the 1960s fight for equal rights and empowerment, black women and men grappled with sexism. We college students, like our contemporaries off-campus, struggled to reconcile the demands of women's liberation and black liberation. Even in new organizations like SNCC and BPP, few female leaders were widely recognized and celebrated, despite their critical creative and sustaining roles. In spite of Ella Baker's central role in the 1960 founding of SNCC and her mentoring of its young male leaders, in 1964, even Stokely Carmichael, future SNCC chairman, could joke that the only position for women in the movement was prone. By 1968, Frances Beal and others found it necessary to form the SNCC Black Women's Liberation Committee to begin to articulate and address the oppression of women within the organization.

Similarly, when BPP was founded in 1966, its rhetoric and militaristic image proclaimed the Party to be for men only. In 1968, a series of articles in *The Black Panther* newspaper maintained that black women's place was to "stand behind black men" and be supportive. By then, women already made up the majority of BPP membership, and they were largely responsible for successful community organizing and implementation of the Party's social service programs. The Party's slogan soon evolved to "The Black Woman's Place Is in the Struggle." Although BPP rhetoric declared sexism to be counterrevolutionary, this new perspective would require a major paradigm shift and dramatic behavioral changes. There weren't many young men whose life experiences prepared them to appreciate and thrive in non-sexist, collaborative relationships. The Seven Sisters found their brother, Harold, to be unusual in that way.

The movements of the day opted to call for a unified front against oppression by race and class, while leaving sexism to simmer on the back burner. We would do the same at Swarthmore. Although we seldom called out sexism and patriarchy by name or explicitly referenced the Women's Liberation Movement, these tensions affected our approach to leadership. We knew that women could and should lead, but we believed we would be more respected if the image of our organization was strong by patriarchal standards because its men were visible and in charge. The Seven Sisters ignored or downplayed frictions with male classmates and camouflaged our strengths. We perceived public leadership as a zero-sum game not to be played at the expense of black men. At Swarthmore, our solution to the dilemma was not unique. The Seven Sisters and a Brother led as a group composed primarily of women who supported black men as the more visible representatives of our community.

Not Just Student Issues

Signs of political progress emerged with the passage of the Civil Rights Act in 1964 and, three years later, the election of black mayors in Cleveland, Ohio and Gary, Indiana and the appointment of Thurgood Marshall to the Supreme Court in 1967, but there was much more to be done. As the first chairman of SASS, Sam Shepherd, put it:

> Black people look forward beyond the Civil Rights Act and the black professionals and see that 47.4 percent of black people and 59.6 percent of black children are classified as poverty-stricken. They see that the few who have made it are unable or unconcerned with doing anything about the others, and that they either deny or superficially affirm the racial aspect of themselves.[6]

Although SASS would be best known for demanding a black studies program, a black cultural center, and a greater number of black students and faculty, we did not limit our work to student-centered concerns. One of our earliest actions was to speak out about the lack of respect afforded to the College's black employees. We were struck by the absence of black supervisors among the College's blue-collar workers. It mirrored the previously uncontested absence of blacks on the faculty and in white-collar and administrative positions. The beautifully manicured rolling lawns of the campus looked much like idyllic representations of Southern plantations where those who tended the lawns, cleaned the buildings, and prepared the meals were all black and all dressed in service workers' uniforms. All of their supervisors were white.

We realized that many of the black workers were underemployed. They worked in jobs that didn't reflect their capabilities or the roles they played as parents, family members, caregivers, religious and civic workers, and leaders in the communities in which they lived. No matter how well they did their jobs or how senior they were in age, they were called by their first names while their white supervisors were "Mrs." and "Mr." Even Harold Hoffman, a particularly capable and distinguished black man on the custodial staff, was thoughtlessly called "Harold." He was polished and responsible and everyone, white and black, looked up to him, though not enough to respectfully call him Mr. Hoffman. We asked him and his co-workers what their last names were and spread the word to other black students, insisting that the black workers be addressed accordingly. We had been taught by our families that the "help" were due respect, just like our parents and our church ladies and elders. Eventually we got the administration to add last names to their badges and to call them "Mr." and "Mrs." just like their white supervisors. We agitated successfully for Mr. Harold Hoffman to become the first black employee to be made a supervisor. Like Mr. Hoffman, several of our parents were blue-collar workers. If we had been born at a slightly different time or place, we could have been working beside those employees who maintained our splendid campus rather than enjoying the fruits of their labor.

More Than Friends

At Swarthmore, maids changed our bed linens each week. We enjoyed meals that were far superior to the cafeteria fare most college students complain about, and we dined in the magnificent chalet-like Sharples Dining Hall. As we entered Sharples, we off-loaded our heavy books, book bags, sweaters and coats onto unsupervised racks in the lobby. The New York and Boston women among us found this especially remarkable. Big city girls never left their pocketbooks unattended. We quickly adjusted to the unspoken norm that, no matter how long we lingered over our meals and conversations, when we finally left the dining hall, we would find our belongings safe and undisturbed. Swarthmore was a trusting place where students were regularly allowed to borrow college vehicles for personal use. We made good use of that resource as well.

Yet Swarthmore lacked the comforts of home. At home, no matter what challenges school might bring, we each returned to families and friends. The foods we ate at home reflected our rich African American and Caribbean culinary cultures. We danced our own dances to the beat of rhythm and blues and calypso. Our local black barbershops and hair salons were specialists in disguising our natural hair to approximate European standards of beauty. We attended churches where worship was more social than the solitude of the Swarthmore Friends Meeting House. On campus, we had to create our own community of friends.

Aundrea, Bridget, Jannette, and Myra entered Swarthmore in fall 1966 and quickly bonded with each other in the dormitory. They were soon befriended by Joyce, who was already in her junior year, Joyce's official "Little Sister," Marilyn H., and her sophomore classmate, Marilyn A. Harold, who was Joyce's and Marilyn A.'s fellow math major, became a brother to the seven women. The four classmates cooked home-style comfort foods in the dormitory kitchen and, especially after holidays, shared "care packages" of homemade baked goods and other treats. When we all gathered for meals in the dining hall, we talked about the issues of the day amongst ourselves and with the other black students who gravitated to our table. After breaking bread together, we often continued the fellowship by singing spirituals together despite the consternation it caused among some of our white classmates.

More than friends, the eight of us felt like comrades in arms. We spent a lot of time together with little distinction between our social and political activities. We studied together, supporting each other academically even when we were studying different subjects in different majors. In the self-taught black studies course we designed for ourselves, we diligently fulfilled our responsibilities to do the course work well to make it a meaningful experience for each other. We traveled together to attend black studies courses at other colleges, black activist meetings in Philadelphia, New York, and on other college campuses, and to see black performers in Philadelphia. We planned and executed a host of events to bring black artists and speakers to the campus. We went together to nearby Chester to tutor younger students and attend church, and to Philadelphia to take African dance lessons. Those who could sew even set up an assembly line with sewing machines brought from home and made dashikis for all of the black male students so that they could be properly dressed for a Black History Week dinner that we had organized. By the time SASS was ready to challenge the College by occupying the admissions office, we had already engaged in many successful ventures together. In so doing, we created our own community and proved the power of collaboration.

Black Is Beautiful

When we started college, we were not that different from most "Negroes," who had been taught to be ashamed of their own physical features and embarrassed by their African heritage. The high school yearbook photos we provided for the *Cygnet*, Swarthmore's freshman directory, were remarkably similar. We looked as much as possible like our white peers—women with straightened hair and men with hair cut low. By the time we formed SASS, we thought and looked differently. In photographs taken in our final college years, we are wearing our natural hair. Some of us even went beyond the eventually stylish afro, and created elaborate West African-style hairdos like neat grids with a puff of natural hair in each section.

Adding to the permanence of our transformation, most of us went into town to have our ears pierced so we could wear a variety of traditional and ethnic-inspired earrings to accompany our newly natural hair and African-style dresses. More than simple fashion statements, our choices were self-conscious, political assertions that "black is beautiful" and that we were proud to be connected to Africa.

Blackness became a desirable quality in the 1960s. Africa and Africans—leaders of newly independent countries, public intellectuals, and fellow students—provided positive points of reference. They were political, cultural, and aesthetic role models. We identified ourselves as part of the African Diaspora, "Afro" Americans. "Black is beautiful" was our American parallel to "Négritude," a powerful, anti-colonial affirmation of African values and aesthetics. That concept was most closely associated with Senegal's First President, poet Leopold Senghor. Like Senghor in Senegal, President Julius Nyerere of Tanzania exemplified the political import of culture. Nyerere gave us the Swahili word *ujamaa* to signify extended family, brotherhood, African socialism, and cooperative economics. It was a political concept that asserted that a person becomes a person through the people or community. The collaborative leadership that characterized SASS in this era was an affirmation of these values.

In the highly-charged environment of the late 1960s, even the College romances of the young women of our group were of political consequence, whether it was the rare involvement with a white activist or relationships with African students. When a contingent of African students from historically black and then all-male Lincoln University descended on campus for a meeting with us fledgling activists, they discovered among us a group of black female students, each one brilliant in their eyes, amazingly unattached, and mostly open to the possibility of cross-national relationships. The African students were older, more experienced citizens of the world and more mature and sophisticated than most of the Swarthmore men. They were from Eastern and Southern African countries that had only recently won their independence or were engaged in a liberation struggle. Through them, some of us gained a much more intimate understanding of African politics and liberation movements as well as validation of our own activism.

Images of struggle had bombarded us all of our lives. We found ourselves in college in the late 1960s, when it had become a norm for college students to speak out and act out against war, racism, and discrimination. We were very much products of our era. We would make the most of our time at Swarthmore with its opportunities to be independent, responsible, and assertive activists, and most of all, to grow as young black men and women.

THE TAKEOVER

Day One

DAY ONE
Locked Inside

> Members of the Afro-American Students Society took over the admissions office of Swarthmore College today and vowed to remain until they [were] given a voice in policy-making and more Negroes were admitted. About 40 students filed quietly into Parrish Hall, began locking doors and refused admittance to anyone...."The police were not called in and I hope we never have to call them," said the College vice president...[he] said he hoped the dispute would be "solved amicably." Swarthmore has an enrollment of 1,024 students, 47 of them Negro.[7]

On a cold but gloriously sunny day in January 1969, a small cadre of black students took control of the Swarthmore College Admissions Office. We entered at lunchtime when most employees were on their breaks. While Harold began securing the doors, Aundrea and Marilyn A. approached each person still at their desks and asked them individually to leave. They had both practiced what they would say and how.

> No one will get hurt. Please take your personal belongings. We are taking control of the office and it may be a while before you're able to return.

They were all white women who were much older than we were, and they grabbed their coats and purses and scrambled out of our way into the hallway, leaving their paperwork behind. They had no idea that it would be more than a week before they would see their desks again. Neither did we.

A more non-threatening group of college students would have been hard to find. We were all in reasonably good academic standing at, arguably, the best small college in the nation. We had to prepare for fall semester final exams. We carried our books along with us, so we could keep up with writing final papers and test preparation in case the sit-in took a day or two longer than the one or two days we had anticipated.

Other SASS members waited at the back entrance for the signal to come in. Once all the office employees had left and Harold had secured the front door, Aundrea and Marilyn A. hurriedly unlocked the chained rear door and let in the rest. A flurry of activity followed as each one took in the premises and began settling in.

> What needs to be done?
>
> Help Harold tape the black paper to the windows and push the wedges under the door.
>
> Organize the survival kit stuff and put it in one spot. We need to know how much we have so we can figure out how to make it last. How many cans of sardines did we list on that planning sheet?
>
> Aundrea and Jannette will be in charge of food distribution to make sure we don't run out. We know how to make food stretch.
>
> Put the first aid stuff here, flashlights and batteries.
>
> I brought my record player and Nina Simone, James Brown, Aretha, gospel music. Anyone else brought records? Put them over there.
>
> Harold, do you have that guard duty schedule ready?
>
> Yes, everyone has to take a turn at guard duty, all day

and all night.

Two hours at a time. At the doors or at the window ledge.

The *New York Times* in 1969 was wrong in its estimate. It would actually be several days before the number of student protesters would reach forty. A 2019 *New York Times* profile of Ruth W., one of the freshmen occupiers, cited her fifty-year-old memory as counting twelve occupants. Perhaps twelve entered in the first hour, shortly after those who first secured the premises let them in. Before that first night ended, there were at least twice that many members of SASS who had brought sleeping bags, books, and enough snacks and personal essentials that would allow them to be away from their dorm rooms for a day or two. Other freshmen besides Ruth came inside on day one, despite some worrying about what their parents would say when they found out.

Setting the record straight may take decades. The official campus newspaper, the *Phoenix*, also got it wrong in many ways. Its coverage of the start of the admissions office occupation identified almost none of the students who led the action and invented an implausible narrative of the chain of events that claimed the spokespersons negotiated with the College dean to access the premises.

What we would later call the "Takeover," but what the College administration dubbed the "Crisis" had just begun. While it was carried out under the auspices of SASS, in actuality the protest was the brainchild of a group of students known as the Seven Sisters, plus one Brother.

None of the media's photographs or articles recognized that it was women who had organized and led the Takeover. No press accounts named or showed a woman. We had intentionally asked some brothers to be the media spokespersons. It's likely the reporters never asked them who planned the Takeover, where or when.

Since its founding, Swarthmore College has had a mission of not just educating students academically, but of educating them to make a difference in the world. Swarthmoreans call it their "Quaker values." It has historically been students of the College who have spoken out and protested about the apparent discrepancies between Quaker values and the College's investments in things that don't improve the planet, such as apartheid and fossil fuel. We were a part of that tradition when we peacefully took over the College Admissions Office in 1969. Little did we know that forty years later, the College administration would call our action the single most consequential event in its 150-year history. What they called the "Crisis" was the cataclysmic event that forced college administrators to wake up and respond to our demands for respect. Respect for black people. Respect for black history. Respect for black culture. Black students refused to be invisible.

The College would be put to a test of its values like never before. It had failed more than once in earlier tests.

The Swarthmore Experiment

HAROLD S. BUCHANAN

Experiments

Swarthmore College is a small, private, coed liberal arts institution located about 11 miles southwest of Philadelphia. The idyllic campus of more than 400 acres, shared by approximately 1,000 students during our years there, doubles as a free public arboretum complete with a creek and hiking trails through the private woods. The meticulously maintained rolling grounds and majestic stone buildings create a landscape that was the deciding factor for many of us to attend college there.

In 1864, one year before the end of the Civil War, prominent Quakers founded the College. Its founders included noted women's rights advocate and abolitionist Lucretia Mott. One of the distinguishing features of the Quaker religion is the emphasis on individual responsibility. In examining ideas and seeking answers, everyone is free to speak until a consensus is reached.

Swarthmore College remains heavily influenced by Quaker values and traditions. Consistent with those beliefs, seeking and testing the *truth* is the basis for what Swarthmoreans call "academic rigor." The Quaker quest for truth has historically extended beyond academics to social justice and led the founders to create the College as a "grand experiment" in coeducation, that is, teaching men and women together.

Quakers had a long history of fighting against slavery and participating in the Underground Railroad. When we arrived on campus in the late 1960s, we were surprised to discover that ours were the first classes with more than a handful of black students. Certainly, this socially conscious community with its long history of fighting against slavery and for the rights of blacks would not deny equal opportunity to attend their institution. It shocked us to later find out that the absence of blacks was intentional. Around 1920, concerned members of the community tried to get the College to correct its de facto exclusion of blacks. They found a qualified black student and money to pay for her education, but the president declined to admit her, citing other priorities. Later in the 1920s, the College accidently admitted a black athlete from Philadelphia. When the College discovered the error, it went into crisis mode and found a way to rescind his admission. Finally, in 1943, after years of pressure from students and others in the community, the Board of Managers determined that there was no actual policy to bar blacks and admitted the first black student. Over the next twenty years, through 1963, Swarthmore admitted fewer than thirty black students, an average of little more than one per year.

In 1964, in the midst of the Civil Rights Movement, the Rockefeller Foundation and other organizations gave grants to Swarthmore and other colleges, essentially paying them to find and accommodate black students. Swarthmore would not have to tap into its rich endowment for a second experiment with black admissions. It never occurred to the College that it might benefit from this endeavor even more than the blacks that they somewhat reluctantly sought to help.

Our group of seven sisters and a brother did not go to Swarthmore to change the College. Our aim was simply to get a good education and enjoy college life, but it didn't take long for us to discover inconsistencies in the Swarthmore story. Elite colleges pride themselves on their rich heritage and time-honored traditions, and Swarthmore was no exception, priding itself on the number of Rhodes Scholars and Nobel Laureates it had produced. In the 1960s, there were other traditions, such as mandatory attendance at a weekly meeting called "Collection," similar to an assembly in high school. Upon graduation, tradition permitted senior women to pick a rose from the Dean Bond Rose Garden. Swarthmore's de facto policy to deny admission to black students was also a tradition and part of its heritage, but one that was wrong and contrary to the College's espoused values.

With the catalyst of external funding, larger numbers of blacks began to arrive on campus. Our group came to Swarthmore with varying degrees of academic, social, and emotional preparation. We were all stellar students in high school. Our secondary schools were rural, urban, public, and private from Northern and Southern states and the Caribbean. Most were integrated, some only recently, and whites vastly outnumbered blacks. In the afternoons, we all went home to our families and black neighborhoods where we laughed, played, worked, and led "normal" lives. Most of us did not mix socially with white students—no sleepovers in each other's homes, no movie dates, no camp roommates. We had occasional telephone talks about homework assignments or missing classroom notes. Even Harold, who had close social ties with white friends, retreated to the security of his black neighborhood at the end of each day. All of this made immersion in the white traditions of Swarthmore a challenge for most of us, yet the administration had not anticipated a need for resources to ease our transition into the College. In contrast, the College gave some thought to easing the transition for white students into this grand experiment in racial coeducation. Many of us discovered that our roommates had been solicited and had agreed to accept a black roommate. None of the blacks received a questionnaire asking for our consent to have a white roommate.

When the class of 1970 arrived with only half the number of black freshmen as compared to the previous year, many black students became concerned. We met with college officials who told us how difficult it was to find qualified black students and faculty. For us, it was difficult to comprehend how they could not find qualified blacks with many urban population centers such as Philadelphia, New York, Washington, DC, and Boston within a day's drive. Our view was that with the right resolve, the College could find them.

Oberlin College is a private liberal arts college in Ohio. It was founded in 1833 and has regularly admitted blacks since 1835, although it segregated its students from 1882-1910.[8]

> Oberlin continued to be an important institution for African Americans for the next century. By 1900, one-third of all black professionals in the US had undergraduate degrees from Oberlin.[9]

Oberlin also participated in the Underground Railroad, the Abolitionist Movement, and equal rights for women, but that college went a step further in putting its beliefs into action. If Swarthmore had an actual history of educating blacks, it would not have needed to go looking for them. Instead, qualified blacks would have been attracted to the College.

Aloof Faculty

Swarthmore had no black faculty when we arrived. Under the Northern system of racism, Jim Crow laws were not necessary. Like so many Northern employers, colleges and universities could easily justify why a particular white candidate was better than a black one. Whether fully intentional or not, the only blacks on campus, other than students, were service workers. Sometime after we arrived, a black librarian appeared. Two years later, the first black professor was hired—temporarily—to replace someone on leave.

We arrived at college without much experience in engaging faculty or seeking mentors, and not many professors reached out to us. A perception among black high school students was that only low-achieving students met with teachers at lunchtime or after school to get assistance with their work. Even if they had questions on the content presented in class, high achievers would simply study harder at home on their own until they "got it."

Few of us remember having more than short conversations with our professors while at Swarthmore. We have forgotten most of those faculty members. We rarely took advantage of faculty office hours. Fortunately, we often studied together, discussed reading assignments, and helped each other with mathematics problems and science concepts. Two of us did make significant and rewarding connections with professors who are remembered for specific and rare moments of exceptional teaching. They were the ones who inspired us to examine scholarship more critically and affirmed us, valuing our perspectives and insights.

At times, it seemed that the majority of professors were not comfortable speaking with black students. Their lives in this idyllic community of Swarthmore separated them from any meaningful interaction with blacks, other than servants. The gap between us was widened further by the changes in our superficial appearance. During the 1966–67 school year, as we let our hair grow naturally and sometimes wore African-style clothing, we began to resemble the students who were sometimes seen shouting in protest on TV. As the presumed adults in the situation, it was incumbent upon those who were assigned as our faculty advisors to look beyond the surface and connect with us. If bonding with faculty had occurred for all of us, we could have grown intellectually, learned about other perspectives and world views, and possibly gained allies who would work with us on the pressing issues for black students at Swarthmore College. When we return to the College today or meet alumni in other situations, we frequently hear that the most rewarding aspect of their Swarthmore education was the ability to connect with and be mentored by faculty. Their memories of the Swarthmore experience differ greatly from ours.

Negro History Week

In February of 1967, Swarthmore College celebrated Negro History Week for the first and only time under that name. This was the first visible sign that black students were organizing as a group. It was early in the development of a formal group that the official pronouncements were about "Negro" students, not "Blacks." Organizations of black college students had been developing for some time prior to this, and an inter-college meeting of black students at Colombia University just a few months before had urged the formation of such groups by blacks on predominantly white campuses. This was part of the new Black Power movement, but participants had not yet fully identified themselves as black. By the next year, we rebranded our celebration as Black History Week as the term "Negro" gradually disappeared from the campus lexicon.

The agenda for Negro History Week began strategically with a folk concert in an intimate setting. In the late 1960s, folk music was popular, and the genre included black and white artists. What better way to create a conversation than with a black folk singer who could sing about current events from a black perspective? As had been the tradition at Swarthmore, all events were free and open to the public. This event took place only hours after the Student Council had formally approved SASS as an official student organization. The next event, and perhaps the highlight of the week, was a soul food dinner in the College dining hall. The College had only one dining hall, so every student and many faculty were exposed to this event, co-sponsored by the dining hall administration. If the main goal of SASS was to create an awareness of and foster dialogue about a different culture than was most prevalent on the campus, the dinner certainly accomplished that.

As Sam Shepherd explained in a letter to the school newspaper, it was not without a great deal of discussion that the organization came into being. A significant number of blacks saw no need to create an organization of this type. They had not come to a progressive, "integrated" college to separate themselves from the majority. Even among those who saw some justification for a black organization, disagreement on its goals generated intense discussions.

The Black Experience

As we learned and grew, the number of "Negroes" on campus gradually diminished as black spirits began to soar. Dean of Admissions Fred Hargadon commented that the rise of black consciousness was a deterrent to some Negro students who were looking for an integrated campus environment.

> A militant "black student" group which dominates the Negro subculture on a campus may be a deterrent to attracting some Negro students to enroll here. Many Negro students are interested in finding an "integrated" situation at college.[10]

We argued that some black students might be deterred by the fact that Dean Hargadon referred to them as "Negro." The dean had increasingly become the symbol of resistance to our advocacy for black awareness on campus.

We came to Swarthmore in all shapes, sizes, and colors and with many diverse perspectives on how we identified with the African American community or did not. Some grew up in predominantly white communities, some in predominantly black communities and some in foreign countries. Some brought a knowledge of black culture with them, others had minimal knowledge of it. Some were quite comfortable with and embraced the cornucopia of white cultural options available to them and some felt awkward and out of place in navigating those options.

In the '60s, the discussion about blackness went far beyond skin color. As we began to define ourselves as black rather than Negro or colored, heated debates often ensued on what defined our blackness. Those who were comfortable with the status quo were categorized as "Uncle Toms." At the other end of the spectrum were those who embraced the struggle and chose to actively participate in dismantling racial oppression. The majority of blacks fell somewhere in the middle, believing that any changes should be slow and orderly. Blacks at Swarthmore paralleled this continuum of the larger society, and we engaged in discussions on who was black enough.

One of the most frequent topics of debate was about the "black table" in Sharples Dining Hall. We used to say that if more than two blacks gathered together in discussion it would attract attention and conspiracy rumors would abound. You can imagine the level of discomfort that we caused when groups of black students started eating together at the long tables in Sharples. There was no conspiracy to plot an uprising, just a desire for community. With so much change going on within us and around us, we had much to discuss. Discussions about the black evolution (or revolution) took place throughout the campus and even included non-black students, but it was always easier and more productive to have these discussions with people who, although diverse, shared the common experience of growing up black in America.

As we settled into college life, the lack of black upperclassmen confirmed that we were pioneers. Although the College was one of the best endowed in the country, it shocked us to discover that it took an external grant to bring about an improvement in black admissions. The College had not lived up to its espoused core values in the matter of racial integration. SASS was not founded specifically to address the College's shortcomings, but when black students came together in this organization, it was inevitable that the persistent inconsistencies in the College's policies would be brought to light.

Some in our group had chosen Swarthmore explicitly because of its Quaker affiliation. Others were attracted to the overall image of the College as a place that was not just an education factory. When we arrived on campus in the late sixties, white students were already actively engaged in protesting the Vietnam War on and off campus. Several in our group supported the anti-war movement and even participated in protests. Over its history, Swarthmore had developed a reputation as an activist college. Activism was not restricted to students, as some professors were also activists in the anti-war movement.

In contrast to its Quaker values, the College aligned with the American mainstream in supporting a de facto caste system. One of the first grievances that the Seven Sisters addressed with the administration was the treatment of the College's black service workers which helped us develop a special relationship with them. We cannot speak for all black students who were at Swarthmore during those years, but our small group had a closer relationship with the black service workers than with the white faculty. They could not advise us academically, but they did listen and give us emotional support. One of the first SASS confrontations with the College was the publication of a list of demands and a press release titled *Why We Can't Wait.* In this document, we exposed the College's history of segregation and its liberal hypocrisy.

> ...because its students tutor Chester Kids, lily white Swarthmore automatically assumes it's [involved in] the racial scene and doing the best it can. White liberal Swarthmore has been content to push for racial justice and Black self-determination in Chester, or Philadelphia, or Media, rather than in its own backyard. Black Power is good in Chester, but bad on campus.[11]

Admissions

In September 1968, Dean Hargadon published a report on the status of recruitment and admission of "Negro" students. The report discussed the successes and shortcomings of the effort to enroll black students primarily funded by a $275,000 grant from the Rockefeller Foundation. The report contained personal demographics of students who had been admitted along with easily identifiable details. When the College placed the report in the library for public review, we learned that Swarthmore viewed our admission to the College as an experiment. The redacted information in Table 1 showed the family income and number of employed parents for each student. Since names were not listed, the College felt that this table was okay.

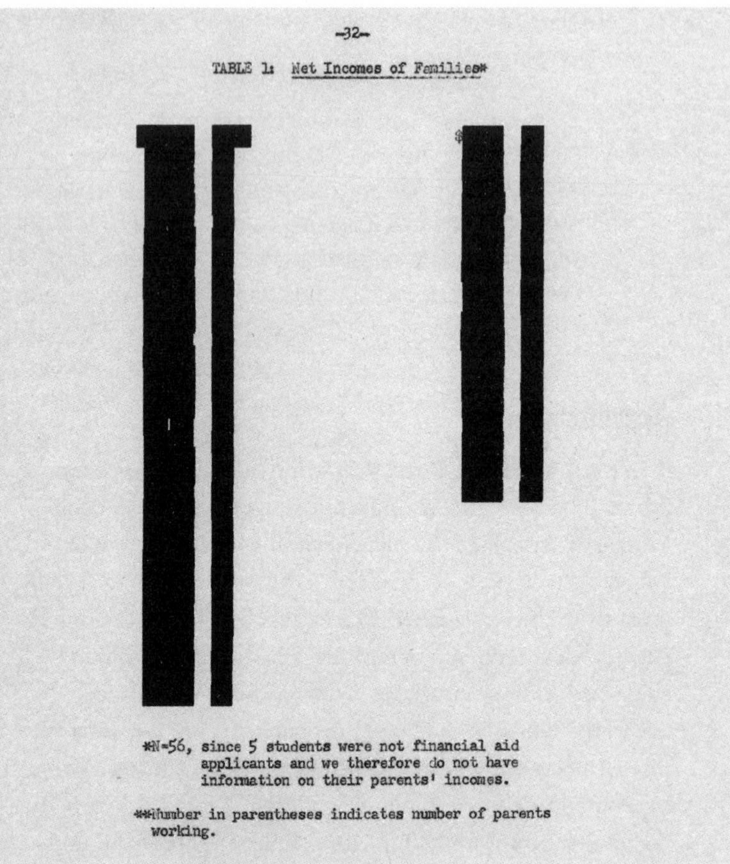

-32-

TABLE 1: Net Incomes of Families*

*N=56, since 5 students were not financial aid applicants and we therefore do not have information on their parents' incomes.

**Number in parentheses indicates number of parents working.

Page 32 of the Admissions Report, showing data that has been redacted.

The report detailed the breakdown of SAT scores as well as the grades achieved by men and women in each class. The class of 1970 had only three black men, so if you were one of those three, you could figure out the grades of the other two. Although no students were named, the report, analysis, and tables presented a detailed look at the education, family structure, and family income of this small population. The study detailed students' academic results and grades, the number of students required to withdraw, and other academic data. Rather than focusing on admissions, Dean Hargadon seemed interested in denying our basic right to privacy.

We felt disrespected not only by having our personal information made available in the library for anyone to see, but also by finding that we had been test subjects in an experiment and treated differently from the other students on campus. This action by the College, and Hargadon's refusal to change course when challenged about it, galvanized many of those black students who had been ambivalent about the goals of SASS.

Professor Legesse

One of the indirect results of the creation of SASS was the appointment of the College's first black faculty member. Asmarom Legesse was one of the twenty-two new faculty members hired for the fall semester of 1967 who were announced in the campus newspaper on May 5, 1967. The "Negro Ethiopian," as he was misidentified by the *Phoenix*, was initially hired as a temporary faculty member. [12] Some of us took Professor Legesse's anthropology courses, which were an opportunity to explore concepts like culture, civilization, and social change from a non-European perspective and to incorporate them to our own activist rhetoric. But his presence beyond the classroom was even more important to us. As an African and the only black faculty member, he was very noticeable. Like so many of his Eritrean countrymen, he had a warm demeanor and spoke softly, but with intensity. A cigarette often clung to his dark lips, never falling or dropping its ash. He seemed worldly, yet accessible. He and his Afro-American wife welcomed us into their home, and he participated in our efforts to create a black studies concentration. For white students, it was common to be welcomed into the homes of faculty, but this was a rare opportunity for us.

Black Studies

At Swarthmore, students could pursue a full major in Russian language and culture, but the College did not offer a single course in the history, language, or culture of any nonwhite people. In 1965, the Sociology & Anthropology Department did not exist, providing no mechanism to study non-European societies. It was possible to complete a baccalaureate degree and graduate believing that the only history worth studying about people of African descent was the legacy of colonialism and slavery, and even that was taught with a Eurocentric bias. We believed that applying the usual Swarthmore academic rigor to black studies would be helpful to all.

Kujichagulia (pronounced koo-jee-cha-goo-LEE-ah) is the Swahili word for self-determination. It means "to define ourselves, name ourselves, create for ourselves, and speak for ourselves." It is one of the Seven Principles embraced by the Black Nationalist Movement emerging as we were coming of age in college. *Kujichagulia* taught us that we didn't have to wait for permission from mainstream society to validate our history, culture, and contributions. If we were not satisfied with the educational experience at Swarthmore, it was up to us to correct it.

Before we began setting up a curriculum, we got basic training on black studies by attending meetings and lectures in nearby black communities. SASS regularly invited speakers and performers to campus to enlighten the student body. Many of us spent enough time in Philadelphia to become familiar with the local leaders of the Black Nationalist Movement: people like Walter Palmer, Playthell Benjamin, Father Paul Washington, and John Churchville. On the heels of a major riot on Columbia Avenue in 1964, community organizers were visibly active and vocal. When Walter Palmer and others came to campus, they treated us like a part of their community and worked with us to become educated on Black Nationalism. We, in turn, respected them for their knowledge and did not require that they have a PhD in order to share what they had learned.

Our next steps toward rectifying the omission of black studies was to begin enrolling in single courses at nearby colleges and petitioning Swarthmore to count the transfer credits toward our baccalaureate degrees. A copy of the syllabus in the Swarthmore library documents a course that several of us took titled "African Civilization." It was offered in spring 1967 by Haverford College and historically black Lincoln University and was taught jointly by professors from those institutions, Harvey Glickman and Richard Stevens, who were both white. In other semesters, we took classes in Philadelphia at Temple University and the University of Pennsylvania. We were thirsty for knowledge about African religions, African politics, and African American literature.

As a testament to our determination, a few of us piled into the College van for a weekly round trip of over two and a half hours to attend a course in Negro Literature at Lincoln University. Historically black Lincoln is located in rural Oxford, Pennsylvania, and we had to go through Ku Klux Klan-friendly territory to get there. On one occasion, we ran out of gas in the center of Oxford. It must have been late at night, because the only gas station we could find was closed. Out of desperation, someone came up with the idea of trying to siphon any gas that might be left in the hoses. There we were, a group of black college students, attempting to drain gas from a private business in the center of Oxford. There had been cross burnings in the area, and we wondered how we would fare if the police came along. Somehow, we got enough gas to reach our destination and did not get burned on a cross, lynched, or even arrested. That course was taught by an elderly

African American professor, J. Saunders Redding. He was distinguished-looking with his receding mixed-gray hair and tiny goatee. Harold has a photograph of us having lunch with Dr. Redding in Sharples Dining Hall, so, obviously, we had established a much better rapport with him than we did with Swarthmore professors. He, too, appreciated the extra effort we had to expend as students in an unsupportive environment and accepted our invitation to visit us at Swarthmore.

Our Swarthmore experience was very different from what we imagined after reading about the impressive history of the College and being captivated by the picturesque setting. The prestigious college had been similarly unprepared for us. Perhaps if they had been funding this social experiment with their own money, they would have done some research and invested more thought into how to accommodate students like us.

THE TAKEOVER

Day Two

DAY TWO
Raising Our Profile

It was hard to sleep that first night. The reality of actually being inside the admissions office was sobering. We had rehearsed what we would say and how we would say it to the office staff when we took over. That part was executed pretty much as we had envisioned it.

Harold had created a schedule for guard duty. The rear door and a window in the office had to be guarded at all times. Everyone had to take a turn, and each person would be on duty for two hours at a time. Jannette did not look forward to being the first to guard the rear door. Far away from the rest of the group, it felt dangerous back there because of the possibility of a surprise invasion by the administration, most likely in the middle of the night when people would be asleep, scattered around the carpet. Black students in a non-violent protest in the South had been attacked and killed less than a year before. We couldn't rule out that some rogue elements in this community might attempt vigilante actions.

Everyone tried to wait until the designated times to use the restroom, which required the guard to unchain the back doors and ensure that no outsider was near the stairs to the lavatories on the lower floor where there was little traffic. We had tipped off the custodial staff the day before that something was about to happen and, once they realized we were staying, they had surreptitiously re-stocked the restrooms with extra toilet tissue, paper towels, and powdered soap each day for as long as we would be there.

The black janitorial staff may have put their jobs at risk by alerting us to security procedures so that we could use the toilets regularly and safely during off hours. The relationships that we had built with them and other black service employees paid unexpected benefits. We had always treated them with respect. After all, they were the only black adults around.

Once daylight came, and we made it through the first night of the Takeover without anyone charging the premises and trying to remove us, we exhaled.

Keeping an eye on the one accessible window was the much more interesting guard assignment. With a ledge about a foot-and-a-half wide and four feet above ground, whoever was on guard could actually sit on the windowsill and observe campus goings and comings when the sun was up. If someone approached, the guard would lift the window. If any admissions office occupiers needed something from their dorm rooms, they could slip in and out, climbing through that window, so we wouldn't have to unlock the doors unnecessarily.

By the morning of day two, a Friday, we got a clearer idea of just how far the news of our action had spread. We had seen members of the local press show up on campus later in the afternoon of the day we took over the admissions office. But, heading into the weekend, the national and regional papers already had us in headlines.

After only twenty-four hours inside, the window guards began making frequent announcements that supporters were approaching and signaling that they wanted to communicate with us.

We didn't realize until later how word about our protest spread like wildfire. SASS founding Chairman Sam Shepherd had graduated, and the founding Co-Chair Clinton Etheridge had assumed the mantle. He and Co-Chair Don Mizell spoke to a group of reporters and community organizers who appeared on campus on the first afternoon we entered the building. Four days later, the *Washington Post* would claim, incorrectly, that black militant outsiders were directing us and other students at "known liberal colleges" in what "had all the earmarks of a revolutionary conspiracy."[13]

They had no idea that the so-called militant outsiders who laid the foundation for the action were really a small group of young women, dubbed the Seven Sisters, and a Brother who understood how to build a family to get a difficult task accomplished. Not a conspiracy to destroy.

Not in Kansas Anymore—Myra's Story

MYRA E. ROSE

Flood Gates of Memory

After my father died in 2008, I was going through his things and found a letter that I had written to our family. Although the year was 1969, the letter is incorrectly dated January 31, 1968 and starts out:

> January 31, 1968
>
> Dear Everybody,
>
> I finished my last exam yesterday so now I finally have time to write to you. I know you were all concerned over my actions and their possible consequences in the past month, so I am writing this letter to try to explain.
>
> When I first entered Swarthmore College, I did not know what to expect. True, I had gone to a white high school before coming here but somehow I expected it to be different. For about two months my roommate and I went everywhere together, the whole bit strictly "integrated." I saw other black people on the campus but did not associate with them. Although [she] and I did have a few things in common I never really felt comfortable and felt very lonely. Then I met Bridget, Aundrea, Janette and other black girls who were freshmen. Being with them was just like being at home and things began to look up. Also, during this semester SASS (Swarthmore Afro-American Students Society) was formed. I believe I wrote you all about that. Since that time (Fall 1966) SASS has been trying to effect changes on campus for black students. Nothing really radical like a black dorm or things like that, just simple things like course(s) in Afro-American history, literature, philosophy, etc., that would benefit the whole school.

When we bring speakers to the campus, white students come in droves, they even outnumber us. SASS also asked that they be consulted about anything on campus that affected black people. The school did not do this. Last year they had a South African (white) speaker that everyone was supposed to hear. Black students staged a peaceful walkout on the speaker at that time and still the school refused to listen to our requests and continued to walk over us. We were called "militants" and given all kinds of labels—even in the national news because we refused to listen to that man.

This year things really came to a head.... The Admissions Policy Committee, headed by Dean Hargadon, issued a report on black admissions... did not consult any black students when writing the report...and proceeded to write a very subtle racist document. What I mean is he used confidential information about our family backgrounds, incomes, etc., which really served no purpose and put them in the report (we could all identify each other).... Needless to say, all the black students on campus were very upset. An expert in black admissions, a woman from NSSFNS (a Negro scholarship group that helps black students get into white Ivy League colleges) offered to come down from New York to talk to the committee about the problem—they refused to see her. Their behavior indicates that they do not respect us enough to consult us on basic issues that concern us. They were ignoring our requests. Finally, we issued a set of demands in November about our grievances. The Student Council even endorsed our demands. The Dean of Admissions wrote them a scathing note saying in effect that he was sorry that he had let them into Swarthmore. President Smith asked for a further clarification of our demands... just one of their techniques to stall us. The final re-clarification was made just before Christmas and presented to the administration as non-negotiable demands. We still were given no answer. Two days after the deadline we held a meeting with the whole school to further express our grievances. The next day an effigy of the school was burned. The next day we occupied the admissions office...

Our occupation did what it was planned to do. We had finally shocked them into some action. Faculty meetings were held every day—an unprecedented fact. Administration efforts to alienate white students from us failed. Most students were in agreement with our demands. Others saw that the success or failure of our efforts had definite implications for student power. People from the black community helped tremendously and brought food and anything else we needed especially the moral support. ...[Through] the news media we have been called everything from extremist black militants and murderers (as if we had control over Smith's heart) to being a part of a Communist conspiracy. They will do whatever they can to discredit you and make you seem like an extremist when in reality SASS is one of the more conservative black student groups. I am enclosing a copy of the Phoenix, the school newspaper. It has the most accurate coverage of what really happened.

At any rate, we have not given up our objectives and we continue to press for them. The faculty is meeting at least twice a week now to bring about a settlement of the issues. I will tell you if anything new develops.

Our scholarships are not in jeopardy. The administration would look bad in the students' eyes if it did something like that.

My arm is getting tired of writing, so I guess I will stop...

Keep the faith babies!!!

Myra

After reading the letter, I realized that now it's an artifact, a hand-written record of what happened and why we did what we did. I read and re-read the letter and immediately telephoned Marilyn A. "You'll never believe what I found," I told her. That letter opened the flood gates of memory.

We were known as the Seven Sisters back then, but were actually the "Seven Sisters + Harold." My experiences with this band of believers at Swarthmore pointed the way for me professionally as I learned to always seek the truth, stand for what is right, and model collective leadership long before I had heard of the concept.

Growing Up

I had a happy childhood and was the oldest of four children raised by Joseph and Ednae Rose. I was "the different one." I was the brown one, the fat one, the ugly one who did not look anything like either my father or my mother. We lived in Liberty Park in Norfolk, Virginia, a Depression-era, pre-war housing project of pasteboard homes. The houses were connected with ribbons of asphalt on tar-based streets that wound through what had once been a large wooded area complete with ditches, winding streams, and lots of trees. We even had our own elementary school and city-run recreation center. The only black hospital in town, Norfolk General, was next to both the edge of the projects and one of the in-town enclaves of the black middle-class.

I never knew my maternal grandparents as they had died long before I was born. My mother and her four sisters were left to raise each other beginning in their late teen years. Ednae is my stepmother, the only mother I have ever known. She was short, light-skinned with full lips, a big nose, no hips, and short nappy hair that she did not like, but she was the prettiest woman I have ever known. She was a great dresser and the very definition of "style," although she made almost all her clothes. She was never seen without makeup until her later years. I did not know that she had full dentures until I was a teenager. The fact that she was my stepmother only bothered me in that I did not look like her and did not have her style, her beauty, or her way of existing in the world. Ednae was an outgoing, gregarious person who "never met a stranger." When she was in college, she was voted Miss Morgan State. Her confidence was awe-inspiring, and if she had any major insecurities other than some of her physical attributes, she hid them well. When her hair did not please her, she colored it or wore a wig. She was a master at makeup and had some foam rubber inserts that fit into the girdle that all women wore those days to give her hips. She was something else and my father loved her.

My father was a plasterer who learned the trade from his father. He did the best housing construction and decorative circle ceilings. He owned his own construction company. He was a true Renaissance man, born in the country, who later migrated to the city with his family. He graduated from college with a degree in animal husbandry, was a member of the Navy shore patrol during World War II, and organized and played with the Brown Bombers, one of the pre-integration black football teams. Daddy always took care of his birth family. He spent a lot of time helping my grandmother, who in my early childhood years lived with two of her daughters and my three cousins in a four-room house. We saw Grandma nearly every Sunday at Sunday School, church, and sometimes after church. She was a mother of the church, a deaconess, and quite formidable. Daddy was always respectful to his mother whom I later learned was largely responsible for my being raised by my father.

My real mother was named Marian and died in childbirth at the age of thirty. Her family lived across the water in Hampton. I never knew how my biological parents met, but I understand that she was a schoolteacher. They had been married for a few years before I was born. I look just like her, as people who knew her said—like she had spit me out. My parents' wedding photo looks like my father could have been marrying me with an old-fashioned hairstyle. For most of my life, I believed that my mother died in the throes of childbirth without ever getting to see me. I later learned that I was born via C-section and that my mother died of complications a day or so later. So, she probably got to hold me and name me. My father gave me this information when I was middle-aged. I cannot tell you how it comforted me to know that I was not a truly motherless child.

Apparently, her death was a big surprise to the doctor and my father who was called in the middle of the night and told that his wife had died. He walked around in a daze for several days and forgot that I was in the hospital. There were plenty of people who were willing to take me and raise me as their own. Apparently, I was quite the prize because I was an exceedingly adorable baby. Daddy was so distraught that he was really considering these options when Grandma told him to bring the baby to her. I lived in my grandmother's house for the first few years of my life. Grandma wanted to keep me, but when Daddy remarried, Ednae stated that I was to come home with them. I think that this was the only family battle my grandmother ever lost.

So, I had a happy childhood: loving parents, one sister, and two brothers. I was the oldest, but definitely not the leader of the pack. That title will always belong to my sister Joanne, who to this day is the boss of us. I was the smart one, the quiet one who stayed in the background, the one who read all the time. I felt invisible in this family of extroverts who were physically beautiful and gifted in their own right. My brothers were excellent football players: Allen, the high school quarterback in a predominantly white high school, and Don, who excelled in college and went on to a short career in the pros.

The world we grew up in was Southern, segregated, and insular. We lived in public housing until I was fifteen. School, church, buses, the eating establishments that we could frequent, and our hospital were all black. The mailman, the bus driver, the teachers, local shop keepers, the staff at movie theaters , amusement parks, beaches—everything and everyone was all black except the white department stores downtown and of course everything on television. We were aware of the white world, which we had to interact with from time to time. This was always anxiety-provoking because you knew that they had the best of the best (they showed that on TV) and ultimately all the power over you. Nonetheless, we were happy. My father had his own business and was able to support his family. We grew up safe and protected in the projects. We had a car, a sandbox and picnic table in the back yard, a three-foot-deep plastic swimming pool, a green Plymouth convertible, a pickup truck, a console radio and record player, and a television when they became available.

This was a time when people who were black middle-class lived side by side with others who were on welfare. Our family was part of the black bootstrap generation that pulled itself up by its own efforts. Both of my parents were college graduates and higher education was always stressed and assumed. As the "smart one," I always knew that I would go to college and that I would need a scholarship. I excelled in my segregated public school and was offered advanced placement to skip a couple of grades. My family wisely declined as other intellectual prodigies in the community did not fare well, developing "nervous breakdowns" and never quite living up to their early promise. I spent a lot of time in the library in elementary school to keep from being bored. I participated in local and statewide sponsored enrichment programs from junior high school onwards.

In addition to running his business, organizing/participating in early black football, and serving as a deacon in our church, my father was a prolific writer, philosophizer, and wannabe politician. He was concerned about the plight of the Negro (as we were called in those days) and was active in the community. He wrote and published a book in which he proclaimed that the solution to the race problem would be solved with miscegenation. He sent free copies to anyone that he thought might have some power or concern over the situation including every POTUS and major politician he could access. He wrote letters to the editor of the local white paper, wrote opinion articles for the *Journal and Guide* (the local black newspaper), and had a talk show on local black radio called "Joe Rose—Tell It Like It Is." We had lots of lively conversations from which I learned to think critically and seek to understand issues at their most fundamental levels. He encouraged me academically and helped me get a couple of writing assignments from the editors of the *Journal and Guide*. Some of my fondest memories are of sitting around the kitchen table reading and reviewing his writings while I was in high school as well as on breaks from college.

My mother encouraged all of her children to excel in school and participate in social and extracurricular school activities. She encouraged me to sing in the church choir, sing in a local operetta (which I did), and join black middle-class social clubs like Jack and Jill (I did not). I was never a social butterfly and declined most of these activities, though I did become a debutante during my last years of high school. My mother made time to pursue postgraduate educational opportunities in oceanography and eventually returned to teaching in the only black high school in town. She was an excellent biology teacher and was one of the first black teachers to integrate the white high school in my hometown.

The integration of the public school system was a major event in Norfolk; white schools closed down for a year or two rather than submit to desegregation. After fifteen years in my insular black world, my parents decided to move out of the projects to a more suburban setting. White flight was out of control and previously unavailable housing areas were open to black families. My father moved us when I was preparing to go to Booker T. Washington High School. I was upset to learn that instead of going to that Mecca of black teenage life, I would have to go to the local white high school. Talk about culture shock. Up until then, I had limited contact with white people, but would now be surrounded by them. There were only ten black students in the tenth grade class, only two of us were in AP classes, and I had only one class that had another black face. Even though I was never a social butterfly, I did miss being a part of the black world.

I was largely ignored in high school. I learned to adjust to a different style of teaching and learning. I had taken two years of French in junior high school, but imagine my surprise when my high school French teacher only spoke French to the class and gave homework and all instruction in French. I failed the first "dictée" largely because I did not know what was happening, but I eventually caught on. Most of my other classes were uneventful, and I did well in high school without any validation or encouragement from most of the teachers. By the time I started looking at colleges, I had decided to apply to schools away from home.

Applying to Swarthmore was pure serendipity. I was sitting in the guidance counselor's office—she thought I should go to trade school—when I saw the College catalogue, picked it up, and thought it looked nice, so I decided to apply. I had never heard of the school, nor had my parents. As far as I knew, no one in Norfolk had heard of the school. I applied to seven or eight schools and was accepted to each one. The final decision rested on the scholarship money that was offered. Swarthmore offered full tuition and two hundred dollars for books, so they got me sight unseen.

The Road to Swarthmore

Going to Swarthmore was to be the big adventure of my life. I always knew I would go to college, but never anticipated the path I would take. I always thought I would go to one of the Historically Black Colleges and Universities (HBCUs) like Howard University or Hampton Institute, which was right across the water from Norfolk and was essentially a local college. I knew that I could meet academic expectations anywhere with no problem, but I was never socially adept and basically felt like an outsider wherever I was. I was not looking for a husband or the usual social life that was an integral part of the HBCU experience.

Leaving home was harder than I expected. My brothers were too young to fully understand what was happening, but my mother and my sister did. We all cried and hugged each other several times that morning. My last image of the day I left is of my mother and sister standing outside on the walkway to the driveway, past the white wooden rail fence that my father loved and my mother hated. That is when I first really felt the loss of my family and all the love and security that they represented. I experienced a strange combination of sadness and anticipation.

My daddy and my uncle brought me to Swarthmore. They packed up my uncle's big green Cadillac for the road trip. We left early in the morning and drove until we reached the Pennsylvania countryside. I had never been that far from home. The campus was beautiful with rolling hills and lots of trees. We arrived sometime late in the day. My daddy and uncle unloaded all my stuff in my room on the third floor of Willets Hall. Swarthmore had previously sent me my room location and the name of my roommate. Susan was already there and had placed her stuff on the left side of the room, so I took the right side. My daddy and uncle kissed me goodbye and headed back home. Then I was really alone.

All first-year women were required to meet with Dean Barbara Lange in the Quaker meetinghouse for some type of orientation. I had never been in a meetinghouse. It was spare, cold, undecorated, and not at all like any of the Baptist churches I had visited over the years. If there was a cross there, I did not see it. The wooden benches were hard and uninviting.

Dean Lange was a middle-aged white lady with white hair, a blue suit, and pearls. I felt like I had been transported to June Cleaver, no, Donna Reed land. Dean Lange embodied the spirit of those true representatives of the white women of middle America, portrayed on late 1950s' black and white television, and I felt like I was in a foreign land where I barely understood the language. House dorm rules for freshmen were discussed. She talked about how fortunate we were to matriculate at Swarthmore. That Swarthmore was equivalent to Ivy League schools like Harvard, Yale, and the Seven Sisters women's colleges, but with a smaller, more select student body.

That was the first time I realized what kind of reputation the school enjoyed. When I looked in the *Cygnet*, the freshman handbook, complete with pictures and school of origin, most of the students were from the Northeast and had gone to Country Day Schools and prep schools. I had graduated from the public school system and attended segregated schools until the tenth grade. At that point, I felt like Dorothy from the Wizard of Oz and knew that I was not in Kansas anymore. I was disoriented and apprehensive. It became clear just how fortuitous it was that I applied and was accepted to Swarthmore College, unless you believe in destiny, and of course, I do. Dean Lange's cold, ruling-class demeanor and her declaration that Swarthmore's academic rigor was comparable to Harvard's had scared the bejesus out of me for sure. The pressure to succeed became real to me.

I bonded with my roommate, Susan, who was from Ohio. We were both science majors and had many of the same introductory science classes. She was going to medical school, and I was going to teach high school chemistry. Susan was the person who would eventually introduce me to my best friend, Bridget, the first black person I spoke to at the College. Bridget was also studying to be a doctor and was taking the prerequisite science and math courses. For a while, the three of us associated mostly with each other as Bridget also lived in the same dorm. First semester of freshman year was intense for everyone as we were all trying to prove that we belonged there, could do the work, and most importantly for me, that I could keep my scholarship.

College Life Before SASS

My science classes began at 8 a.m. and afternoon labs were always required. My roommate and I went to dinner and attended several social and musical activities together. I was focused on doing well in class and tried to fit into college life as seamlessly as possible. The early part of the first semester was filled with learning my way around campus and meeting all academic requirements.

I was seventeen years old and I loved being alive. Magill Walk perfectly captured the majestic campus scene lined with oak trees and steps cascading down to the train station and the tiny commercial strip called the Ville. I have lots of memories of climbing the hill beside Willets Hall to get to campus for science classes. I have always loved the early morning sun, fall season on campus with leaves beginning to fall and blow around everywhere, me carrying the green drawstring bag full of heavy science books, dragging the bag up the hill behind me.

My green Swarthmore book bag was square camouflage green with a drawstring. It was waterproof and could hold all my textbooks along with several spiral notebooks and other school supplies. I remember thinking that you could always tell the science majors from the social science majors—the science majors all had a hump in our backs. It was sometimes necessary to change shoulders or drag the bag along because it was so heavy. Remembering that green book bag makes me feel that I have always been prepared to carry the load, whatever it might be.

Susan played the cello, which I had only seen occasionally on TV. I loved music, all kinds of music, and tried to be open to whatever music was around: organ music at Collection, bagpipes, hootenanny, even white rock and roll, but the string quartet concerts were my undoing. Susan loved the string quartet classical music concerts that were given in Bond Hall. At first, I thought these gatherings were okay. The music was melodic, peaceful, and played with passion by the student musicians. I tried to follow along and thought I did fairly well for the first couple of concerts, but then my mind began to wander, and I almost fell asleep during one of the recitals. Science courses and labs took up all my time, and I think that an innate appreciation of classical music was not in the cards for me. Susan soon realized this, and I stopped attending those recitals with her. Occasionally, I could pick up an R&B radio station from Philadelphia on my clock radio, so she soon figured out that I was much more appreciative of this type of music. She even told one of her other acquaintances that she had a roommate who also loved this music genre. This acquaintance eventually came to our room to meet me, but lost her enthusiasm at possibly finding a kindred spirit when she discovered that I was a Negro. Susan thought that this was funny, but also very hypocritical of her acquaintance, whom she never mentioned again. I think that this was also around the time when B'nai B'rith, the oldest Jewish service organization in the world (who had written a letter to welcome me to the campus before I arrived and before our pictures were printed in the *Cygnet*), also rejected me by not initiating any further contact after they realized that I did not fit the expectations raised by my surname. Fitting into campus life was going to be harder than I expected.

My response to African and Caribbean music was entirely different. I felt as though I was at home. Through Bridget, I met Jannette who introduced me to music from NYC and the islands that I had never heard before—calypso, soca, and black American artists like Arthur Prysock, Nina Simone, Lou Rawls, and Nancy Wilson. The music of my childhood was southern R&B—James Brown, Carla Thomas, Otis Redding, Motown sounds, blues singers like Ray Charles, Ella Fitzgerald, and, of course, gospel music. When I finally got to hear African music and see African dance, I knew that I had found the original source of the music and rhythm that I loved. One of the first things that I bought with my own money was a record player, followed by albums. I picked up the habit of grazing record stores on a regular basis, a practice I continued throughout medical school, well into my late twenties.

At the end of my second month at Swarthmore, on my eighteenth birthday, I was still hanging out with my roommate from Ohio, wearing my "preppy" clothes and penny loafers, and trying to find my place at Swarthmore. I came back from my afternoon classes to find a surprise that I have not forgotten after all these years. I even have a picture of it: me in an A-line, sleeveless, green floral dress, a permed, mid-length page boy cut hair with bangs, and a forest green glass vase/jar that was placed on the top of my dresser in the left-hand corner. I was smiling a big, open-tooth smile and blowing out the candles on a cake that had been delivered for my birthday. My mother had arranged to have a birthday cake complete with candles and a birthday card delivered to my dorm room. I was pleasantly surprised and pleased that my special day had not been forgotten. I remember how grown up and loved I felt.

I came to Swarthmore to study science, preferably chemistry, because my mother taught high school biology and I saw myself as destined to teach high school chemistry. My mother had a good life as she went to work, made money, and had some level of independence in spite of having a husband and four children. I never saw myself as being married or having children—that was for the normal pretty girls. I knew that I would always have to take care of myself and thought that teaching high school would do the trick for me. I loved science, and still do, but I was surprised at the joy and opening of the spirit that I felt in English class.

The great awakening occurred in second semester of sophomore year: fourth semester of math, calculus, second semester of physics, and second semester of physical chemistry. I barely made it out of those courses alive. These courses would "separate the men from the boys," the true scientists and mathematicians from the wannabes. It was clear that I was not a real scientist. As I looked around for another path, my friendship with several of the postbaccalaureate students (most of them were HBCU graduates who were spending an academic enrichment year at Swarthmore, usually as a pathway to additional degrees), showed me the way.

Female physicians were unknown in my world and seemed mythical to me, even if Bridget and Susan had originally expressed interest in this profession, but I thought that if a post BACC could get into medical school and become a doctor, so could I. I changed course and took biology classes, eventually earning majors in both chemistry and biology. The path was smooth and the detour almost imperceptible, but I knew that medical school was the way forward.

Sharples Dining Hall and the Beginning of Black Consciousness

Sharples was a beautiful dining hall near the edge of the central Swarthmore campus. There was plenty of multi-use space with large common rooms, tables for two, semi-private rooms, and closed small meeting rooms that could be reserved. The serving line was a thing of wonder with fresh salad, hot yeast rolls, drinks, desserts, and several entrees. I had never tasted real butter, broccoli, or asparagus before. Several other food surprises like matzo balls and corned beef that did not come out of a can were certainly not anything I had ever experienced: it was a culinary adventure land. Most days, lunch and dinner tended to be leisurely affairs, except for us science majors who often had afternoon labs that interrupted many an interesting conversation.

Sharples was where I met most of the other black students. Some I only knew by sight. Others would actually sit down and share a meal with fellow black people; some never did. These group dinner experiences were a thing of beauty. Sharples was where we became the "Seven Sisters."

The seven of us were a nuclear family, and I thought of us as such with Joyce as our mother. The Marilyns were our older sisters, and the four freshmen were excited teenagers who had finally gotten free of our mothers and could come out to play, learn, study, and experience true freedom for the first time. Sam Shepherd, a thoughtful, quiet upperclassman, noted our girl group affinity and started referring to us as the "Seven Sisters," a thinly veiled homage to the Ivy League's Seven Sisters women's colleges of New England. The name stuck.

At first, the stories we shared were about our families, home, and the different lives that we came from. Harold, a sophomore math major from semi-rural New York, was the only male who became an integral part of the group. We thought of ourselves as the "Seven Sisters + 1." Other black students came and went from the table, but Harold stayed.

Group conversations were the norm—exuberant and rowdy. We eventually gravitated to a semi-secluded, medium-sized dining alcove just off the main dining area where we felt free to be ourselves with ourselves. Some called it the "Black Table" and stated that we were segregating ourselves, but eating meals and socializing together just seemed natural. I never thought of the table as self-imposed segregation. It was just family having a family meal. In many respects, it was like my family gathering at home in Norfolk with people coming in and out, ebbing and flowing like the tides. Everyone at the table had different experiences, and I loved it. Black students at Swarthmore accepted me as I was, and that was a great feeling.

People largely accepted you for who you were at Swarthmore. I never felt that I had to conform. The cool kids were just as individualistic as I was. I was definitely no longer the smartest person in the room, which was an entirely new feeling for me. I was glad to know that there were people who were as smart or smarter than I. Smart kids in my hometown were estranged from most people, and the school herd mentality leaves the academically gifted isolated, set apart, knowing that there is something different about them. At Swarthmore, I was just a regular student, as bright as the rest.

As the dining room circle expanded, the outside world intruded, especially the events of the Civil Rights Movement. Stories of the contrast between raw Southern racism and Northern and Midwestern racism resonated with all of us. Black consciousness became a part of life. We educated ourselves and each other through conversation, reading suggestions, and meetings at Swarthmore as well as off-campus. Without my sisters, I felt alone and surrounded by the same indifference I had experienced in high school. In the presence of my sisters, there was warmth and understanding. We could talk about hair, fashion, politics, schoolwork—anything. My birth family was reconstituted with the Seven Sisters and Harold.

Formation of SASS

SASS grew out of the friendships, group experiences, and education that we tried to obtain together. Most black students were fully aware of the lack of diversity in the cultural and social offerings from the College. We decided to form a student group to correct these omissions. Marilyn A. obtained information on the availability of school resources to support student group activities. She prepared and submitted a budget to support our projects, and the funding was approved. All black students were invited, and everyone was welcomed.

Although the Seven Sisters were the core group, none of the women wanted to be the leader. This type of sensitivity was very common during this time. In addition, we felt that the existing power structure was more responsive to male voices. The majority of the visible leaders of the Civil Rights Movement were male, and we wished to maintain this appearance. I do not feel that black women felt as disempowered as white women felt, and so expressions of "girl power" were not as important to us. Our leadership style tended to be more expansive and inclusive versus personality driven. Sam Shepherd, the first SASS chairperson, was even-tempered and could build consensus, considering everyone's thoughts and opinions. Clinton Etheridge was vice chairperson and succeeded Sam as the second chairperson.

All decisions were collective decisions. Students were always free to do their own thing. This way of operating carried over into the "Takeover" with all written and verbal communication being crafted by the group and presented by a designated spokesperson. This style of collaboration was an invaluable model that I have carried with me throughout my professional life and has served me well.

Contrary to news reports from that time, SASS was a home-grown organization and there were no outside influencers/provocateurs of any consequence, at least as pertains to SASS activities on campus. We did have frequent visitors, some with pan-African ideology, who presented a worldview of African peoples that was new for me, but entirely consistent with what I knew about America and its brand of racism. Learning about the different peoples and cultures in Africa—some geographical, some tribal—was eye-opening. I saw this more as a cultural exchange as opposed to politicization.

There were a few people who came to SASS meetings for political purposes. There was a guy who some thought was an FBI operative, and a student from a nearby college who always seemed to be on the edge, wanting political action beyond the point where Swarthmore black students were willing to go.

Individual SASS members participated in other political activism on campus against the Vietnam war, for civil rights, and for women's rights. SASS, however, aspired to introduce black culture and black studies to Swarthmore as an academic interest and to offer a cultural alternative that showcased all we are as a people.

College Life After the Formation of SASS

Getting away from Swarthmore was always a treat. Although the campus was extraordinarily beautiful, it could also be stifling and insular. Riding the Media Local to Philadelphia was exhilarating. I can still hear and feel the rhythm of the rails. The Media Local was my first train ride ever, and the ride was peaceful and intoxicating. Each holiday or school break, some campus organization would charter buses to major cities like New York City, Boston, and Washington, DC. I visited all these places with classmates over several of these breaks and got to experience the freedoms of the road and sightseeing in places that I had only heard about.

When a group of black postbaccalaureate students from HBCUs started coming to Swarthmore, it was a breath of fresh air. Because my home was near several HBCU colleges: Norfolk State, Hampton Institute, and Howard University, I understood the types of cultural experiences and socializing that occurred at these schools, so post BACCs felt like my cousins. They were older. Some were serious and goal oriented, while others were still looking for the party. One person in particular, "Ed," was the consummate partier. Whenever he decided to let go, he brought all of us along with him. Ed drank like a fish at these parties and introduced several of us to its pleasures.

It would be an understatement to say that our college was not known to be a party school. For black students, dating opportunities were limited. The social events sponsored by the College were oriented toward the dominant culture and didn't feel welcoming to someone like me. Typically, only three or four black males were in each class and at least double that number of black females. Couples that did find each other could be seen walking across campus, dining in Sharples, and attending movies, dinner dances, and other College-sponsored social activities. Some relationships were long-lasting and resulted in marriage and family. Not all of us were that lucky. Although a few interracial couples did exist, they were rare in that day. The black women who were uncoupled often found that the black males on campus were either not interested or not willing to approach us. That left us to socialize with each other, to organize SASS-sponsored parties in available campus spaces, and to travel when we could.

Although Bridget was the only one of the Seven Sisters who experienced a lasting relationship at Swarthmore, all of us were supportive of the black males as leaders among us. We were careful not to disparage them and to lift them up where possible, protective of their leadership position as representatives of the race. Whatever challenges we had partnering for dates, when the black students began to meet and organize, participation in group activities was always open and inclusive with everyone sharing their ideas and concerns.

I never had a personal relationship with any of the faculty and don't remember much about them. There was an African sociology professor who mentored several students and even had us over to his house for dinner. A visiting history professor, J. Saunders Redding, taught one of the few black studies seminars that I attended. Interactions with administration, for me, were limited to the written notification of grades and scholarship offerings. I didn't have a faculty advisor or mentor and was left to navigate my education by myself with help from my friends. In that sense, Swarthmore was just like being in high school where I was left to figure out what I wanted all by myself.

The Takeover and Beyond

I was not a part of the planning for the Takeover of the admissions office, but when the plans for action were discussed, I was all in. No one in SASS was in favor of violence, and we all knew this was a principled action that was largely a reaction to a pattern of disrespect from the College administration toward black students. It was the middle of my junior year.

I was not afraid of the action we were taking. If we had not expected it to be peaceful, we would not have taken our valuables—books, record player, music albums, personal items, bedding, and toiletries. I was not a leader in this action, but was content to be a foot soldier. I had confidence in our generals. They were brilliant, principled, and focused, and SASS had always crafted written and oral pronouncements to the College community and media, collectively and by consensus.

Perhaps it was strange that I did not think that the Takeover was endangering my grades or my scholarship. I felt that the white people of Swarthmore were somehow different from the ones I had grown up around in Norfolk. Swarthmoreans were intellectuals, not stirred by the racial polemics of my childhood. There was a civility about Swarthmore, perhaps because of its Quaker roots, that led me to believe that there would be civilized discourse—no dogs, fire hoses, guns, or rabid police. In spite of this conviction, deep down, I concluded that this was not the world where I belonged. Being treated more like the subject of an experiment than a student at the College confirmed my mistrust of mainstream America. I came from a black world, and I discovered that I preferred to live in a black world. I continued to be educated in predominantly white institutions and met all academic expectations, but the black world is ultimately where I have made my home and given my talents.

After the Takeover, our group concentrated on finishing our courses and resuming our individual lives. It was as if we had been stunned by the recent events and scattered to get onto the next phase. We continued to participate in SASS, took classes in black studies, and brought in outside speakers and entertainers, but our mood and sense of urgency changed as we realized that time was short. Maybe we had to get on with the job of fully growing up.

I disappeared into my books taking enough biology courses to major in both chemistry and biology and prepared to take the MCAT and applied to medical school. Medicine offered more human interactions, which I discovered I also craved as opposed to what I perceived as the isolation of pure science. In a way, I think that I was practicing my withdrawal from a group of people who were critical to the beginning of my understanding of myself and how to operate in the world. I had learned that leadership was a skill, did not have to be megalomaniacal, and could occur from a position that was not necessarily on top. I learned to value collaboration and respect for all persons. I learned that a great idea can come from anyone and that it should be shamelessly praised and improved through discourse.

I never wanted to be a leader. I tried to avoid the spotlight, but eventually had leadership thrust upon me because of skills I did not even know that I possessed. SASS was spiritually led by women who allowed the men to come to their own level of black consciousness and encouraged them to explore their leadership skills. The Seven Sisters were individually very different, highly intellectual, and the smartest women I ever met. Being part of the camaraderie and collaboration that occurred so frequently within this group changed me forever. It was a privilege to know them, love them, and grow with them.

By the fall of 1969, my senior year, only three of the original group were left: Bridget, Aundrea and me—although it felt as though Aundrea had already left due to her class schedule and frequent trips back home to Boston. We became the de facto representatives of the old guard. There were many more black students at Swarthmore by that time. I felt so old compared to the eager young faces that were everywhere.

SASS still existed on campus, attempting to institutionalize the gains that had been made the prior year, with new leadership. This new leadership continued to push for change and organized another major confrontation with the College administration and a sit-in that led to the establishment of the Black Cultural Center.

This phase of institutional development has always been less exciting to me rather mundane and lacking the fire and heat of original creation - the soul and guiding principles of a movement. Institutionalization needs the right kind of leadership to identify the right goals, assemble its soldiers, and mobilize others to follow. Neither Bridget nor I was ready to lead. We both were focusing on what was to come next for our professional development. In addition to the usual class work and lab courses, we had to take the standardized graduate school entrance exams, apply, attend interviews, and pray for acceptance and scholarships. We managed to participate in whatever SASS social events were available. I remember doing a lot of knitting that year and falling in love with the music of Roberta Flack. I did the best I could, but did not feel that I had any wisdom to impart to the next generation of black students at the College.

Becoming a General

After the MCAT exams had been taken and medical school interviews completed, I began to appreciate the power of a Swarthmore education. I was accepted into four schools and received scholarship offers, but settled on Tufts University School of Medicine in Boston.

The work and reading in medical school, while intense, was not much different than what was expected at Swarthmore, except that I didn't have to write any papers, and there was no time for activism. I did find time, however, to join the campus and Boston chapters of the national black medical professional associations and work in high school student enrichment programs run by the Nation of Islam.

Many who remember my persona at Swarthmore and in the first half of medical school have wondered how I morphed into the outspoken, largely unfiltered person that I am today. I had never had any academic deficiency in my life, until a letter from the dean in the middle of my clinical rotation in the third year summoned me to his office, threatening my academic progression. One of my evaluators had questioned my mastery of the subject matter because I did not interact well in rounds and other student conferences. I remember being stunned. The dean simply stated, "the squeaky wheel gets the grease," a phrase that has stayed with me and pushed me to change. If I needed to talk so that people would not think that I was stupid, I could do that, and believe me, I did. I came out guns blazing and let everybody know that I knew my stuff. A classmate who had been on a previous clinical rotation with me, several months later appeared dumbfounded when she saw the change in my medical clinical persona.

After graduation, I did my internship and residency in internal medicine followed by additional training to specialize in hematology and medical oncology.

During my fellowship, several life-altering events occurred—I broke my foot, ruptured my appendix, and met my future husband, who had two sons who eventually became my family. Marriage disrupted my plans to return closer to home. I got pregnant on my honeymoon.

I had to have an emergency C-section and nearly died. I was thirty-one, one year older than my biological mother when she died in childbirth. My son did die, and my life would never be the same. I never did have any other children and threw myself into my career and raising our two sons. Ednae had taught me how to love and care for children who were not my own, and I did the best I could to mirror her unconditional love and steady guidance with as little judgment as I could muster. Life is so circular.

Following fellowship training, I went into private practice. I was the first black hematology-oncology physician to practice in the State of Georgia. After a few years, I eventually joined Morehouse School of Medicine (MSM) as one of its first clinical faculty and discovered that teaching was still my passion, although I continued to provide direct patient care.

MSM was a fledgling medical school (of predominantly minority students and faculty) that had limited resources and a mission to train physicians to provide medical care to the underserved. I became consumed by the mission. After a few years, in an unprecedented recognition of my leadership skills, the faculty elected me department chair. I helped design and write the residency program, recruit the core faculty and staff for the Department of Medicine and led the entrance of MSM internal medicine into Grady Hospital, where MSM was in competition with a more established medical school that was unwilling to cede any power. Morehouse had to be present, we had to be good, and indeed, we had to be better to show others the way and prove that we belonged there. We built a creditable residency program.

My experience with black activism at Swarthmore pointed the way for me professionally. In SASS, I had seen collective leadership modeled. The same values carried me through my journey at Morehouse School of Medicine and helped set me up for success. Believing in our mission gave me and my colleagues at MSM the stamina to seek the truth, stand for what is right, and persevere for change.

So I got to teach science, except it turned out to be the art and science of medicine, for more than thirty years, a career that I love and seems to have been made for me. The loving cocoons of my family and the "Seven Sisters + Harold" clearly set me up for success and professional fulfillment. I have never worked a day in my life.

THE TAKEOVER

Day Three

DAY THREE
Flavors of Support

Once daylight came on the third day, we realized that the College administration was not planning to force us out—at least not yet. It was Saturday, and we figured they were unlikely to feel the urgency to resume business as usual on the weekend. Little did we know that they were working around the clock, trying to contain the unexpected publicity and scrutiny they had begun to receive from supporters and detractors of our action.

Additional black students joined us after their classes ended for the week. Some climbed through the window, sheepishly, after the sun had gone down, avoiding the press cameras. Others brought possessions with them and we had to unlock the chains to let them in. The size of our group would continue to grow each day as the environment on campus became more polarized. Students whom we had never before thought of as supporters suddenly showed up to join us. It started as a trickle and was quickly becoming a bustling encampment. So far, there was enough space for us to be comfortable, even when we all stretched out to sleep. But would these newcomers stick it out?

Different kinds of supporters began to arrive from other quarters. We had no idea then, but we would find out that ordinary black citizens were not deceived by the hostile press accounts. People may have had no idea of our names or what our protest was about, but they knew we were standing up for black people and began quickly coming to our aid to make sure that we would not be mistreated.

As an example, a year later, during a follow-up SASS sit-in to secure unfulfilled promises from this takeover, eight black employees signed an open letter of support for the students, several of whom had been part of the 1969 action. One of them was Harold Hoffman, highly respected by his peers in the local black community, and over-qualified as the de facto leader among the maintenance staff. He and the few other black employees are the “we” in their letter:

> We went to them tonight to inform them of our support, and came away revitalized... We take this opportunity to express our confidence in them... no matter what the national press and silent majorities say....[14]

Perhaps these adults were even more inclined to publicize their support of the student protesters because of how we had handled ourselves the year before. Quietly, delegations of black citizens brought us edibles much tastier than the sardines and peanut butter that we had packed in advance. We were pleasantly surprised when the first cooked meals arrived. Several communities of black people in nearby Media and Chester also brought food. Total strangers to us, but perhaps church families of black service employees at the College, they cooked hot meals that didn’t need refrigeration, like large pans of macaroni and cheese, and drove to campus to deliver them through the window that was our portal to the world.

Perhaps most surprising was being sent meals by a small group of sympathetic faculty and white students who had raised money to buy us food and have it delivered.

Ironically, and unknown to us until after it was over, a group of four black students had committed to a hunger strike as an expression of their support of our action even though they had not joined the actual sit-in. While they pledged in an open letter to the College community to abstain from regular meals until the situation that precipitated our action had changed, we on the inside were beginning to worry about the abundance of food that was arriving for us.

By the end of day three, we realized that we might eventually have so many occupants and so much food delivered that we'd have to figure out a whole new set of logistical concerns we had never anticipated. How would we keep the premises and ourselves clean and safe?

We Had to Do Something!—Aundrea's Story

AUNDREA WHITE KELLEY

Early Influences

My Irish high school guidance counselor told me not to bother applying to Swarthmore because—according to her—I would never get in. (Today I would characterize this attitude as an example of the soft bigotry of low expectations.) But I was enamored with its beauty. The poster on the bulletin board outside the guidance office depicted a grand, gothic-style building sitting at the end of a gently sloping, tree-lined walkway. In reality, the campus was grander still—one of the most beautiful places I had ever seen. Its beauty reminded me of nature, of camp—those summer camps like the ones that gave low-income, inner-city kids like me a chance to experience fresh air.

I was born an Army Brat in Tokyo, Japan. Daddy called me Tokyo Rose. I smiled when he called me that—he was the brightest flower in *my* garden. He was a proud captain in the US Army. Mommy and Daddy, Flora Belle and Jack, were born in Mississippi, the deepest of the Deep South. One constant in my early years was that our home—whether on a military base in Japan or Germany, or at a US post like Fort Knox, Fort Campbell, or Boston, where we finally settled—was open to all—early Cuban immigrants, former Holocaust survivors and, yes, even white Southerners. Daddy believed strongly in family values, and from his perspective, the family extended beyond his wife and five children. He always said, "Always treat everyone the same. Share what you have. Don't turn people away."

He was forever seeking out new cousins, aunties, and uncles—those who remained in the south or who moved north during the Great Migration—for us to get to know and love. Our house on Alaska Street in Boston became a halfway house as one by one, Daddy brought his extended family up from the Deep South to a better life. He brought his twin sister to Boston and became the surrogate father to her three children. He made sure every child in the family—including his five and her three—was present for picnics and outings. Even if he had to make two car trips to bring along all the family members, he always made a way.

Daddy was the embodiment of World War II's "Greatest Generation." He worked harder and with more boundless enthusiasm, determination, energy, wit, positivity, and caring than anyone else I knew. He was blessed with exceptional intellect, vision, and ability to accomplish. He was proud and humble at the same time. Daddy's father, Tobie, could read and fought in WWI. For a while when their twin children, Jack and Priscilla, were young, Tobie and his wife Lillie lived in rural Alabama. Tobie left the family when my father was about eleven or twelve. My grandmother Lillie could not read or write and could barely survive financially even with the help of extended family nearby. When my father was thirteen, he finished the eighth grade, quit school, and worked to help support his mother and sister. He joined the Civilian Conservation Corps, which was a cornerstone of FDR's New Deal to pull the nation out of the Great Depression. Later, he enlisted in the US Army to fight for his country in World War II. This young black man with an eighth grade education went from chef to company commander and became a father to many of the soldiers he commanded.

As a young army soldier, Daddy came home on leave to visit my mom in Laurel, Mississippi. He had performed honorably in the frozen tundra of Alaska where severe frostbite injuries left him with lifelong pain in his legs and hands. I remember Daddy's emotional pain each time he recalled what should have been a triumphant return. An elderly white man sitting in front of a general store stopped the young Jack White strolling proudly, resplendent in his military uniform.

"What's your name, boy?"

"I am Sergeant Jack White, sir."

"I said, "What's your name, boy?' "

Attempting to accommodate this first confrontation with the past, Daddy responded as a man and looked him in the eye: "My name is Jack White!"

Not satisfied, the old timer barked, "Boy, I said 'What's your name!' "

Dad finally got the message and responded meekly, "Jack." This experience was pivotal to his decision to make his career in the US Army, to do everything in his power to make his country better for all, and to uplift others regardless of their situation or the color of their skin.

Undaunted, Daddy persevered to become a leader of men and women, and he was honored in his lifetime. He received a battlefield commission for leadership and bravery at Normandy, and among his many awards is the Bronze Star, which he donated to history by having it placed in a time capsule that is scheduled to be opened in 2050. Daddy was the original creative problem solver with a solution for everything. He got the black officers' club closed down and cleverly figured out how to integrate the Fort Campbell officers' dining hall by getting one black officer to sit at each table before the white officers arrived. He was the first to integrate officers' housing at Fort Knox by maneuvering into the base's newest housing section. He even worked with both the prosecution and the defense at various times in the US Army Judge Adjutant General's Corps!

Shortly before I came to Swarthmore, and after a hiatus of forty-one years from the time Tobie had left the family, Daddy found his own father sharecropping in the Louisiana Delta and brought him, his wife, and his stepdaughter to Boston, encouraging the stepdaughter to go to school. He traced his grandmother's whereabouts and found her in upstate New York when she was 103 years old and still working full-time as a domestic. It was nothing for him to bundle all of us up in his big car and drive fifteen hours to visit relatives in the Midwest and up and down the East Coast. He drove those long hours without stopping because few motels accepted blacks and he never wanted his children—accustomed to the comforts of the quasi-integration of the military—to be accosted by the harsh realities of racism. Daddy didn't let others see him down. "If you fall off the horse," he'd say, "get up and get back on it."

(As we discussed our families during the planning process for this memoir, one striking common chord was the strong impact of our fathers in our lives. Black Dads Matter!)

From the outside, our home was an ordinary Roxbury multi-family duplex. We settled there when I was in kindergarten and just before our family shipped out to Germany. Alaska Street was a small, one-block street bordered by busy Blue Hill Avenue on one end and Perrin Street, where the neighborhood elementary school was located, on the other. In 1956, the neighborhood was just beginning to experience racial change. Most of our neighbors were white, as was my kindergarten teacher who lived in a red brick apartment building on the end of my street closest to the school. There were a few black families on the street, and at least one was headed by a ranked police officer. A few years later, when we returned from Germany, two-parent black families had started replacing many of the white families. I lived there until the day

I got married, and by that time, black residents populated the street almost entirely.

Next door to us, to the right of our family of four girls and one boy, were Mr. and Mrs. T. who had four boys and one girl. To our left lived a female friend of the man who came to be known as Reverend Ike. Mr. W, a driver for Wonder Bread, one of the Hostess brands, lived across the street. Daddy got a job as the first black route salesman for Hostess. Being a route salesman meant that every morning, before dawn, he was up and out of the house, delivering products to local stores well before the sun rose. Over time, he became a supervisor. He kept meticulous books and regularly sat at the kitchen table to enter and review his figures. I realize now that he likely got his job via the referral of our friendly white neighbor, Mr. W.

When I was in fifth grade, my mom started doing domestic work for a lady who lived in the nearby Jewish enclave of Mattapan and who encouraged her to pursue further education. This caring Jewish woman told Mommy to check out a government-sponsored program called Model Cities. Mommy followed through and became plugged into a network of education and training opportunities targeting "disadvantaged" families. With Mommy working and my older sister in college, it became my responsibility to get my three younger siblings dressed, fed, and off to school on time.

Emily's, the corner store, was the source for most of our staples—milk, bread, bologna, eggs, and other food items. Sometimes we didn't have the money and I had to ask Emily, a warm Italian lady with large brown eyes and brown hair beginning to gray around the edges, to put the amount down as "owing." She never said, "No." I never thought to ask my parents how the accounts got settled. When I did pay cash for something, Emily would put the change in my hand and not throw it on the counter like most white store clerks in Boston did.

Growing up in Boston meant learning quickly which ethnic group lived where. Jews lived in Mattapan and Roslindale, Yankees lived downtown and in Jamaica Plain, Eastern Europeans lived in West Roxbury. Italians lived in East Boston and the North End. Black folks lived in Roxbury. Irish folks lived in South Boston. I learned where the boundaries were that I had better not cross.

When Mommy was ten, her father, John, died of a ruptured appendix near the doors of a white hospital that refused to treat him. My grandmother Josie was devastated. John had been the sole support of the family. He could read and was a foreman at the local mason plant as well as a respected church deacon. With his death and the country falling into the throes of the Depression, my grandmother was in despair. The government had given aid to local preachers to distribute to families in dire straits. Since my grandmother refused to "put out" for the local preacher in charge of her area, she did not benefit from that aid and survived by taking in laundry—washing and ironing—and through the support of friends and family. My mother—just a little girl at the time—went to the fields and picked cotton to help out. Her father had named her Flora Belle, which means "beautiful flower." Still, she felt rejected and looked down upon by others because her skin was darker than that of her brother and sister. Her father lavished attention equally on all three of his kids and at the end of the workday would run down the verdant hill from the mason plant and pull from his pocket candy surprises for each.

Mommy was proud that she and her siblings graduated from Oak Park High School in Laurel, Mississippi. Flora Belle always went to a segregated school with all colored teachers and administrators who looked out for their students. She often recounted the time when the famous colored scientist George Washington Carver had been invited to speak to the white schools in town. The colored principal they sent to pick up Mr. Carver arrived early and brought him to Oak Park High School where he addressed the colored students. He wanted them to have the same opportunity to hear this famous scientist as the white teens and figured out a way to make it happen.

I was a teenager when, after their mother's murder, our "cousins" came to live with us as foster kids. Our household became eligible for a monthly allotment of these gigantic portions of "government food" all wrapped in plain white labels with big letters printed in bold typeface for all to see: CHEESE, MEAT (it was really more like Spam), BUTTER, DRIED NONFAT MILK. Each package must have weighed five pounds and didn't fit inside a bag, so that anyone who saw you transporting them from the pickup location would assume you were poor. Somehow, Mommy figured out how to put these items to good use. When our fresh milk ran out, we turned to canned milk, and when the canned milk ran out during a month, we had the dried milk to fall back on. She drilled into us perhaps her most favorite maxim: where there's a will, there's a way!

I turned fifteen the summer Mommy first took us by train to visit Laurel, Mississippi. We spent time with relatives and enjoyed simple pleasures like gathering in the kitchen with cousins to snap freshly picked green beans. I enjoyed seeing the farm animals, including a somewhat scary-looking bull that I was glad to see enclosed behind a locked gate. I also experienced another first. We kids were walking home around dusk, and while crossing a field, a white man cocked his gun and yelled at us to get off of his property. We ran away as fast as we could. A few days later, we went into downtown Laurel to go to the movies. For the first time, I saw water fountains and restrooms with signs labeled "white" and "colored." A sign on the theater's main entrance directed coloreds to a side entrance where we had to climb stairs to watch the movie from the balcony, even though we paid the same price for admission as the white kids. I was stunned by this, but my excitement about going to a movie (it was only the third time in my life that I had gone to a movie theater) overcame my astonishment. Nevertheless, the insulting image of that sign, "COLORED," with an arrow pointing to the side entrance, is burned into my mind.

Ironically, the overt racism in Laurel, Mississippi was much like Boston's racial environment—except in Laurel, there were signs. Although there were no "whites only" signs on Carson beach or elsewhere in the Irish enclave of South Boston, if you were "colored," you knew if you tried to swim or shop or walk in South Boston streets, there was a tangible risk of being heckled, chased, or beaten up. The animosity was palpable, and the entire country eventually came to see that hatred when court-ordered busing arrived in Boston.

Tourists loved walking Boston's Freedom Trail, but I loved going to Freedom House—a Boston non-profit established in 1949 by black activist social workers Muriel and Otto Snowden to promote integration and self-help for low-income people of color in the city. Freedom House provided a neutral location—not officially affiliated with a particular church, union, or political party—for helpful community services: information about educational and employment opportunities, help with completing forms, tutoring, and social capital—i.e., connections with influential Boston area people of color—pastors, educators, law enforcement, and connections to government figures. The Snowdens were a world away from the blue-collar folks who came through 29 Alaska Street. The Snowdens were college-educated, well-dressed, politically aware, light-skinned with silky hair, and articulate in their impassioned advocacy about the black community's concerns. I can remember seeing their photos many times in Boston's newspapers and a couple of times on television news. Eventually, Muriel Snowden was named a MacArthur Fellow for her transformational civic leadership and community organizing. Freedom House was a meeting ground for parents, too, although I was always in the youth programs and didn't know what the adults talked about. During the fight for better education, parents—including my own—pulled us out of regular public school, and we went to Freedom House for classes offered by educators from the community. I loved the energy that shot through my core when we marched in the streets carrying signs demanding an equal education. Even though I was young, I felt a sense of pride and determination as I internalized the messages in our freedom songs:

> Ain't gonna let nobody turn me round, turn me round, turn me round,
>
> Ain't gonna let nobody turn me round,
>
> I'm gonna keep on a-walking, keep on a-talking, marching into freedom land.

When the Boston Schools Superintendent Louise Day Hicks, a politically connected Irishwoman from South Boston, defied the integration of the schools, we had the biggest march of all—singing louder than ever the updated words of our theme song:

> "Ain't gonna let Louise Day Hicks turn me round!"

It was Roxbury vs. South Boston, "colored" vs. white, poor vs. poor. The courts ordered supervised integration, including busing where necessary to achieve racial balance among the schools. The white Irish, except for the poorest families, fled to towns south of the city like Quincy, Weymouth, and

Marshfield. They were not going to force their kids to go to school with kids like me. It was a confusing time. I wondered what was wrong with our being in the same school.

Boston was noted for education–home of the first public school, the first university, the teachers' education movement, the best private schools, and Boys' Latin and Girls' Latin, the highly praised, six-year exam schools. What better school system to attend, right? I was one of eight black girls in my class at Girls' Latin. During my first year at Girls' Latin, I felt uncomfortable being the only black kid in my classes. But that experience certainly prepared me for my minority status in so many Swarthmore classes.

It wasn't until I got to Swarthmore that I came to understand the shortcomings of the Boston Public Schools and began to reflect on the attitudes toward black kids some of my teachers displayed—contemptuous attitudes like those of my fifth grade teacher, Mr. C, who regularly lined up all the black boys in class and hit them painfully with the rattan. (I could never figure out what the infractions were.) There were careless attitudes like that of my sixth grade teacher who regularly put two students, my friend A., and me, in charge of our classmates while she went out of the classroom for lengthy unexplained breaks. Then there were the condescending attitudes like those expressed by ninth grade English teacher Ms. T, who, in trying to give me a compliment, insulted my background and community as she raised her thick Armenian eyebrows, peered over her dark-rimmed glasses, and said in her high-pitched voice, "Even a rose can grow in dung!"

Although like Boys' Latin, Girls' Latin boasted six years of a classical high school curriculum, we girls endured under-resourced facilities, pared down science labs, and worn, outdated textbooks. Although students at both Latin Schools were overwhelmingly white, it was as if Boston Public Schools had decided that the boys were more worthy of the best BPS had to offer. At Girls' Latin, success in most subjects depended on memorization and regurgitation. Teachers seemed to care less about encouraging or rewarding creative, independent thought in the classroom.

Fortunately, my education was not limited to the classroom, and my active life growing up helped prepare me for my activist life at Swarthmore. Mommy's philosophical principle about child raising was to keep us busy. In fact, Grandma used to tell her that she kept us *too* busy, but Mommy believed in structured activities as a way to keep her brood of five out of trouble. Daddy was always working, and Mommy didn't drive, so when some place was too far to walk, we took the bus or subway. Boston was home to one of the nation's earliest mass transit subway systems. As long as we stayed away from South Boston where it was not safe for us, black kids could use public transit to get to pretty much anywhere notable in Boston or Cambridge. I loved going to the Egyptian exhibit at the Museum of Fine Arts which first got me interested in archaeology. I loved the exquisite dollhouse collection at the Children's Museum, which helped me imagine how exciting it would be to live in a perfect house with fine furniture. In high school, my best friend A. and I sometimes would ride the subway to Boston Common or Harvard Square and "people watch." We delighted in seeing passersby do a double take when they heard the two of us speaking fluent German! Using public transportation helped contribute to my emerging sense of confidence, adventure, and independence.

Just as happened at Swarthmore when we left campus to learn more about black culture, when I was growing up, my world was not confined to the geographic limits of how far my feet could carry me. Just as the books in my local public library transported my mind, the MBTA transported me to a rich variety of places and people, places like Arlington Street Church and people like M. Goldyth Myers, director of the Camp Fire Girls group my sisters and I belonged to. Mommy didn't feel that the Girl Scouts in Boston were welcoming and inclusive of brown kids, so she put us in Camp Fire Girls. Ms. Myers had done graduate work in social work and we, her Camp Fire charges, were the beneficiaries. Camp Fire had a big impact on my life. We met every Saturday during the school year in the basement of the historic Arlington Street Church located downtown near the renowned Newbury Street shopping district. I was a Camp Fire Girl from elementary through high school. Camp Fire's structure and program reflected elements of Native American culture. I couldn't wait until I reached Horizon Club level so that I could wear a Native American-style fringed garment! We earned specially-designed beads and emblems for completing assigned projects. In this way, we competed against common standards instead of against each other. Camp Fire's motto was WoHeLo—shorthand for Work, Health, and Love. Every meeting began with singing or reciting the Law of Camp Fire:

> Worship God, hmmmmm
>
> Seek beauty, give service and knowledge pursue
>
> Be trustworthy ever in all that you do
>
> Hold fast on to health and your work glorify
>
> And you will be happy
>
> It's the Law of Camp Fire.

Just as much as the words of the songs I sang every week at church, these words became ingrained in me, and I truly sought to live up to their meaning—before, during, and after Swarthmore.

The historic Charles Street AME Church was my hub away from home. I was at the church three or four days each week. Sundays started with 8:00 a.m. morning worship, followed by Sunday School at 9:45. If the children's choir was also scheduled to sing at the 11:30 a.m. service, we stayed for that one—which ran until 1:00 or even 1:30 on a first Sunday. We walked home for Sunday dinner and then headed back to church for Youth Group at 4:00. Weekly choir rehearsals, planning meetings for special events, and rehearsals for musicals, plays, and seasonal church presentations filled out our weeks. Every Sunday I was in the choir stand—usually passing notes to my best friend A. (once the sermon started!). Although I may have missed the point of some of pastor's messages, the words of the Decalogue with each command followed by the incantation, *Lord have mercy upon us and incline our hearts to keep this law,* penetrated my heart and shaped the person that I was becoming.

It was only later in life after I began working with church kids that I realized the sacrifice of time, talent, and social capital given by the role models who volunteered to work with the youth of Charles Street AME. Mrs. Bagwell directed operettas—like *Cinderella*—and gave a girl with brown skin the chance to be the star. Her son played classical piano at a time when few African Americans went to Symphony Hall. She ran her own day care center, and all of her children became college-educated professionals. Our pastor, Rev. Walter C. Davis, was well connected and led a large, politically active, growing, responsible congregation. There were special afternoon and evening services when we sang freedom songs, always ending—swaying and with hands clasped one over the other—with the song "We Shall Overcome."

I loved music and always wanted to play the piano. I signed myself up for free solfège and piano lessons at a United South End Settlement House and tried my best to master the keyboard. We didn't have a piano at home, and since I knew we couldn't afford one, I tried to practice on the pianos at church whenever I could by arriving early for choir rehearsal and youth group meetings. Much as I tried, I couldn't get in enough practice time and gave up on the lessons. I tried to satisfy my love of music by singing in the church youth choirs, school glee club, All City Chorus, and Elma Lewis' performing arts groups. I also loved competition and, for me, that meant participating in competitive sports: community track (100-yard dash and 4 x 100 relay), basketball (a terrible shot, but fierce defender, and I could pass), and volleyball (no one could return my serve, and my high school team won the All City Championship my senior year).

Reading was my passion and anytime I wasn't out of the house for one of my never-ending activities, I would read the *Encyclopedia Americana* or *Merriam-Webster Dictionary*, random fliers, cereal boxes—anything in the house that had words on it. From the time we got back from Germany, I walked to the small local public library weekly. After reading through nearly all of its collection, I began walking to the larger library, which was about twice as far away, but which contained books I had not read. After going through that larger collection, I started taking the MBTA to Boston's esteemed main library at Copley Square.

Swarthmore

At Swarthmore, I was so excited about my first English assignment because the professor asked for *my* interpretation of a poem. I was crushed at the comments and the grade I received when I gave my interpretation. I felt pretty defeated because—

despite my outstanding grades, high SAT performance, and personal efforts to drink in all the knowledge I could, in and out of school—something must have been missing from my academic preparation.

A feeling of aloneness descended on me gradually during my first few days as a freshman college student at Swarthmore. My activities were like those of any other college freshman. I moved my meager belongings into the one-room double shared with my roommate, attended orientation, stood patiently in lines to register for classes, and learned about the College's athletics, student organizations, and other extracurricular activities. As a first-generation college student, each of these experiences was foreign to me. But I was eager to plunge into the College life. There was a flyer announcing a mixer sponsored by one of the big fraternities. The one experience I thought typified *college* more than anything was the College mixer. The mixer represented liberation from the strictures and structures of my sheltered life. Off I went! But when I got to the mixer, I stood next to the wall.

The hall was packed with students talking, dancing, laughing, and enjoying beer flowing from giant kegs. Apart from me, everyone seemed to be chatting easily with someone else, comfortable and relaxed. I didn't know a single soul in the room. I didn't see any other students who looked like me. An introvert by nature, I mustered up the considerable courage it took to try to make eye contact and strike up conversations with fellow students, but responses never went beyond a polite hello. In those days, the guys asked the girls to dance and not the other way around. That didn't happen, and I couldn't get the girls to talk with me either. Feeling simultaneously ignored and as if I were standing out like a sore thumb was a strange phenomenon for me. To get away from the wall for a few minutes, I went to the ladies' bathroom, where I encountered girls throwing up—from beer, I imagine. I was horrified! At that point, I left the ladies' room, brightly lit and with pink accents, and I left the mixer with its multi-colored, rotating lights. I was downcast at not having been able to connect with any fellow students.

I was the only black student in my classes and in my dorm, Parrish Hall. My roommate, Debbie, was a pleasant, quiet, dark-haired Quaker girl from a nice leafy town nearby. Debbie brought a record player from home and when she was studying, played classical music on vinyl 33s. I learned to enjoy Bach and grew especially fond of one of Debbie's favorites, "Jesu Joy of Man's Desiring."

Sitting in my dorm one evening during those early days at Swarthmore, I began to feel a sense of doom. Debbie had gone home for the weekend. I was alone and disappointed after the mixer. My throat began to close up. My tongue felt paralyzed. I needed help. It was dark out, a mild fall night. I didn't see anyone else as I hastened toward the health center. With each step, my sense of dread intensified. I wondered whether I could keep breathing long enough to make it to the Center or if I would pass out and die—utterly alone—along the way. Gone was the comfort of the familiar replaced by strange spaces, strange people, strange ways, and now a strange and never before felt sense of absolute fear. I kept walking.

Somehow, I made it to the student health center. When the nurse asked me questions, the paralysis of my tongue caused me to struggle with my responses. I couldn't articulate what I was feeling. I couldn't explain aloud what was wrong with me. I wondered what she thought of me. Eventually she gave me some medication to relax and had me lie down in a plain, quiet room. Slowly, I began to recover from what I now recognize was a panic attack and, in a few hours, returned to my dorm room. It was still dark outside.

When the next day dawned, I wondered, "Why did I feel alone—apart?"

It's not as if I was uncomfortable around people of difference. Being a person of color in Boston always felt like being part of an unwanted, barely tolerated minority—in school, at the city's retail establishments, at sporting and cultural events, in the workplace, or just walking down the street in one of Boston's white neighborhoods. But at the end of the day, home, church, community, friends, and family always beckoned—welcoming me, appreciating me, and wrapping me in the comfort of the familiar. Was that comfort the source of the confidence I had always been able to muster? From whence had my strength come?

Connections

After a couple of weeks, I began to connect with other Swarthmore black students at Sharples Dining Hall and during the mandatory Collection in Clothier Hall.

I felt an immediate connection to Joyce. We were both from Massachusetts, played basketball in high school, had grown up in large families, and both ended up at Swarthmore. Joyce was like a sister, anchor, and friend all rolled into one. I also found solace in Marilyn A.'s room listening to James Cleveland—especially *Peace Be Still.* Despite the Quaker milieu in which Swarthmore was steeped, for me, Marilyn A. was more of a spiritual touchstone. Like Marilyn A., Marilyn H. was one class ahead of me. I saw them both as genius-level leaders. Marilyn A. was naturally gifted to energetically spearhead strategic planning—I visited her house in New York during school break in the fall of '68 to help plan the Takeover. Marilyn H. seemed to always have exactly the right words when we worked on drafting statements. She also had a rare, spellbinding oratorical delivery and presence when addressing a group. I viewed Harold as a Renaissance brother. He was always aware of the latest—the latest music, special events, and interesting speakers—and willing to help transport his Swarthmore pals in his stylish, shiny green, vintage 1953 Chevy Belair auto, whose cast iron engine hummed smoothly as it carried us along highways and city streets.

Bridget, Myra, Jannette, and I were in the same entering class. I began to spend more time with them enjoying the camaraderie and laughing at common experiences, both in our upbringing and as students at Swarthmore. I found myself spending more time in their rooms in Willets Hall. It wasn't that I intended to exclude students from other racial backgrounds; it was more the sheer delight of finding kinsmen. Our laughter helped sustain me. The College may not have been able to provide us with the comfort of home, but we began to create our own. After some time, our desire to have our people and culture represented and included in meaningful ways at Swarthmore led us to become a cohesive group. I began to thrive. I stopped feeling alone.

How would I have survived Swarthmore without my adopted "siblings"? Jannette's wit was (and is) incomparable. We were studying—of course—but oh how we laughed and talked about experiences with secondary school mates, former teachers and authority figures, and siblings and parents—and laughed some more! Myra was the first southern belle that I came to know. She was beautiful, graceful, circumspect, easy to talk with, and—like the other Swarthmore sisters—exceptionally smart. Bridget, like Myra, was another brilliant science major who spent the majority of her afternoons in the lab. She was the first person I met from Guyana and the first person whom I knew with three middle names. The four of us from the class of '70 were close. We studied together, laughed together, talked about guys and politics and justice and the swimming requirement and what we felt Swarthmore needed in order for black students to have a genuine academically and culturally complete college experience.

Because of my Swarthmore siblings, I experienced a sense of normalcy. I began to understand what my professors wanted and returned to achieving the solid academic performance that I had been used to pre-Swarthmore. Our dogged pursuit of knowledge about black people broadened my horizons in ways I never expected. Looking back, I wonder—how could it have been that I, a voracious reader since primary school, had never encountered tomes that delved into the rich history, culture, accomplishments, and intellectual thought of Africa's children, no matter when or where they were in the world? As the Takeover unfolded, the courage and determination of early black activists inspired me. I was so motivated by what I was learning through our black studies course that I chose the topic "Garvey and Garveyism" for my senior thesis.

Love Story

During a Kappa boat ride in Boston Harbor the summer before my freshman year at Swarthmore, I met Bob. Bob was an engineering student at Tufts University near where he grew up. Despite being in different states, we began to correspond and visited each other whenever we could. We had so much in common—our dads had both been army officers and our families had both lived in Germany when we were in primary school. Our mothers were active in their churches and communities. We enjoyed live music and nature and sports. As we visited each other's campuses, we got to know each other's friends and eventually fell in love.

Whenever I heard the song, "Gee Whiz," I thought of Bob.

> Gee whiz, look at his eyes; Gee whiz how they

> hypnotize...he's got everything a girl could want, man oh man, what a prize!

I played this 45 vinyl record by Carla Thomas over and over and over until it finally warped! Years later, I learned that Carla was the sister of Vaneese Thomas, a Swarthmore alum and founding director of its famed gospel choir. After that, Bob met Vaneese at a performance of the choir and told her about the impact of her sister's song on our love story.

In our frequent letters and occasional phone calls, Bob and I exchanged information about the activist "goings on" at our campuses and spent many hours discussing socio-political issues with our college friends. Tufts's black students moved in parallel fashion to Swarthmore's to demand greater support from their campus administration. As happened at Swarthmore, the students created black studies courses. Bob was a founding member and officer of the Tufts Afro-American Society. During his senior year, he became the first residential advisor for the men's dorm section of Tufts's newly-established Afro-American Cultural Center.

Bob, an audiophile, seemed always to be on top of the latest songs and groups that served as the backdrop of our young lives. One group of studio musicians, the Funk Brothers, were not widely known as individual artists, but he could always distinguish their unique style on Motown's biggest hits, songs that were the rhythm of young activism:

> Bet you're wondering how I knew, about your plans to make me blue...
>
> well I heard it through the grapevine.

As black students, we had our own grapevine. Moreover, like the Funk Brothers, Swarthmore's black cafeteria and custodial workers were engaged behind the scenes, their contributions unacknowledged and their names and voices unknown to most. How ironic that inside the admissions office the musical sounds of the underappreciated Funk Brothers uplifted us, even as the unnamed black employees at Swarthmore were working behind the scenes to feed us, encourage us, and look after our safety. (Years later, I was truly moved by seeing one of Swarthmore's caring black workers recognized by the College and hearing *her* voice as she addressed the vast audience assembled for the inauguration of Swarthmore's first black president.)

Takeover Memories

By the time of our planning session at Marilyn A.'s house, our patience with the College administration had run out. By the numbers, the black student presence at Swarthmore was under threat of perishing. The presence of black faculty, administrators, and staff had never gained traction. The presence of black studies in the College curriculum was absent. Meanwhile, the presence of the Hargadon Report in the library represented yet another glaring example of the College's disrespect of its black community. Could the public dissemination of the report have been a form of retaliation against black students for raising our voices about our concerns?

I felt driven, yet resolute, calm, and focused. I didn't know what a Gantt Chart was in those days, but our approach to planning was just as meticulous and thorough. We had tried to prepare for every eventuality, and we managed to remain on top of things throughout, even in the face of that singular event we would encounter that we could not possibly have foreseen.

In the days before the Takeover, I had zero fear and absolutely no hesitancy about the action we were about to take. And once inside, that peaceful mood continued, no matter how turbulent it was outside the admissions office. We worked on getting the College to respond to our demands, studying all the while. We truly were, as Jannette once characterized us, peaceful nerds.

Where did this assurance come from? Was it the naiveté of youth? Or had our common struggle engendered a tight bond among most black Swarthmore students? Or could it be that we were undergirded by our faith in God and in the justice of our cause? As Marilyn A. and I, serving as the advance guard, spoke quietly to the administrative staff in Parrish that first day, the words of James Cleveland's "Peace Be Still" were ringing through my mind.

> Carest Thou not that we perish?
>
> How canst Thou lie asleep
>
> When each moment so madly is threatening
>
> A grave in the angry deep?...
>
> No water can swallow the ship where lies
>
> The Master of ocean and earth and skies
>
> They all shall sweetly obey my will, peace, peace be still

I didn't have a sleeping bag. Instead, I had fashioned my own, sharing with fellow students the technique I learned as a Camp Fire Girl: roll a blanket and sheet tightly around your pillow–neatly of course–and loop a belt around the roll to hold it securely in place and use as a convenient handle.

I always enjoyed taking notes and had plenty of experience doing so in the classroom, but also from serving in that role in church and community organizations. Who would have thought that the summer typing course I took for fun before my junior year in high school, or the mimeograph machine I learned to use at church, would come in so handy in preparing SASS announcements, flyers, and statements? I used composition notebooks for my SASS notes.

When I prepared to come home in the spring, those notes, along with all of my worldly possessions, were stolen. The night before leaving, I had packed my car so that I could get an early start. What was I thinking? Because of my student teaching practicum, I lived in North Philly and should have been more aware of the possibility that loading my car in full view of my neighbors was not wise. That car contained my clothes, books, letters, records, school papers, and my precious SASS notes. I was leaving school early because I was physically sick, but when I came outside the morning of my planned departure and saw that my car was gone, I was crestfallen. The police came, took a report, and even drove me around looking for the car, but there was not a trace. Many years later, after reading the FBI file and learning that we black students had been under surveillance by the FBI's Media Field Office (the same one involved in the Watergate burglary), I wondered whether the FBI had anything to do with the theft of my car and my irreplaceable SASS notes.

Post-Takeover

When I returned to Swarthmore for my senior year in the fall of '69, I was a de facto commuter student. I scheduled my classes from Tuesday through Thursday to make it easier for me to both keep up with my studies and spend long weekends with Bob when possible. While on campus, I continued with post-Takeover SASS, including serving on the College's Ad Hoc Black Admissions Committee which met in the fall semester and issued its report in January. It was comprised of five students and five faculty—including Dr. Legesse—and administrators (including the first black assistant dean, Dean William Cline), and its existence was a direct outcome of the Takeover. In addition to recommendations on black student recruitment and admissions, the Committee's work led to the publication of a brochure called "Black at Swarthmore."

During spring semester, I had an education internship at a North Philadelphia elementary school and lived off-campus near the school. I was assigned to assist the teacher in a special ed classroom—in those days there was no mainstreaming—with about ten students—all black boys, as I recall. Although I had enjoyed working with students all my life until that point—from tutoring primary kids in phonetics when I was in elementary school, through my college years when I tutored high school kids as an Upward Bound Counselor—these students displayed behavioral issues that were foreign to me. I became disillusioned and convinced that the classroom was not for me. Yet, I remained interested in education. My parents had drilled the importance of education into me and my siblings. Swirling in the background was the fight for a quality education for *all* of Boston's public school kids. That education was key to opportunity is a concept that has pulsed through me since I can remember.

As I watch students today decrying gun violence in Parkland, Florida, I see that their sentiments are similar to those we experienced at Swarthmore. I see that same spirit: teens feel they have to take it upon themselves to do something because the adults in positions of power have not been able (or willing) to create change. Who would have thought that fifty years later, the country would be in a situation that required students to advocate for themselves? I remember the feeling in 1969 that nothing was going to change. That no influential adults were listening to us. That *we* had to do something.

My class at Swarthmore had ten black students. The class before had twenty. Nothing was changing. Our parents were caught up in struggles of their own, battling other issues of the era. Swarthmore College demonstrated no sense of urgency when it came to considering—let alone resolving—our concerns. As our small planning group met at Marilyn A.'s house to finalize logistics, we were resolved. We had had enough of waiting on the College to address our concerns seriously. We had to be our own advocates. We had to take it upon ourselves to create change. We had to take a stand.

Post-Swarthmore, I experienced several "firsts" as an African American in the professional workplace. Why was this? It was the many lessons learned growing up at 29 Alaska Street and growing up some more at Swarthmore. I didn't rule out any position of interest just because I was a person of color. Somehow, despite majority culture views and stereotypes to the contrary, I didn't view my color as a limitation. I felt confident in my degree from the top-ranked liberal arts college in the US. I had been the lone African American in so many circumstances and wasn't hesitant to interact with whites.

My lack of preparation in the Boston Public Schools became a motivational factor for me in my professional advocacy for aligned, high-quality education from preschool through college and career.

The Takeover crystallized for me that ordinary people—no matter their age—have the ability to push for justice. I learned the importance of careful planning, a diverse set of skills, and teamwork. To paraphrase George Washington Carver's message to my mother's high school class, "God has given you two hands and one brain and that's all you need."

My experience working in teams at church, Camp Fire, and at Swarthmore helped shape my ability to cross boundaries and quietly steer, manage, and encourage others to pursue a goal from concept to implementation. Eventually, I earned an MBA and an MS in Public Policy, both from the University of Massachusetts Boston. SASS's collective approach to problem-solving meant listening carefully to each other's perspectives and understanding and acting on agreed upon policy positions and roles. This approach helped shape my own approach to public service. When I had the opportunity to create my own unit and title, I chose "Deputy Commissioner for P-16 Policy and Collaborative Initiatives." In this role, I was able to—for the first time in Massachusetts' state education agency history—formally bring together the Commonwealth's education boards to collectively address issues across the education continuum. I also broke ground in my public policy career by rising from graduate intern to being named the first African American female to serve as Massachusetts Commissioner of Higher Education.

Given the brilliance, accomplishments, and upbringing of my Swarthmore friends and their families, I had never been sure that a working-class "ghetto" girl educated in one of the worst urban school systems had a story worth telling. But my story interweaves with *our* story. The eight of us. Standing up for change. That's what we are all about.

THE TAKEOVER

Day Four

DAY FOUR
Sunday Morning

It was Sunday morning, four days into what we originally thought would have been a shorter occupation. We had been living together around the clock, defining our version of a sit-in. Aundrea was in charge of the music, and with her stereo played José Feliciano to wake us up in the morning and put us to sleep at night. This morning, we listened to and sang along with gospel songs by the Staple Singers and Aretha Franklin. As the spirit moved, different students shared inspirational thoughts that buoyed us.

Unlike the caricature that had been made of us in the national media as angry, disrespectful haters of the established order, most of the leaders throughout our months of advocating for change were driven by their spiritual and moral beliefs and were adherents of the Civil Rights Movement's commitment to seeking change without violence or hate. We were anti-war and participated in peace marches, but we were not anarchists. Rather than relying on negative emotions, we drew on spiritual and cultural resources to refuel in the face of disrespect, indifference, and even rejection.

Each day since the Takeover began, the atmosphere inside the admissions office was quiet and peaceful. The large sheets of paper taped to the grand office windowpanes shielded us from view day and night. Being serious students as a way of life, we made a point of getting our necessary sleep. We studied throughout the occupation, keeping the faith with most of us not leaving the premises until we were forced to.

Photographs of what went on inside the occupied offices were never sought out by the media. Most of the few that remain were taken by Harold. Although he wasn't the official

SASS photographer, Harold could always be seen on campus with a camera around his neck. His pictures provide most of what visually documents our activities in college.

The Takeover images could have been taken at a large family gathering, with everyone casually interacting. One is of first-year student Roy seated on a desk chair with a classmate, Francis, cornrowing his hair in the subdued light of day. Another shows Myra braiding the hair of Ade, a student from Africa who may have been risking his status as an international student by joining our protest. The other photo of Myra on a stuffed chair at night, lit only by the flashlight she used to study her large textbook, is evidence that we all hoped to take final exams in the weeks ahead. Three dozen or so students lay scattered throughout the cramped living space, all over the carpet in sleeping bags and blankets in a random pattern like pickup sticks that had been throw up in the air. No nightgowns or pajamas here, the same clothes were worn around the clock with infrequent trips to the bathroom for personal hygiene. The black and white images remind us of the newspapers, duffel bags, canned food, crackers, and disposable aluminum baking pans scattered about. One color photo has also survived. In it, Aundrea, Bridget, Jannette, and Myra, the four sisters in the class of 1970, are pictured sitting together in the upholstered armchairs of the admissions office, deep in conversation as they so often were in the times leading up to the Takeover.

It was exhilarating to realize that we had gained the support of nearly all of the black students despite our differences. By the end of the occupation, there were only a handful of black students who had not participated. We welcomed all who came to join. Camaraderie masked any fear we felt. Evenings, after eating, we would relax and retell highlights of the day or week, often chuckling at the irony of it all.

We didn't discuss it, but there was a big elephant in the room on Sunday night. The next morning would be the start of a work week and the last week of classes for the fall term. Would the College continue its virtual shutdown of normal business? The pressure to force us out would be intense. Students needed to complete their courses and seniors needed to get ready to graduate and move on to graduate schools and jobs. Would they turn against us? No matter. We could not turn back now.

SASS—On Our Own

MARILYN ALLMAN MAYE

Black Recruitment

We realized that if we were going to increase the black presence on campus, we could not rely on the personnel in the admissions office to find qualified black students. We would have to find them ourselves and convince them to come to Swarthmore. And most of them had never heard of the place.

We figured that, eventually, they would have to hire a black admissions officer whose job it would be to know where top black students were. We were going to first have to prove that those students were out there.

We discussed looking more closely at the high school students several of us tutored in the Upward Bound program from Chester and the nearby towns. We knew that if some of them had a chance to come here for college, they could succeed.

Joyce was a senior and was applying to Harvard Graduate School of Education for her master's. She had been a dedicated tutor for years and a student teacher at the high school in town. She knew there were talented black students out there. She suggested that we return to the high schools that we graduated from and see if there were at least one or two students who might come to a weekend on campus. If we made it interesting and fun, they might be convinced. She drafted a letter to high school guidance counselors while some of us worked on making sure the students had a great time during their visit.

We decided to put them up in our dorm rooms and get the College to pay their bus or train fares and meals. We identified impressive and inspiring speakers, poets, and artists from Philadelphia or DC. We planned a party for Saturday night that would introduce them to other black students and to our ways of socializing on campus. We realized we would need more than was available in our SASS budget and would have to submit a formal funding request to the administration.

We probably spent at least one evening a week in one of the dining hall meeting rooms with Aundrea taking notes at every session. We debated plans, programs, and educational options, and then ran back to our dorms or the library to finish reading assignments and papers.

Some photographs from our first Black Recruitment Weekend in spring 1968 show high schoolers who would actually go on to apply and be admitted as freshmen before we graduated and become SASS leaders in the years afterwards. Our first effort had been a success.

As far as we know, we were the first to create the concept of a Black Recruitment Weekend which has since become a staple of admissions practices at many predominantly white institutions seeking to attract talented black enrollees. We may never know how much our own schoolwork suffered while we provided hours of unpaid labor to the College's admission efforts. Eventually, they saw the benefit and hired the first of several black admissions officers. In later years, some black alumni became admissions officers, recruiting students of all demographics.

Although none of us earned our advanced degrees in the field of higher education leadership, given our experiences advocating for change in college, it is not surprising that most of the Seven Sisters have spent decades in the field, as professors, administrators, and board members.

Negro History Week Soul Food Dinner Snafu

Not every SASS project turned out as successful as the first Black Recruitment Weekend. A case in point was our first

Negro History Week observance that began with a Soul Food Dinner in the campus dining hall.

"You people cost us hundreds of dollars last night," the food services contractor blared, his face beet red.

His neck was bulging over the top of his too-small shirt collar. Perspiration was glistening on his cheeks.

"We couldn't give away all those pigs' feet that nobody ate. It was a disaster."

This was not a member of the Quaker elite. He looked as though he would have tried to punch us if one of the College administrators was not in the room. The food service contractor was the only male, along with a white female college administrator and two nineteen-year-old African American students, Marilyn A. and Aundrea.

His resistance to our request for a single night with a culturally sensitive menu had been masked when we had first met with him and the dean a few months earlier.

"Our cooking staff know how to prepare all kinds of food. Sure, Dean. We can prepare whatever you want. What is the date?"

"February 7th?" The Dean looked to us to verify the date.

"And you want fried chicken and collard greens? We have never fried chicken for a meal here before. I don't know if collard greens are available that time of year. We may have to substitute another green vegetable if we can't get them in bulk."

"But, the pigs' feet. Umm. We will have to speak to the wholesaler. I've never heard of an order like that. I will have to investigate."

"Well, all the cooks are Afro-American. We're sure they will know how to prepare fried chicken as well as pigs' feet and the black-eyed peas. You should meet with them ahead of time and make sure you have the right seasonings."

We continued. "This will be Negro History Week, and we want to expose the whole student body to the culture and traditions of African Americans and bring the observance to their attention."

We had lessened the impact by calling the event a Soul Food Dinner, not unlike observances of other ethnic celebrations on campus.

"Yes, just like the shepherd's pie and corned beef and cabbage and cake with green icing for Saint Patrick's Day. Everyone notices that it's a holiday being observed that evening."

Then came the microaggression, although we didn't have that word in 1967.

"I have an idea," he offered smiling. "Why don't you Negro students dress up in black shirts and skirts or trousers, with white collars, and help the servers dish out the food?"

He was serious. And he got away with it because we hadn't learned how to threaten to report him to Human Resources for a racially insensitive remark disguised as a friendly suggestion.

We endured the stab we felt in our hearts and politely declined, saving our expressions of outrage for our retelling to the rest of the group when we gathered to report on our Negro History Week project activities. Through the entire interaction, the Dean offered no words of support.

"He just couldn't resist the temptation to put us in our place."

"So, the darkies are supposed to serve the food to the white students in honor of Black History. How's that supposed to look?"

It took a while to calm down, but, as always, we did. We had lots more to plan. We had to confirm the arrangements for the performance of African American folk singer and songwriter Len Chandler. He had marched with Dr. King and we had invited him for the whole college to hear at the Soul Food Dinner. Later the same evening, then-Rhodesian freedom fighter David M'pongo was expected, and we had to arrange for his transportation. We were finalizing arrangements for three more concerts that week—gospel music, African dance, and jazz. And all of us had to complete homework assignments for classes the next day.

A few days after the drubbing we got from the food services contractor over the uneaten pigs' feet, the headline about the event in the *Phoenix* student newspaper credited SASS with bringing awareness of black history to the campus, but relied on a racist meme for front-page eye-catching humor to describe the event.

oenix

ORE, PENNA. Friday, February 10, 1967

Hog Meat

SASS Brings Soul, Awareness; Alma Mammie Gorges, Listens

Headline from the *Phoenix* after the Soul Food Dinner.

We were too busy trying to coordinate three cultural events to respond to the headline's reference to "mammies." If we responded to every insult that showed up in print, both by whites and sometimes a black student not in SASS, we would never have completed our important work of changing the College.

I don't know if we decided then or after the snafu about all the uneaten pigs' feet, but the whole experience left us deflated and unwilling to put further effort into trying to educate and expose the white students to black culinary culture. We'd get the College to buy only enough soul food for the black students, and we would cook it and eat it ourselves in one of the other campus buildings, which is exactly what we did the following February.

Black History Celebration Sewing Circle

Unlike the contemporary ski chalet design of Sharples Dining Hall, Bond Hall was a maze of black one- and two-story medieval stone buildings with thick, heavy, wooden doors and metal-framed windows that opened outward by pushing metal rods attached to the window sills. In the absence of an official gathering space of our own, SASS made creative use of Bond Hall in ways it had probably never been used before.

You could walk from one small Bond building to another through below-ground passageways and uncarpeted spaces big enough for working on an art project or drama rehearsal. On the ground level were carpeted, living room-like spaces warmly lit by lamps and rarely bright even in daytime hours. With a huge grand piano, and, for some time, a harpsichord on one end, the room could host a small audience for a chamber music concert or students gathered to hear speakers, sitting cross legged on the floor as readily as on the well-padded armchairs. At other times, teachers gave music lessons there or groups and individuals practiced vocals or instruments. For us, Bond was a favorite place to listen to reports on the progress of liberation movements in Southern Africa or to jazz artists who sang or played to mesmerized fans.

Other parts of Bond Hall housed upper-level female students in bedroom suites, and by 1968, several of the SASS women lived there. In winter 1968, we saw the possibility of converting an area in the lower level into a hidden assembly line for creating a couple of dozen African-style "dashiki" shirts for our SASS brothers. The shirts would be surprise gifts for each of them at the Black History Week dinner that we were also planning.

It may have been Jannette and the Marilyns who arranged for the College van to drop a group of us off at the shopping area nearest to campus where you could purchase fabric. The shoppers had returned loaded down with a dozen or more bolts. Finding in a mainstream store cloth designs that could be arranged to simulate West African fashion was no easy feat. Artistic creativity was needed to identify fabric otherwise destined to cover throw pillows or to drape windows, and re-purpose it to create bold designs for chest and back that matched precisely at side seams.

We gathered portable sewing machines and steam irons that we had brought from home and set up an assembly line on the Bond Hall basement tables with space enough to lay out fabric, measure, cut, and stitch enough for the two dozen or more black male students on campus. At every step, there was excited laughing and anticipation of the success of this creative endeavor.

Those sisters who were more experienced guided the others, and everyone contributed what they knew. To safeguard the surprise, we hadn't taken the guys' actual measurements, so all the females involved participated in estimating neck sizes, waists, and back height, from memory, for each of the brothers. The cloth cutting was punctuated by hysterical laughter as we selected which colorful design would look best on which brother.

"Does it really take that much fabric to go around Bob?" Laughter again as the rest of us stopped our job stitching or pressing seams to gape in disbelief at the amount of fabric the more experienced, like Joyce and Aundrea, had cut for a more portly brother. Sisters like Myra and Bridget kept track of the inventory, making sure we didn't forget anyone, and sharing and distributing the tasks of machine stitching seams and hand stitching hems.

While the cutting and sewing could have been tedious, we experienced it as a restorative and fulfilling communal engagement, reminiscent of the quilting bees for which black women of the South were famous. While we worked our assembly line, as always, we exchanged funny stories about our families or campus lives and entertained ourselves. We could intersperse the laughter with problem-solving the challenges of SASS and of life on the margins of the campus.

It was projects like this where the legend of the Seven Sisters was likely cemented. We became known among black students on and off campus as much for our intense ideological discussions and political activism as we were for our hard work cooking, baking, sewing, and organizing dinners and parties. There were other mostly younger sisters who worked alongside the Seven. Ava from Chicago, Francine from Tennessee, and several others were committed to our culturally affirming projects. The relationships we forged as we worked hands-on were rich and hard to find in mainstream, campus organizations and extra-curricular activities.

In two or three evening sessions over perhaps a single week or slightly more, in spite of all our other academic obligations, we got the job done. As each brother arrived on the celebration evening and tentatively donned the handmade dashiki with his name pinned on it, the sisters held our collective breath until we saw how closely our estimated sizes had fit. When it worked perfectly, there were oohs and aahs. Here and there was a taller guy whose height we had underestimated with a shirt that ended a little too far above the hips. Or one with a smaller frame where the neck was cut too wide or where the sleeves reached too low. We have a few photographs of brothers just beaming with surprise, seated around the tables, each dressed like African royalty.

Relationships between the male and female black students on campus had sometimes been tense with misunderstandings. This Black History Week dinner and sewing project, among all the activities we experienced together until that point, may have generated the most healing. Looking at photographs that remain of the dinner, the smiles on the faces of the young men that day affirm that we had made real the sixties rhetoric of African unity and economic self-sufficiency; they had indeed become our brothers.

Black Studies Field Trip

SASS members were undergraduates, with no professional training in designing courses. Yet we took on the task of working with college faculty to create courses for the first Black Studies concentration. There were almost no limits to the lengths that we would go to understand our black history. Our field trip to the international headquarters of one of America's most charismatic black leaders was typical.

A van full of black students, all members of SASS, disembarked from the College vehicle outside the side entrance of the Divine Lorraine Hotel in North Philadelphia one evening in spring 1969.

> No Smoking, Drinking, Profanity, or Undue Mixing of the Sexes

Someone noticed the sign and pointed to it, amused, muffling a giggle.

> Wonder what "undue" mixing means?

> We should be careful. We don't want to offend. Prof. Barrett warned us how seriously the people here take their beliefs.

The exploration of Father Divine's Peace Movement was arranged by one of the black visiting professors who was teaching us about mass movements led by charismatic leaders of African descent. Father Divine, one of the most unorthodox of them, had died in 1965, just as many of us were entering college. His success during the Depression at providing jobs, high-quality, lavish banquets, and affordable merchandise for his followers in 150 racially-diverse communal "Peace Missions" around the United States and abroad, had invited the scrutiny of investigators and critics. But we knew there had to be more to his success than the negative rumors we had heard, and nowhere else in our college courses was his name ever mentioned. Marilyn A. knew about Father Divine from people in Harlem where he was best known, but, even for her, a visit to his headquarters was a first and provided new insights into his social justice movement.

Someone muttered under his breath that he felt the place was kind of spooky. He had heard that even though Father Divine had been dead for many years, his followers claimed he was alive and appeared at the meals they serve.

We were so lost in our thoughts, we did not appreciate the beauty of this historic building called a Victorian urban mansion by later historians.

Welcome to Father's private quarters.

The person who met us at the door was quite serious.

We made our way through dimly lit corridors and up to the top floor. There, we were ushered into a huge banquet hall. This was probably the most formal dinner we had ever attended as students. Most of the seats were already filled with regular attendees. Dozens of black and white people were seated at the long banquet table. The mostly elderly people in attendance welcomed us warmly, glad to see young people take an interest in their religion. Each place was set with fine china reminiscent of a State Dinner that the president might host. At the head of the table, there were place settings for Father and Mother Divine.

We prided ourselves on getting access to primary sources, and this was as good as it got—our class attending one of the weekly banquets hosted by Father and Mother Divine. A bell rang whenever Father was about to speak. We could clearly hear a voice, apparently emanating from a pre-recorded source, as he spoke of his mission. Only to the faithful was he present in the room, and only the faithful could see him.

Having black visiting professors was only a step toward ensuring the viability of a program in Black Studies. Our first efforts had required us to travel to different colleges and universities and negotiate for credit toward our degrees through special administrative arrangements. We had also successfully initiated a student-run course, Black Philosophies of Liberation, that we taught collectively, jointly selecting a rich bibliography of primary sources and scheduling and planning evening classes and weekly assignments. We built an innovative feature into that course—that students would come to class dressed in clothing of the period being studied and the presenters would set up the room with music and food of the period as well. Even when we had no African Americans on the faculty to teach the course, each participant took a turn leading—preparing the purple-ink reprographics with historical information, organizing the music, attire, and food, and facilitating the discussion of the reading that attendees were to have completed beforehand.

To ensure the integrity of the courses we helped design, we eventually got involved in recruiting and hiring full-time black faculty to teach them. We hoped these faculty would remain and build a respected academic program and that, over time, black students would no longer have to try to complete their rigorous academic work while also developing and sustaining significant institutional services and curriculum as the SASS founders did.

Fearful to Fearless—Joyce's Story

JOYCE FRISBY BAYNES

Early Fears

I was the first of the Seven Sisters to enroll at the College. Before my class, there were only ten black students in the entire school. Although there were at least ten other black students who entered in 1964, I felt lonely and out of place. In my class and in later years, Swarthmore admitted other black students who were first-generation college students.

I hadn't heard of Swarthmore College until someone from the College Admissions Office came to my high school. I tried to attend as many college sessions as possible because my parents knew little about the admissions process. The Swarthmore representative was very personable, and the photos he showed of the campus were magnificent. Magill Walk, the Rose Garden, Clothier Hall, McCabe Library—all breathtaking! The peaceful nature of the campus and the Quaker tradition about which the admissions officer spoke were the major reasons that Swarthmore became my first choice. I had no idea about the academic rigor, the social milieu, or the financial demands. Swarthmore was too much of a reach academically for most of my high school classmates, but they wished me luck.

My father drove me down to Swarthmore for an interview and campus tour. He saw my fascination with the College and assured me that if I was accepted, he would find a way to pay for it. One day in March 1964, as I left my high school to walk to my job at the Stop & Shop supermarket, I saw my father's car outside of the school. Immediately, I thought something was wrong—a terrible accident, an injured sibling, a death in the family. Slowly, I approached the car and got into the back seat behind my mother. My father handed me an envelope that had

Swarthmore College on the return address label. I tore open the envelope and screamed for joy—I was in!

But I did not know what I was in for!

I had been on campus for three weeks when the gym teacher asked me to jump into the pool and swim. I was terrified. When I applied to Swarthmore, I had no idea there was a swimming requirement for graduation. Before my class entered, Swarthmore College had no beginners swim class. The administration assumed that every student who came to the College knew how to swim. I needed attention to overcome my fear of deep water and learn the strokes necessary for graduation. I took weekly lessons for two years, gained comfort in the water, and learned to swim four strokes and tread water. I faced a number of challenges at Swarthmore; swimming was only one of them.

Growing up in Massachusetts

I grew up in a poor, working-class family in Springfield, Massachusetts. My father completed the eighth grade and my mother was a high school graduate. They were both from Baltimore and got married in 1942. I was the second eldest of five children—three girls, two boys. Before leaving Baltimore, my father had a desire to own a roller-skating rink to provide more entertainment for young people. No bank agreed to help him finance the venture. Hoping for better opportunities outside of Baltimore, my father and his new bride took the risk of moving north to Springfield to join a few friends and family members who had migrated there. He landed jobs as a rigger at the Monsanto Chemical Company and a head waiter for a catering firm. Later, he catered parties for friends, neighbors, and co-workers on the weekends. With the exception of occasional waitressing with my father, my mother did not work outside of our home. There was often not enough money to meet the needs of our family. There were times that we went without heat, electricity, or telephone service. My mother made all of the clothes for my sisters and me until we went to high school. For Easter, some years, we were allowed to choose outfits from a local department store. I remember that the soles of my new Easter shoes were so thin I could feel the stones onto which I mistakenly stepped.

Our family's first home in Springfield was a modest house that we called the Cottage located behind a three-story apartment building in an old section of the city. My father borrowed money from friends so that he could purchase both buildings. As our family grew, we moved to the second floor of the apartment building. Then we moved again to a better section of the city. My father's income had increased with the addition of the catering services that he offered. But he was always in debt, and the struggles to keep up with the monthly bills continued. While my sisters shared a room with twin beds and my brothers had bunk beds, I was finally able to have my own room, albeit a tiny room off the upstairs porch.

Our neighborhood was integrated, and all the children attended public schools. We played outside most of the daylight hours, especially during the summer months. My siblings, cousins, and friends, mostly black, who lived on the block enjoyed jacks, tag, dodge ball, jump rope, and hide-and-seek. After my father arrived home from work every day at 5:00 p.m., my mother called us for dinner. Now, my father was not perfect, but he was always there for his family. He was a product of his times, having grown up in the streets and culture of East Baltimore. That included drinking, gambling, and smoking. Fortunately, at age nineteen, he met and married my mother. He was clearly the head of the family. There was no talking at the dinner table, and I remember hearing, "Let the food fill your mouths," when any of us attempted to have a conversation. Once, my father reprimanded me when I explained that in books I read, mealtime was an appropriate time to share stories, insights, and experiences, and that family members talked about their day and asked questions that were on their minds. My father didn't buy it! Surely, I did not learn the art of conversing over meals in our household.

Nevertheless, both of my parents valued education and were very proud of my academic achievement. My mother was the oldest of three and was smart, responsible, and reliable. Her mother depended on her to settle conflicts between her siblings and to keep peace in the family. After her marriage to my father, she had a stabilizing effect on him in spite of the fact that he was not easily controlled. My mother never realized her dream of becoming a dental hygienist, instead choosing to care for the family and home. My father loved her and appreciated her calm and consistent demeanor. He expected my mother to understand his often-spontaneous actions like when he moved his sister and her husband in with us because they couldn't pay their rent. We made room by doubling up in the children's bedrooms and accepting smaller portions of meals. It wasn't until after my father's death that my mother came into her own. She learned to drive and completed a training program in the insurance field. She became a productive member of the workforce. I admire her for setting aside many of her own wishes to raise and educate all five of her children.

Like my mother, I was never gregarious, assertive, or boastful. Throughout my formative school years, I never thought about race as a factor, positive or negative, in my life. School was an enjoyable outlet where I was recognized for my ability to memorize facts and figures and to grasp concepts rapidly. I was also good at organizing tasks and managing time with little assistance. Later, the rest of the Seven Sisters valued these qualities, and I became a de facto big sister to most of them.

My junior high school years were eye-opening. I wanted to be like my peers who were involved in activities such as organized team sports, music, dance, and clubs outside of school. I wanted desperately to learn to play the piano. I was able to take one lesson, but my parents could not afford more and certainly could not buy a keyboard or piano for me. Once I realized that I couldn't have the same range of opportunities as others, I became quieter and more withdrawn. But I never let my grades suffer. In fact, there was fierce competition for the position of top student in the ninth grade. My chief rival was a boy named Walter who, ironically, became my husband ten years later! Walter lived down the street from me. His mother, a nurse, refused to allow him and his sister to play with us. Walter's parents could afford to take their family on vacations in the summer and they had dessert every night after dinner. The Baynes family was middle-class and the Frisby family was not. Walter played the piano and trumpet and was a Boy Scout.

He taught himself calculus while hospitalized in Boston during his senior year in high school. Brilliant, artistic, and creative, Walter wore thick-rimmed plastic glasses, stood 5'11", and was medium brown-skinned and of average build. As a teen, he had an awkward sense of humor and a slightly clumsy demeanor. I was not attracted to him at all then. Walter and I were both top honors students in our respective high schools. The black community was very proud of us, but I felt that the class differences between Walter and me far outweighed our kinship as black students.

My high school years brought other social challenges and revelations. There was the situation when a couple of friends and I applied for positions at the local supermarket and the ice cream parlor. I secured jobs as a cashier at both places while my two friends were offered positions in the stock room and kitchen. They were both good students capable of operating the simple cash registers at Stop & Shop and Friendly's, but they were darker in complexion than I. It suddenly occurred to me that this might be a factor. The stratification of blacks by skin color was ingrained in the minds of many people.

I worked approximately thirty hours a week at the local Stop & Shop supermarket and was finally able to buy my own clothes and shoes. I was named "Cashier of the Year" during my junior year in high school and was invited to a recognition ceremony in Boston. Stop & Shop hosted a luncheon afterward. I had London broil, which I had never heard of, much less tasted. It was not well-done like all the beef I had previously eaten. I survived and added that experience to the list of "things I never knew before."

In high school, I became fascinated with mathematics. Perhaps this stemmed from my classes with a seventh grade teacher whose depth of knowledge in mathematics impressed me. In those days, subjects like mathematics and science were male-dominated, so I was reticent about displaying my enthusiasm. My girlfriends leaned toward the humanities and the arts, especially the dramatic arts. I felt alone and almost deceitful, hiding my love of mathematics from my friends. I continued to excel and was selected to take calculus my senior year. My father insisted that I take physics for my final science course. What did he know about physics? He was skilled at using information that he overheard at his job at Monsanto, and he gathered that physics was the most challenging science course in high school. Well, his daughter was certainly going to sign up for that course! My father saw college as a path to success in a professional world for his five children, a world that was closed to him.

On the first day of my senior year in high school, my physics teacher looked at me as I entered his classroom and asked if I was in the right class. At Swarthmore, there was no stigma against women majoring in mathematics or science. I felt that I had cheated myself during those pre-college years by hiding my love for the subject, and in later life, as a teacher and supervisor of mathematics, I encouraged young women, particularly those of color, to pursue mathematics and science without fear and without embarrassment.

Worry Upon Worry

At Swarthmore, I was naïve about my ability to "fit in" to such a different culture. Despite the fact that I was never an outgoing person, I had always managed to have a few good friends. I thought that would be the case at Swarthmore as well.

It took a long while for me to feel comfortable in an environment that was very new to me. I didn't want my parents to know that I worried about the difficulty of the courses I selected. I worried about whether I had enough money to pay for the textbooks for fall and spring semesters. I worried about whom to ask when I could not find a classroom. The campus was huge to me and there were students everywhere. Most were white and moved in twos and threes from one venue to another, talking, laughing, never paying attention to this shy, unobtrusive freshman. I kept telling myself "you chose to come here." I didn't realize that things were going to be so incredibly different from life in my formative years.

My favorite cousin in Baltimore asked me to be a bridesmaid in his wedding. The green, V-necked, satin, knee-length bridesmaid dress fit perfectly. During the weeks leading up to the event, I noticed an increasing number of tiny pimples on my skin. Since the age of eight, I had suffered from eczema, although I had had no serious outbreaks in years. By the wedding day, my legs, arms, and chest were covered with a reddish, unsightly rash. The stress of those first weeks at Swarthmore brought on the skin disease with a vengeance.

I was assigned a room in Parrish Hall for my freshman year. My roommate was Linda, a dark-haired Jewish girl who lived in a suburb of Philadelphia. Almost out of necessity, Linda and I became friends. We went to dinner together at Sharples Dining Hall on a regular basis. Unlike me, Linda was accustomed to having a variety of choices and more than one course at each meal. Although my father was a hard worker, it was difficult for him to feed a family of seven. I remember trying to find the meat on the neck bones that my mother prepared for dinner. I wondered why the skin on the pig's feet was so very thick. Some of the best meals we had were the leftovers my father brought home. I could cut the beef brisket with a fork and the chicken breast was tender. (We were accustomed to eating only dark meat because it was less expensive). Soon, I learned the routines at Swarthmore—soup, salad, entrée, and dessert, and took full advantage.

After a few months, Linda started dating a young man who was a sophomore at the College. She went everywhere with him. Occasionally, I missed meals because I was afraid to go to Sharples alone. After months on campus, I was not comfortable introducing myself to students at a table in the dining hall. If I sat alone, I feared that I would be too conspicuous. If someone came over to join me, I imagined that it would be an act of sympathy, not an authentic gesture. Eventually, I met a couple of other black students and we made a point of dining together daily. I was happy to have a few black dining partners, yet I did not consider them to be close friends like my six sisters who came to Swarthmore later. Perhaps it was because of my insecurity, homesickness, or sense of being overwhelmed by the demands of the College that I could not relax and enjoy the company of other students.

My academic experience at Swarthmore was vastly different from my pre-college experiences. At Classical High School in Springfield, teachers rewarded students who could memorize facts, formulas, procedures, chronologies, and rules of grammar without error. I earned A grades mainly because I possess an excellent memory. During a test, I could visualize a page in a textbook that contained the answer to a question posed. At Swarthmore, on the other hand, professors demanded a deeper understanding of fundamental concepts and an ability to transfer skills to new situations.

I graduated near the top of my class from a highly respected public school in Springfield. I always took my studies seriously, often staying up way past midnight to complete assignments. I thought I was prepared for the challenges of Swarthmore. Once on campus I discovered that the majority of the students there had graduated at the top of their class and many came from private and selective high schools, demanding that the curriculum be more advanced than I had expected. One evening, I called home crying about the huge amount of reading I had to do. Even though my father was proud of my being at Swarthmore, he could not bear to hear me cry. He exclaimed, "Listen, you can come home and go to Westfield State Teachers College. You will still become a fine teacher." Unfortunately, he did not live to see me stick it out to the end at Swarthmore. I was grateful for the support of my family during those most difficult times at Swarthmore. I would have appreciated the attention of a resident advisor or mentor assigned to first-generation college students or to black students in need of assistance. The College had not established structured tutorials, mentorships, or counseling to ease the transition from our respective secondary schools to Swarthmore.

I never saw myself as a slow writer until the day when Marilyn A., who had attended private school, and I were in the same room, both writing essays for our classes. For every six pages that Marilyn wrote, I wrote one! Perhaps my writing habits slowed me down—seeking esoteric words, or unusual situations, or just perseverating on how stuck I was. I wondered whether speed of writing correlated with speed of speaking. Many consider me a quiet person. Was my not being verbose causing me to write more slowly? Whatever the reason, I continued to persevere and was successful in every course.

In sports, I was not familiar with lacrosse nor field hockey and, believe it or not, I did not know what a Frisbee was. So, the teasing about my last name (Frisby) had little impact. Basketball was the sport that many black boys and girls played in the neighborhood playgrounds. I wasted no time joining the women's team. I excelled on the court, often becoming frustrated with my teammates who could not anticipate the passes I made.

Our chief rival was Bryn Mawr College, and upon my arrival, we were in a position to defeat them. There was one other black woman on the team, Pamela. She was a sophomore from Westchester County, New York. When we beat Bryn Mawr, I remember the hug of joy between Pamela and me. I was happy that I had basketball as an outlet that first year at Swarthmore.

My family came to Swarthmore for Parents Weekend my freshman year. I had mixed feelings about their coming to the College that spring weekend. I was excited about showing them my dormitory, eating with them in Sharples, and touring the beautiful campus together. I worried about how they would act, what clothes they would wear, and how my six-year-old sister would behave. My father bought a new suit for the occasion, and my parents and two sisters changed in the restroom of a service station on the way down.

We ran into Pamela and she introduced her parents to mine. Both of her parents were doctors, very sweet and down-to-earth. Neither my parents nor I had much to say, so we smiled and continued on our tour. Perhaps I hurried my parents along for fear that they would not be able to converse with a different class of people. Perhaps I felt inadequate in my social skills and did not want to be awkward. Later, we attended a choral concert in a small intimate setting. I was embarrassed by two incidents that occurred there. My little sister exclaimed loudly, "I can't see," and she strutted herself up to the front row and sat down. Several minutes later, I heard someone snoring in the row behind me. It was my father! My mother nudged him gently and whispered to me that he was tired from working all week and then driving down from Massachusetts. Despite these periods of discomfort during the weekend, I was happy that my parents and siblings made the trip to get a glimpse of my college experience at Swarthmore.

Unexpected Crises

My world was about to change forever during the summer following my sophomore year. My father had secured a summer job for me as an accounts payable/receivable clerk at Monsanto Chemical Company. My goal was to earn enough so that my parents would not have to give me any spending money for the ensuing year. I enjoyed traveling to work with my father who was proud of me for deciding to stay at Swarthmore. He often fabricated stories about specific opportunities that awaited me after graduation.

As I sat on my bed reading one night, I heard heavy breathing from my parents' bedroom. I got very nervous. My father was not one to admit feeling ill; he was always energetic and active. I shouted to my mother to come upstairs. When she came out of their bedroom, she said, "I think he is dying," then called an ambulance immediately. When my mother returned from the hospital, I was still upstairs. Upon hearing the news of my father's death, I literally fell down the steps. Someone laid me on the living room sofa, and I stayed there for hours. I felt that I was my father's favorite child. He dreamed of my success in a world he only knew as fantasy. My father was an adventurer who needed little guidance from others, and he found those same characteristics in me. I earned excellent grades to please my father, and I always sought his praise. When I was a teenager, my father told me that he trusted me to make good decisions about friends, school, and work, and trusted me to take care of the other children and to be morally sound. His perception of me was a factor in my decision to become one of the Seven Sisters. Now, at age forty-two, he was gone, and I was left to help hold the family together in the midst of my own grief. My faith in God deepened upon my father's death. I trusted God's Word and relied on Him to love and protect my Dad.

My mother was in a state of shock. She sat in the recliner in our living room day after day following my father's passing. Several times, she said of my father, "He loved me more than he loved himself." My mother had always looked at me as clear-headed, conscientious, and knowledgeable, regardless of the issue. I reviewed all available paperwork and decided how the life insurance after burial costs would be divided, and I applied for the Social Security and Veterans Survivors benefits. I comforted my two youngest siblings. So much responsibility, and where did Swarthmore fit into this picture?

Fortunately, the tuition agreement that my father signed with the College contained a clause that stated that in the case of his death, the remainder of the loan would be paid in full.

My mother was relieved to know that she would not have to pay that $33 a month and that I would be able to continue my education at Swarthmore. My mother enrolled in a local job training program and eventually became an excellent insurance clerk. Back to Swarthmore I went with a strong sense of resolve that I would finish with a degree in mathematics as my father had expected. I put the thoughts of personal loneliness, isolation, and insecurity aside and focused on academic achievement, racial group identity, and spiritual development.

Change of Racial Perspective

In my early years at Swarthmore, several of us sisters gathered in the dormitory rooms of Willets Hall. We discussed everything from recipes and family to politics and society. As we talked night after night, we began to get agitated and angry as we realized the paucity of courses, professors, and activities that related to our backgrounds and interests. I was feeling a change in my own outlook on my life and on what it meant to be black in this country. Those early sessions set the stage for the formation of SASS. At the same time, nationally, Stokely Carmichael was espousing "Black is Beautiful." Our talks in Willets and later in Worth Hall got so animated at times that I remember us asking ourselves, "What are we willing to die for?" We responded with "Black Power." Those dorm room gatherings marked the beginning of a bond that would carry us through challenges at Swarthmore College and beyond. We were definitely preparing to demand radical change at Swarthmore College, not knowing then that the takeover was to be the climax.

In my junior year at Swarthmore, I took German because many original mathematics documents are written in that language. Ordinarily, I was not bold enough to sit right in the front row of a classroom, but I wanted to hear the teacher's accent and diction well. There was no other black student in the class. The professor was a tall, stately, serious woman who was clearly a native speaker of German and looked intimidating. She rarely smiled and glared unpleasantly at any latecomer. I never missed a class. I was doing very well, getting As and Bs on quizzes and tests. One day, after class, the professor asked me, "You took German in high school, didn't you?" She looked so surprised when I told her that I had not. Then I realized that she held low expectations of me.

Recalling that incident now reminds me of one that occurred ten years later at the Upper East Side private school where I was the only black academic teacher. I wrote a letter of recommendation for one of my eighth graders who was applying to boarding school for high school. The headmaster of my school came to me after reading the letter and said, "You write well." I had graduated from two prestigious institutions, undergraduate and graduate. This man had expected much less from my writing. These examples and others served to convince me that I must set my own standards for excellence and evaluate my performance based on those standards.

I was involved in several activities leading up to the takeover in 1969. Swarthmore College had a tradition of inviting speakers to address the entire student body in Clothier Hall. One Thursday each month, we filed into the hall and took our seats in the magnificent auditorium. Attendance was mandatory. March 21, 1967 was the anniversary of the Sharpeville Massacre in South Africa. Seven years prior, scores of unarmed blacks were killed, and many others injured because they were protesting the cruelties of apartheid. Once we learned that a white South African had been invited to speak, a group of SASS members held a meeting. We decided that we would go into Clothier, take our seats, listen to the introduction, and stand up and walk out just as the guest began to speak. Roughly ten black students made that brave move. I was not afraid to be among them.

On the world scene, the Vietnam War was waging, and many of us knew young men who were fighting and dying for no reasonable cause. There were numerous protests across the country. Students at Swarthmore, white and black, decided to travel to New York City to join in the protests against the war. Some of the black organizers mapped out a special route for the black protesters to follow. We black students from Swarthmore agreed to follow that route. White Swarthmore activists joined students from other colleges and universities and marched with them. There was nothing illegal that we were doing in following a second route. Nevertheless, the police took the opportunity to trample us with their horses and to beat us with their batons. The white students experienced no such ill treatment. When one young black woman from Swarthmore was knocked to the ground, others of us came to her aid quickly before the horses approached. We were all shaken when we returned to campus. Our young black men were fighting and dying for a country where racist police brutality reared its head clearly that day.

Steadfast and Committed Leadership

I often wonder how we, the most radical group of black students, Seven Sisters and a Brother, came to be so revolutionary. Few of us were particularly activist-minded before coming to Swarthmore. Most of us were preoccupied with schoolwork, church, family, and a limited number of extracurricular activities. Who were these black Swarthmore students from the '60s era? I met two of them, Marilyn A. and Marilyn H., in 1965, one year after my arrival on campus. They were both barely seventeen years old, having each skipped a grade in school.

Both Marilyn A. and Marilyn H. grew up in Christian households. Marilyn A.'s father was a minister, and he imposed some rigid rules on his children. She was not allowed to dance, go to parties, and certainly not to drink. Her devotion to God and her decision to seek his guidance for her life kept her well-grounded. Marilyn A. went to church in Swarthmore and in one of the surrounding towns on a regular basis. We were all raised as Christians with Marilyn A. being the most committed to her faith. As the years passed, I became more intentional and consistent in my relationship with God.

My friendship with Marilyn A. and Marilyn H. spans fifty-plus years. They came to Swarthmore at a time when I was discouraged and doubtful about myself. Marilyn A. and Marilyn H. helped me to discover new reasons for being at Swarthmore. Stepping into the role of big sister to Marilyn H. showed my ability to nurture others, and my interactions with Marilyn A. gave me a heightened appreciation for the degree of intellectual prowess among us.

Harold also came to Swarthmore in 1965. He was a mathematics major just as I was. We often studied together, and we worked hard to understand the most difficult problem sets. He was calm and patient as a young man, and whenever I saw Harold, he had a camera hanging from his neck. At Swarthmore, Harold's politics became more radical and his recognition of the impact of race and class on blacks in the United States made his allegiance to the Black Student Movement solid. Harold was quiet, but not shy and spoke up when circumstances demanded it. We all appreciated Harold's loyalty to our group. There was never a question that he believed in the actions we decided to take. Harold was such an important part of our group that he attended my wedding in Springfield, Massachusetts and took some wonderful pictures. Harold was comfortable in his own skin and had an inner spirit that permeated his being. The Seven Sisters alone would not have been as effective without Harold.

I met Jannette, Aundrea, Myra, and Bridget in 1966 when they arrived on campus as freshmen. They were all eighteen-year-olds, yet vastly different from each other. Each of these friends had a different accent—none like mine. Western Massachusetts residents did not speak like those from Eastern Massachusetts and certainly not like Southerners or West Indians. I was excited and amazingly comfortable to be among black students whose backgrounds were so varied. A common element in our friendship was the fact that we shared the same beliefs about what we wanted the College to be.

Since I was the oldest member of our group, I tried to "keep track" of the other six sisters. I knew their course schedules, and in some cases, I knew when they had examinations. At vacation and holiday times, I made sure that all of them had off-campus plans because we could not always afford to go home. One Thanksgiving, I took Myra with me to my grandmother's house in Baltimore.

I was aware of the risks that all of us took by challenging the College's policies, but I was steadfast in my determination to take a stand with the group against the College's negligence and discrimination. We did not want to lose our scholarships nor disappoint our parents. In group sessions, we talked about the need to be committed to the cause and to be willing to make some sacrifice on its behalf. I wanted to be certain that each of the younger women in the group felt comfortable with her individual decisions. Their choice of joining the Takeover would later be their biggest decision.

Graduation with Confidence

Who ever heard of an amphitheater! My family was about to discover natural beauty as never before imagined. Granddaddy lived on a farm in Virginia with his second wife. They raised chickens, pigs, and cows and used an outhouse for their bathroom. Nana lived in Northwest Baltimore. As children and teens, we were never allowed to leave her block for fear of getting mugged. I was thrilled to have my grandparents join my mother, my aunts, and my siblings to witness the College graduation of their eldest granddaughter. My grandfather marveled at the way the amphitheater had been constructed right there in the midst of Crum Woods. Granddaddy asked, "How long did it take to create this outdoor setting?" Unfortunately, I did not know the answer. The women hesitated to sit on the rock steps in their Sunday best, colorful dresses, handmade scarves, and old-fashioned hats. Of course, they acquiesced. My brothers and sisters took careful note of the decorum displayed by the other families. They were not fazed. As I approached the stage to receive my diploma, I heard a loud roar and long applause. I knew that my family could not contain their enthusiasm and their pride. Why not celebrate!

My family's cheers were amplified by my Swarthmore black sisters and brother for whom the graduation ceremony was a mixture of pride and also a sobering reminder of the imbalance of representation of blacks in the College community. The bonds created by our core group of eight were truly unique. I did not know that our work would result in a major confrontation in a matter of months. I was proud of the seven of them for leading the Takeover of the admissions office the semester after I graduated. I was even a little envious because I was not among them. By creating SASS, we all had laid the foundation for the actions that followed. I read about the takeover in the newspaper and wondered how the parents of the black students reacted. I prayed for the safety of my sisters and brothers in the admissions office and hoped that the administration would respect them and acquiesce to their demands.

I doubt that many other college alums can count seven graduates from their alma maters as friends. Our eight lives went in many different directions after college. Some of us focused intensively on building and advancing our careers. Eventually, all of us married and many started families and expended tremendous energy raising children. We care for and support each other in times of ill health, tragedy, and unexpected crises. We celebrate each other's joys, whether they be births, graduations, promotions, authorships, or retirements. So, it was no surprise that when we were called upon to become involved in SBAN (Swarthmore Black Alumni Network) events and to write this book together, we all answered enthusiastically. It must have been the passion for and the commitment to the cause of justice and equality for black people that lived within all of us and kept us together in spirit.

Post-Swarthmore Years

The symbolism of the Takeover galvanized me to face personal obstacles and professional challenges that I would have feared earlier in my life. It moved me to take proactive steps when required. It gave me the strength and skills to observe biases and stereotypes that people held toward others. My husband passed away at a very young age, and I raised three sons on my own. I was determined to beat the odds and not have them succumb to the typical expectations—low academic achievement, substance abuse, incarceration, etc.—of black males in single-parent families. I had the courage to stand up for my children in racially-charged situations. Racism was not obvious to their innocent minds. Although I was diligent about observing and addressing injustices regarding my children, I never told them that race would be a burden or barrier for them. They grew up feeling that the world was their oyster and that they could be and do anything within their capabilities.

Their full grasp of the inequities in our society emerged during and after their college years. By that time, each of them had developed a sense of self that was very positive and enduring. In my numerous positions as a teacher, mathematics supervisor, and school superintendent, I never hesitated to point out class, race, and achievement biases to teachers and principals and to demand fairness.

After my graduation from Swarthmore in June 1968, I enrolled in the Harvard Graduate School of Education and earned a master's degree. It just so happened that Walter Baynes, the longtime friend and neighbor in Springfield where we both grew up, was starting a job at IBM in Boston that same summer. He offered to help me move into my small studio apartment in Cambridge. I appreciated the gesture, since my brothers were not available.

Throughout our youthful years in Springfield, I had considered Walter a real nerd and was totally disinterested in any romantic relationship with him. However, as I got to know him that summer, I found his sense of humor engaging and his intellect extraordinary. I didn't have to intentionally lose at board games and cards—he beat me fair and square. Over that 1968–1969 period, we spent many hours together. He was a salesman, then a systems analyst (physics major looking for his purpose in life!) at IBM. He enjoyed hearing about my mathematics projects and the challenges of teaching middle level students. We fell in love and Walter asked me to marry him. We were both twenty-three. I was fortunate to have an advisor at Harvard who took a real interest in my welfare. I wish I had had such an advocate and counselor at Swarthmore College. When I told Dr. Wilson I planned to get married, she exclaimed "You cannot mix mathematics and marriage."

She was not the only person who was surprised by this announcement. Three of the seven sisters, Marilyn A., Marilyn

H., and Aundrea, traveled to Cambridge to grill me over a day and long night about Walter and my hopes and plans for a future with him. These women were leaders of the Takeover only a couple of months prior and had final exams for which to study, and Marilyn A. and Marilyn H. were preparing for graduation in May. Yet they camped out in my tiny apartment and were relentless with their questions and concerns. I convinced them that they should not worry. During their Cambridge visit, these three sisters briefed me on the eight-day Takeover. I was impressed with the strategic planning and the peaceful execution of the event. It was heartwarming to have friends who cared so much about my well-being that they would travel miles to see me during a very difficult semester. I will never forget that grueling weekend. That summer of 1969, those same three sisters were delighted to be bridesmaids in my wedding.

I married in 1969, earned my master's degree in 1970, and started a family in 1971. I had a remarkably exciting teaching job in an alternative school in Roxbury, Massachusetts, and my husband was a medical student. I never thought about returning to Swarthmore for my fifth reunion in 1973, nor my tenth, nor my fifteenth. I had no personal ties to anyone in my class; my closest friends were in the Class of 1969. So when their twenty-fifth reunion came around in 1994, I did return to campus with a couple of friends. Why was I not drawn back to that beautiful campus during the previous twenty-five years? In fact, nearly another twenty years passed before I got involved in any other alumni activity. As a black alumna, I didn't feel attached to the College. I belonged to a subgroup that academically went through the same paces as others, but during my four years there, black students were significantly marginalized. Had I returned to campus for those prior reunions, who would have remembered me, who would have welcomed me, who would have been happy to see me?

Once SBAN (Swarthmore Black Alumni Network) was created, I returned to campus and attended a number of events—all associated with black alumni. I have no inclination to join the wider group of Swarthmore peers at future class reunions. That will probably never change.

The image of the Takeover and all that it meant to me as a symbol of power was a driving force in my life after Swarthmore. It was an impetus for me to assume leadership roles in my educational career. While raising my three sons, I taught mathematics for eighteen years. I spent the next eighteen years in public school administration. My first position was K-12 Mathematics Supervisor in a school district in New Jersey. I was the first black supervisor.

When I became a Chief School Administrator, I was the only black district superintendent in Bergen County, New Jersey, a county with seventy-two school districts. In my last position, before I was appointed, there were no black administrators, teachers, secretaries, nor custodians. Nine Caucasian men hired me as superintendent to run their school district. I was amazed! I am certain that Swarthmore College, the Black Student Movement, and the strength of my relationships with six black sisters and a brother instilled in me the mantra that change is good and necessary, and that I must continue to fight for it without fear.

Now, I am retired with three married sons and six grandchildren. I am grateful that I continue to find time to help parents with their growing children. The world has become more complex over the years and the problems young people face are often complicated. I bring them stories of resilience, perseverance, and faith. They hear about the academic, cultural, and political struggles I had in college. Many of my current young friends are eager to learn about the determination we had to change the direction of a college in the 1960s. I hope that I make a difference in their lives just as experiencing Swarthmore truly made a difference in mine.

Photo Gallery

Cygnet and Halcyon are Swarthmore College publications of freshman and graduates, respectively. They have given permission to use these photos.

Entering College

Marilyn Allman, her high school yearbook

Harold Buchanan, courtesy of Bellport HS Clipper

Jannette O. Domingo, courtesy of Hunter College HS Annals

Joyce Frisby, by SC Cygnet

Marilyn Holifield, at Lincoln HS prom

Myra Rose, by SC Cygnet

Bridget Van Gronigen, by SC Cygnet

Aundrea White, by SC Cygnet

After Transformation

Marilyn Allman, by Weitzmann Photo, NYC

Harold Buchanan, by SC Halcyon

Jannette O. Domingo, by SC Halcyon

Joyce Frisby, photo by Walter J. Baynes

Marilyn Holifield, courtesy of Edward Holifield

Myra, courtesy of Rosalind Plummer

Bridget Van Gronigen, by SC Halcyon

Aundrea White, by Jannette O. Domingo

Seven Sisters and a Brother authors in Panama City, Panama
by Clifford Charles

Campus Life

Marilyn H. at the black table with visiting professor, by Harold Buchanan

Marilyn A and Aundrea with friends on campus, by Harold Buchanan

Harold and Marilyn H. in the dining hall, by Marilyn Holifield

Marilyn A. and Aundrea on campus, by Harold Buchanan

Bridget relaxing on dining hall patio, by Jannette O. Domingo

Marilyn A. carrying books, by Harold Buchanan

Jannette on Parrish Walk, by Jannette O. Domingo

Harold on campus, by Marilyn Holifield

Myra and Bridget on campus, by Jannette O. Domingo

Sisters on lawn with male friends, by Marilyn Maye

SASS Dinner, by Marilyn Maye

Bridget and Jannette with friend, by Jannette O. Domingo

SASS members at the train station with prospective students, by Marilyn Maye

Marilyn A. and Joyce at the train station, by Marilyn Maye

Marilyn A. and Marilyn H. at graduation, by Marilyn Holifield

Scenes from the Takeover

Student entering Admissions Office through window, by Harold Buchanan

Aundrea climbing in Admissions Office window, by Harold Buchanan

SASS members talking with the Deans, by Harold Buchanan

Marilyn A. and Aundrea on guard, by Harold Buchanan

Myra combing a brother's hair, by Harold Buchanan

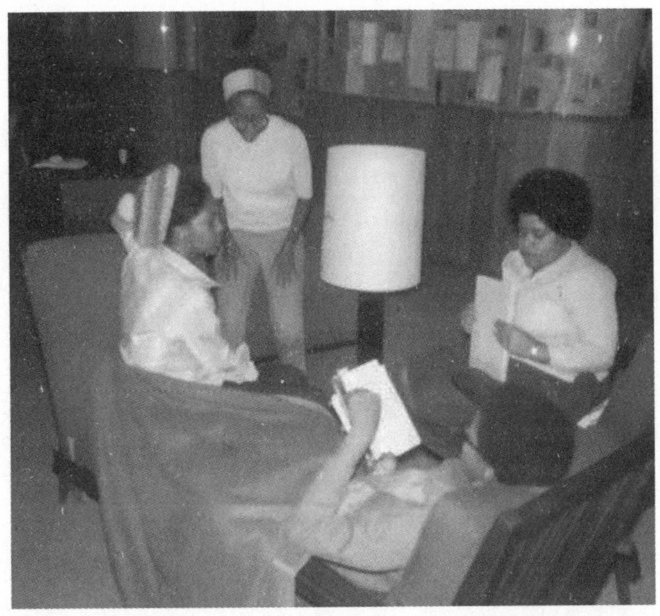

Bridget, Jannette, Myra, and Aundrea in the Admissions Office, by Marilyn Maye

At the desk in the Admissions Office, by Harold Buchanan

Black students inside the Admissions Office during the Takeover, by Harold Buchanan

Black students sleeping inside the Admissions Office, by Harold Buchanan

THE TAKEOVER

Day Five

DAY FIVE
Meeting the Press

Day Five was a Monday, the start of a new week, and we found ourselves in demand, being called on to explain ourselves and to respond to proposals that might bring our action to an end.

Since they were the visible representatives, the SASS spokesmen were frequently asked by faculty and administration, the campus newspaper, and other student groups to meet with them to answer questions and respond to offers of compromise on our demands. The spokespersons would return to report to the larger group and give their recommendations, and the debates among us were often vigorous.

> We agree to no resolutions adopted by the faculty or administration without us all discussing it first.
>
> Classes are suspended 'til next week. The faculty and administration are meeting every day, and as late as three in the morning, arguing about whether to concede to our demands. The radical students have supported our demands, and many of the others as well.
>
> The faculty and administration are all very divided on how to respond to us. Some worry about setting bad precedents by giving us a say in who gets hired to administer black admissions and to recommend which students get admitted to the College. Others worry that so-called "at-risk" students are going to degrade the College in some way.
>
> That "at-risk" label is insulting anyway. Look how well most black students are doing despite what they

> consider risk factors in our backgrounds. They're just embarrassed because they know we can find qualified black administrators and students, and we will take away their excuses.
>
> The College violated our privacy and treated us like subjects of an experiment. Any reasonable person can see that the Dean of Admissions was insensitive and then stubbornly refused to back down.
>
> That's why we had to add another demand, that Hargadon be replaced as Head of Admissions if his conduct doesn't change.
>
> And what are the odds that he's going to be able to change?

We spent the week in parallel realities, two teams united in the same cause, but experiencing it in at least two different ways. The spokespersons engaged the opposition outside the admissions office, and the leaders inside made sure our operational headquarters were secure and worked on writing statements of our positions. One of the major discussion points among faculty and administration was their claim that we had used "force," rather than "civil discourse" without a time limit, to seek change. We believed that talk without time limits would amount to de facto denial of our goal. We would not be on campus another year to see change possibly arise.

One of Harold's photographs of freshman Mike H. sitting in front of a 1960s manual typewriter reminds us how many hours we spent each day articulating, transcribing, and typing our viewpoints for the spokespersons to share. Aundrea recalls capturing key points during our excited discussions and then repeating them as we edited to ensure that nothing crucial was omitted.

A *LIFE* magazine photograph of two SASS men addressing a press conference would later become misleadingly iconic, the defining image of the Takeover. Their poses were reminiscent of the Black Power posture in the famous 1968 Olympic photo. Dashiki-clad, afro-wearing, the black male students dominated the attention in the room. Don Mizell is standing on a chair that raises his head at least two feet above everyone else's, looking down as if reading aloud from a document in his hand. Clinton Etheridge holds a microphone up in a fully extended arm toward Don's mouth, while himself facing away as if to avoid distracting attention from the speaker. Almost everyone else in the room appears to be white, some sitting cross legged on the floor, others sitting on chairs or standing, many taking notes. Silently holding sway over the gathering, however, is a giant oil portrait on the wall directly behind the reader of a seated, nineteenth-century Quaker founder.

These young men played their role well as visible representatives. Meanwhile, inside the admissions office, the Seven Sisters and a Brother continued to coordinate the action and draft public statements. Those in the picture had the leadership titles, but the soul, hands, and feet of the operation were predominantly women, and the media never photographed or interviewed them.

Not from Around Here—Bridget's Story

BRIDGET VAN GRONIGEN WARREN

From South to North America

I got a real education at Swarthmore College. In addition to the scientific knowledge gained as a biology major, I learned what it was like to be black in America.

I was a relatively recent immigrant when I started studying at Swarthmore. I had arrived in the United States in 1963, just as I was beginning my last years of high school. My mother continued the nursing profession she had practiced back home, but my father's failing eyesight made it impossible for him to proceed similarly. Instead, he made the necessary adjustments that permitted him to move on from his position as the Chief Pharmacist of Guyana to becoming trained to function as a blind person, which he did admirably until his death at ninety-nine years of age. My brother, sister, and I had to quickly adapt to American curricula and school environments, quite different from the system of education at that time in a British colony that would become Guyana at independence in 1966. In addition to being part of the British Caribbean territories, at different points in the country's history, French and Dutch colonial powers also ruled the area, and as such also contributed to the cultural mix. Guyana is on the northeast mainland of South America and is bordered by Venezuela, Brazil, Suriname, and the Atlantic Ocean. Nevertheless, as the only country in South America where English is the official language, and as a former British colony, we are often referred to as part of the British West Indies.

In many ways, my experience of race and ethnicity in the British Guiana of my youth was quite unlike what I would encounter in the United States. Guyanese of East Indian descent are the largest ethnic group. Guyanese of African descent like me are the second largest group comprising approximately a third of the population, proportionately a much larger minority than African Americans in the United States. The indigenous Amerindian groups comprise about 10 percent of the population, while most of the remaining Guyanese ethnic milieu includes Portuguese, Chinese, and Europeans. Exploring the reasons why this last group does not officially include the Portuguese would be better served if treated as a separate topic.

As might be expected, there was quite a bit of ethnic/racial mixing so that these groups are not quite as neatly defined; DNA testing could probably confirm this. This admixture is also made evident by the culinary preferences included in many Guyanese daily and celebratory activities. The racial/ethnic mix that was a consequence of the European arrival in the New World brought colonialism, slavery, and indentured labor to British Guiana. These colonizing measures resulted in demographic, political, economic, and cultural dynamics that are quite different from those seen in the United States. Race and ethnicity have played and continue to play an extremely divisive role in the country's political and economic development.

The 1960s were just as turbulent in British Guiana as in the US. We were very much a part of anti-colonial struggles that would culminate in the independence of countries in the Caribbean and Africa. While the Civil Rights and anti-Vietnam War movements raged in the United States, in our corner of South America, we were most concerned with dealing with British colonial authority and competing amongst ourselves for political and economic control of our soon-to-be-independent nation.

When I left home in the mid-1960s, the rivalry between Indo- and Afro-Guyanese political parties and their allies was fierce, acrimonious, and sometimes violent. By the time I graduated from high school and entered Swarthmore in

1966, an Afro-Guyanese-led coalition had won control of the government and British Guiana had become Guyana.

Having grown up in this South American country, I learned about the United States from news reports, books, and magazines. Television would become a part of the local scene shortly after my family's migration. Unlike the rest of our group of seven sisters and a brother—all of whom grew up in the US, I did not grow up considering myself to be one of a small minority. Even though Guyana was not yet independent from Great Britain in my youth, it was quite normal for me to be aware that people of African ancestry were highly visible at all levels of society.

When the time came to make decisions about college, I was able to visit three of the schools that I thought I might be interested in attending. I was impacted by the physical beauty of Swarthmore. The highly wooded country setting reminded me of areas of my homeland. I had spent my childhood there because of my father's professional responsibilities which included establishing a mobile health unit to take care of the health needs of the indigenous communities in the northwestern sector of the country. I liked the small size and the academic programs that were offered at Swarthmore. I was interested in science, biology in particular, and the College's curriculum coincided with my interests within a liberal arts structure. I didn't see any black students when I went for my interview on campus. My tour guide told me that there weren't many, and that was the situation when I arrived as a freshman in the fall of 1966. At that time, I could walk from one end of the campus to another without ever seeing another black student. Yet, interestingly enough, with my class, the campus had its largest black population ever up to that time.

Swarthmore always treated me as both a foreign student and as a black student even though I had been living in

Brooklyn, New York during my last years of high school. As a foreign student, I feel that I received special attention from the Dean's office. I remember having sprained my ankle and the foreign student liaison checking up on me in the infirmary to make sure I was okay. My roommate, who I met prior to arriving on campus, had specifically requested a foreign roommate and she got me. Somehow even my father got involved in my education in an unexpected way. He was able to put Dr. Weber, my entomology professor, on the right track in Guyana so that he could collect specimens for his ant collection.

Attending Swarthmore was truly special. Maybe it was just a matter of destiny that I happened to be at Swarthmore and learning about life in the United States during a crucial time in the Civil Rights Movement. It is definitely ironic that I would learn so much about black Americans on a predominantly white campus. As I got to know other black students, I learned more about the subtleties and nuances of being black in a white environment in the US. I was present during the process that culminated in the formation of SASS, the first Black organization on campus. Because of SASS's efforts, the College opened up its academic offerings to include Black Studies, and I was able to take courses such as the one on Black Mass Movements with Visiting Professor Barrett that helped me to better understand the race situation in the US. Due to the time restraints imposed on me as a science major (all those hours spent in laboratory), I was not as free to take off-campus courses as I would have liked, but some students traveled to Lincoln University and other nearby schools for courses that were not available on campus.

During my four years in college, schools like Swarthmore were beginning to see increasing numbers of black students on campus. For the first time on these campuses, traditionally white colleges like Swarthmore were beginning to see students of color all together in larger groups. Maybe because of this, conflicts arose, which during my time resulted in protests that included the black students' occupation of the admissions office. I believe there were differences in the expectations of all parties involved which did not allow for a seamless blending of the black student population into the predominant college culture. Through SASS, one of the results of the admissions office protest was to incorporate studies of black culture into the College's academic offerings which would be available to all students.

Turning Point

My name is associated with the Seven Sisters, but I wasn't nearly as active as my six other sisters. We became friends and we ate and talked together—a lot. After returning to campus after a break, we could skip the cafeteria and share food from home in the dorm. We threw our ideas at each other and maybe because of this, we were seen as a unit, some kind of powerful entity.

All this was occurring within an environment that led to the formation of SASS. I do remember many meetings, some of which I would attend. I listened carefully to the issues, some of which I didn't know existed, some that I could let pass, and others that I didn't consider to be very important. Maybe as a newcomer to the US, I did not feel that I was in a position to provide leadership on resolving many of the concerns of other black students. If there was a turning point for me, it was probably the study on the black students that came out of the admissions office. I felt that we were being studied like lab rats! I felt naked. SASS was influential in helping everyone see that black students really were experiencing a Swarthmore reality that was different from that of the white students on campus and that there was a perspective that needed to be respected and included.

All this led to the 1969 Takeover. Once it began, I joined other students to publicly support the group in the admissions office after the initial sit-in had started. There were plenary sessions in Clothier Hall where members of the general student body gathered to discuss the situation. I recall joining a group of students in issuing a letter of support for the students protesting in the office, but I reached a point where I felt that I needed to join them, and I was not alone. I can't speak for all the other students who joined the protesters, but one of them, Ferdinand Warren, a black student from Panama, became my husband three years later. Like me, he also began to feel a need to do something.

During this period, there were continuous negotiations with the College, but things took an expected turn when President Courtney Smith died. When that happened, we considered it prudent to remove our protest from the campus. We got support from area churches and community members from nearby media who provided transport, lodging, and food until the protest was formally ended.

I was a junior when the occupation took place in 1969, so I was there for a whole year afterwards. Immediately after the event, there was the friction that is to be expected among the various factions when something like this happens. Yet, there were visible changes on campus. Swarthmore's lone full-time black professor was Dr. Asmarom Legesse. Once SASS was fully active and the black student occupation of the admissions office had begun, he was our liaison with the College, and became SASS's official faculty representative. As a result of this protest, new academic courses—some of which had been designed by black students—formed the basis for what would become a concentration in Black Studies. There was a Black

Assistant Dean of Admissions[15] and the College created—with input from SASS—an Ad Hoc Committee on black admissions. Not everything happened right away, but there were students in my graduating class, and the one just prior to mine, who were able to receive traditional degrees with an additional concentration in Black Studies. This was something that was never available before. When these students couldn't get all the courses they needed for the Black Studies concentration on campus, they looked for classes at nearby universities and colleges and took them there.

When I look back, that Black Studies concentration was the beginning of many other non-traditional studies programs that came along after my time. Fortunately, this was happening not only at Swarthmore, but also at other colleges and universities. For the first time, it was seen as something that was necessary, important, and positive—to have varied cultural perspectives on campus—especially at a college with the stature of Swarthmore. Many years later, when my daughter applied to Swarthmore, she was told about the Latin American Studies program. That can be considered to be one of the direct outgrowths of SASS's actions of so many years ago.

Was the occupation of the admissions office effective in achieving a more socially just institution? Maybe we should ask current generations of students this question. The activism that prompted Swarthmore's 1969 protest was going on all over the United States in various institutions of higher learning. I do think it was an action that produced something good. It worked slowly, but it worked. It is good that it has also opened the doors for other groups to develop their own organizations without being perceived as threatening. I think our activism is something to be admired.

After completing our studies in the United States, my husband Ferdinand and I settled in Panama. So, in addition to learning about science and about the vicissitudes of life for blacks living in America, I also continue to learn about the person with whom I am sharing my life. Our daughter memorialized our relationship through a surprise assemblage of photos for a recent wedding anniversary. The feature photo she chose was a profile of me taken during my senior year on the lush lawns of Swarthmore by my future husband.

The lessons I learned at Swarthmore about how to handle injustices facing black Americans and those about how to coexist in multiethnic Guyana helped prepare me to navigate Panama's own racial, ethnic, social, and political complexities. After Swarthmore, I did my graduate studies in medical microbiology and immunology at Temple University and, upon relocating to Panama, I joined the faculty of the Medical School at the University of Panama. One of my most significant challenges was that I had to learn and then teach in Spanish! After many wonderful years in higher education, I switched to the industrial sector and worked for the latter part of my professional life in water quality control in the Panama Canal. I am recently retired, but do some work for the animal care committee of the Smithsonian Tropical Research Institute in Panama. I also take part in and have served on the board of directors of the Society of Friends of the West Indian Museum of Panama.

To See the World—Jannette's Story

JANNETTE O. DOMINGO

To See the World

"Join the Air Force and see the world." The announcer's commanding voice seemed to speak directly to me from our black-and-white television with the rabbit ears antenna on top. TV was mostly a family affair back when I was just starting high school, so my younger brother, two sisters, and my parents would all probably have been watching along with me. But somehow, it seems only I really heard that particular message. It seemed like a follow-up to the poetry that I had absorbed in my Harlem elementary school. John Masefield's "Sea Fever" was a staple in every substitute teacher's repertoire at PS 57. My classmates and I had regularly proclaimed, "I must go down to the seas again."

Masefield probably had not intended it, but to me, the seas included the Caribbean Sea. Everyone in my circle of extended family and friends had Caribbean roots. Almost all were from the Virgin Islands. Mommy came to New York City from St. Thomas, Virgin Islands in her late teens and Daddy's parents had come as young adults a generation before. Virgin Islands-born aunts, cousins, and family friends had also come to New York to work and raise families. Friends and relatives often talked about going back "home" to the Virgin Islands, and somebody else was always just arriving.

Someone might exclaim enviously, "He goin' home for Carnival!"

Another might ask, "When the las' time you went home?"

And sometimes it was a bittersweet farewell when a loved one returned home to stay. I hadn't visited St. Thomas since I was a toddler, so the gift of spending the summer between high school and college in St. Thomas was a very grand graduation reward, indeed. It would be an exciting adventure, and the first steps toward leaving the nest.

The world also spoke to me from the African dance and drumming classes my mother took my younger siblings and me to from the time I was six or seven. Like the anthropologist with whom I studied dance when I got to high school, those first teachers were culture bearers, whispering to their students that we were part of something and somewhere beautiful and great. When we little ones performed in the vivid costumes our mothers had sewn for us, we felt that we were not only accomplished artists, but African royalty, a connection that had been missing from earlier tap dance and ballet classes. Our drummers were among the performers featured on Nigerian percussionist Babatunde Olatunji's seminal *Drums of Passion,* one of the first record albums I bought myself, and the first to popularize African music in the United States.

The message that would eventually become "Black is Beautiful" was reinforced by many voices. As a teenager, I read every issue of *Ebony* magazine from cover to cover. It was a staple in most Negro households. In addition to uplifting articles about American Negro accomplishments in the arts, sports, and civic organizations and advertisements for the latest Negro beauty products, *Ebony* featured glowing reports of newly independent African and Caribbean nations. I learned the mellifluous names of Nigerian leaders like Nnamdi Azikiwe, Amadou Bello, and Sir Abubakar Tafawa. *Ebony's* black and white photos of Northern Nigerian horsemen in majestic white robes and turbans were awe inspiring.

I can also see a young Jomo Kenyatta, the first post-independence premier and future president of Kenya, on the cover of the book I borrowed from atop Daddy's dresser. I liked to appropriate his books once he put them down. They were usually otherworldly science fiction novels and short stories by the likes of Isaac Asimov, Ray Bradbury, and Arthur C. Clarke, but there was also Jomo Kenyatta's classic *Facing Mount Kenya: The Tribal Life of the Kikuyu.* Although I remember the cover photo in great detail, I'm sure I didn't get far with the text. The academic anthropological treatise was not at all as romantic or exciting as the cover photo of the author with a spear and an animal skin draped across his bare chest.

South Africa truly captivated me. While most Africans were winning their independence from European colonialism in the early 1960s, South Africans were fighting against an apartheid system with chilling resemblances to our own. The 1960 Sharpeville Massacre and the treason trials and imprisonment of Nelson Mandela and other African National Congress leaders brought South Africa into our American consciousness with a unique intensity.

Singer Miriam Makeba personified South Africa for me. With her short natural hair, she was a striking role model. She was among the women featured in an *Ebony Magazine* article about the radical movement toward natural hair. The fact that my parents thought such a hairstyle meant that the wearers were too aggressive in no way diminished her appeal. The movie *Come Back, Africa* featured Makeba's South African "jazz" and introduced me to South African penny whistle music. Its depiction of somber urban landscapes, masses of black workers commuting to work in overcrowded trains, ragged young penny whistle street musicians, and chanting work crews reminiscent of black chain gangs in the American South also made South Africans seem more like people I might know.

Daddy gave me a secondhand copy of a Smithsonian Folkways recording of South African freedom songs entitled *This Land Is Mine.* Although the liner notes translating the songs were missing, the militant sentiment was clear. I sang along and memorized the Xhosa and Zulu lyrics phonetically.

I recognized Mandela's name in the song "Tshotsholoza Mandela (Go Underground Mandela)," but it was not until I got to college that I learned that "U Sobukwe Ufuna Amajoni (Sobukwe Wants Freedom Fighters)" referred to Robert Sobukwe, another important leader in the anti-apartheid struggle, and that "Nkosi Sikelel' iAfrika (God Bless Africa)" was becoming a pan-African anthem.

When I arrived at Swarthmore, fresh from my post-high school summer in St. Thomas, I brought my love of African dance and my *Drums of Passion*, Folkways, and Miriam Makeba albums with me along with my Air Force aspirations. I believed that I was on the way to seeing a wider world. Swarthmore would soon arm me with new friends and offer me unforeseen ways of engaging that world and an unexpected academic and professional direction.

East Harlem Mosaic

We lived on East 115th Street, halfway between Park and Lexington Avenues. Our Park Avenue was not the iconic avenue of movies and magazines. That was downtown, a wealthy, fashionable world away. In East Harlem, Park Avenue meant tenements and housing projects and the elevated tracks on which commuter trains thundered out of the city to mysterious suburban destinations. Park Avenue meant five block-long structures under the tracks from 111th to 116th Streets where hundreds of vendors sold everything from Caribbean produce and fresh meats, fish, and poultry to clothing and household goods and hardware. In the shadow of the tracks, we shoppers were unseen by the equally invisible commuters who sped by over our heads.

Many of our neighbors were like us, black families with Caribbean roots. There were other islanders, mostly Puerto Ricans, who insisted on identifying themselves as "Spanish."

We also had a few neighbors from the South like the building's super and his wife. The strange little cylinder on our apartment doorframe was the receptacle for a mezuzah, a prayer scroll, left behind by the Jewish tenants whose neighborhood East Harlem had been a few decades before our arrival. Although the shopkeepers and policemen and most of the teachers were white, there were no longer any white people actually living on our block. But there was Gerault, the one white child in my sixth-grade class.

Gerault lived a few blocks away in the Little Italy enclave close to the East River, on Pleasant and Paladino Avenues. Two decades earlier, Daddy and his friends had taken the crosstown bus from their West Harlem homes to start attending Benjamin Franklin High School on Pleasant Avenue. On the first day, they were met by an angry Italian mob. They did not get off the bus. Those black students from across town needed a police escort to enter the school on the second day of classes. A few years later, in 1945, Frank Sinatra famously went to the school to try to soothe the continuing racial tensions with music. Daddy didn't tell us his story until many decades later. Nevertheless, although we hadn't known about such incidents when we were children, we understood the boundaries of our neighborhood.

We lived on 115th Street until Julia, my second little sister, was born, and Daddy had saved enough for a down payment on a modest row house in the Bronx. We moved in January 1960. From January to June, I traveled an hour by bus and subway to finish the school year at PS 57 in Mrs. Simpson's class.

Public School Days

All of the sixth-grade classes were in the schoolyard for recess when Mr. Marx confiscated a plastic water gun from one of his students. In a fit of rage, his eyes bulging, he threw the toy gun to the ground and jumped on it, stomping it to bits that flew in all directions. Mr. Marx was a middle-aged, balding white man with an unhealthy complexion and a paunch. Much like his unruly students at the bottom of the school hierarchy in Class 6-13, he was always frustrated, angry, and yelling. I felt sorry for his class. It seemed that the weakest students also got the worst teachers.

At the other end of the spectrum, my Class 6-1 had the wonderful Mrs. Carrie Simpson. Like the neighborhood, the students in my elementary school, PS 57, were mostly black with a few Puerto Ricans. Teachers and administrators were mostly white. Mrs. Simpson was one of the few black teachers. She was an elegant young woman whose fashionable red lipstick reflected her warmth and positive attitude. She believed that her students could be poets and scientists and even learn foreign languages, although such things were certainly not part of the prescribed curriculum. Mrs. Simpson was also determined to get some of her girls into Hunter College High School, one of the city's most selective public schools. Over the course of several months, she spent her lunch hours tutoring a small group of us for the entrance exam. Near the end of the semester, a monitor brought Mrs. Simpson a note from the principal. After reading it, she ran out of the classroom crying. We were all stunned. We waited apprehensively for her return. After a few minutes, she came back, composed again and smiling. She announced that I had passed the exam and would be admitted to Hunter's seventh grade in the fall. Her generosity and belief in her students had elevated my academic prospects for the foreseeable future. I never had another teacher like Mrs. Simpson, so I've carried her with me ever since.

Mrs. Simpson sent me on to a junior/senior high school that was like a foreign country. Hunter College High School was in affluent midtown Manhattan, miles from my working-class neighborhood. It was untouched by the 1964 boycott and other protests of segregation in the city's public schools. Only one of my Hunter classmates, the child of activist parents, ever expressed any interest in or even seemed aware of the Civil Rights events of the day. For all of my six years there, I was one of just a handful of black students. Nevertheless, some of my teachers could never distinguish me from the other five black girls in my cohort. In a small school where teachers generally knew their students' names, I was not a recognizable individual to them.

New York City had not yet declared the High Holy Days to be school holidays. Nevertheless, almost all of the Jewish students stayed home to observe them. On such holidays, it might be just me and two or three other non-Jewish students in a classroom. The occasional care package of Passover Seder macaroons that thoughtful classmates brought me were well-intentioned, but they also highlighted the cultural divide since I could never imagine what actually happened at a Passover Seder in their homes. Ironically, even the school's innovative Integrated Arts program was alienating. While it skillfully wove together the classics of European history, literature, and the arts, it ignored Africa and the African Diaspora. I was grateful for the cultural lifeline offered by Pearl Primus, one of the school's few black alumni. Primus had graduated from Hunter almost thirty years before and had become a celebrated dancer and a respected dance scholar and anthropologist, researching and recreating Afro-Caribbean and African dances. She recruited three of us black students from her former high school to take dance classes at her studio. This was an amazing opportunity. Her other students included professional dancers, some of whom went on to create their own dance companies.

At Hunter, intellectual gifts were taken for granted. Nevertheless, some classmates expressed surprise when I exceeded their expectations. We all anxiously checked our grade point averages and class rankings after midterm and final grades, assuming that we would be competing with each other for college admissions. Negotiating the rigorous curriculum and cultural differences of that elite high school prepared me well for the intensity and challenges of college.

Leaving the Nest

We were speeding down the New Jersey Turnpike toward Philadelphia on a Greyhound bus. Mom and I sat shoulder to shoulder peering out of the window. The Turnpike was a very new highway in 1965 and this was our first Turnpike trip. Little money had been wasted on landscaping. So, once past the smog and the industrial wasteland of Elizabeth, New Jersey, the vistas were uncluttered and open, largely barren. We had left our Bronx home at the crack of dawn to take a city bus to the subway to the Port Authority Bus Terminal in midtown Manhattan, just west of the still sleazy Times Square. We were dressed for the occasion in Sunday best—stockings and low heels, probably hats, possibly even gloves.

This was the first time we were traveling out of town together since we had returned from a year in St. Thomas when I was only two years old. With a younger brother and sisters, and parents who each worked at least one job, there were not many occasions when I had a parent all to myself. That alone was enough to make it a memorable day, but it was also the first time either of us was visiting a college campus.

In Philadelphia, we made our way from the bus terminal to the commuter train for the short ride from the familiar city environment out to the suburbs and the Swarthmore College campus for my pre-admissions interview. The Swarthmore train station was at the bottom of a gentle hill. We walked briskly up McGill Walk, the long tree lined corridor from the train station to Parrish Hall, the stately building that occupied the crest. As we walked, we were dwarfed by the towering trees that announced that this was a magnificent and historic place. Beyond the trees, we could see imposing stone buildings and a vast lawn and garden-like landscape that extended as far as we could see. In the distance, a few students strolled casually, seemingly oblivious to their wonderland. When we finally entered Parrish Hall, we were subdued by the formal parlors and the hushed, softly lit halls en route to the admissions office.

My interviewer was Dean Barbara Pearson Lange, impeccably coiffed and tailored with a cool handshake and reserved manner. Somehow, the Virgin Islands became part of the conversation. Perhaps she detected my mother's accent, or maybe I had mentioned my heritage in my admissions essay. In any case, she warmed to us as she shared recollections of her father and his service as Governor of the Virgin Islands in the early 1930s when my mother was a young child. Mom listened and chatted politely, but when we left the office, she told me that Governor Pearson had not been very popular. Although his administration was undoubtedly more enlightened than the aggressively racist occupation by the US Navy that preceded it, his was still a colonial administration and to many Virgin Islanders of my mother's generation, his legacy was largely one of fiscal mismanagement and liberal paternalism as he attempted to bring culture to the "natives."

Although clearly well-meaning, the governor's daughter was oblivious to the possible chasm between her perceptions and those of a "native." I had experienced such dissonance before. After all, I had gone to a selective public high school in New York City where I was one of few working-class, non-Jewish students and one of even fewer black students. So, when I started at Swarthmore in the fall of 1966, the issues facing black students seemed familiar. While Swarthmore had decided to admit more black students, we were confronted with unacknowledged contradictions: more black students had been admitted, but the number remained too small to significantly impact diversity; despite its liberal Quaker traditions, microaggressions and indignities were common; and although Swarthmore was one of the country's most highly rated academic institutions, the canon on which its curriculum was based was too narrow. Nevertheless, I believed that Swarthmore was well-intentioned, and I was sure that it would provide the knowledge and credentials I needed to have a successful life and career.

My parents hadn't really wanted me to go away for college. They could never have afforded private college tuition and they didn't know just how generous elite scholarships could be. They were also concerned about the perils of too much independence and too little supervision in an environment beyond their experience. Perhaps on some level, they also knew that I would never truly come back home. In those days, the distance between the Bronx and Swarthmore seemed much greater than it does today. Working-class Bronx girls like me did not have their own cars, and frequent Greyhound bus or Pennsylvania Railroad tickets were not in the budget. With the exception of the holidays, I don't recall ever going home during the school year, and I can only remember one visit from my family. I became completely immersed in a life that was largely separate from theirs. I told them about my Swarthmore friends and a little about our African companions from Lincoln, but they seldom actually met them.

When summer vacations rolled around, I found jobs in educational opportunity programs that foreshadowed the career I would pursue. These jobs also kept me away from home. After freshman year, I worked in a Temple University program in North Philadelphia. After my second and third years, I worked in a residential Upward Bound program at Columbia University. And then I got married. Although the marriage didn't last, it never occurred to me to move back to my parents' home. My friends and I cherished our independence, and we had every expectation that we would make it permanent, even in the face of the challenges we knew were bound to come and hardships we could not anticipate. It seems the times in which we came of age and our youthful experiences, including our Swarthmore activism, made us more self-reliant and resilient, more prepared for adversity, and better equipped for struggle. Although we were not among the entitled, we knew that we were able and definitely worthy. After college, I never again lived in my parents' house.

Sisters

I met my first-year roommate when we were assigned to room together at a recruitment weekend at the College. She was from an affluent suburb of New York City far removed from my working-class Bronx neighborhood. She had also lived in Europe. Her father was a WWII conscientious objector, the first I'd ever met. He drove a bottle green Jaguar, also the first I'd ever seen. After the recruitment weekend, she called and asked me to be her roommate. I gladly accepted. Having a roommate who had actually chosen me was a relief. We got along well. She didn't ask ignorant questions or make insensitive remarks as I heard some white roommates were prone to do. In our room, I introduced her to the Miracles, Tito Puente, and Miriam Makeba. She introduced me to the French icon Charles Aznavour. But I don't recall doing anything at all with her outside of that space.

In that first year, I had already forged much stronger bonds with the Sisters and our Brother. Our dinner table and dorm room discussions had quickly evolved from such concerns as where to find hair salons and barbershops that could straighten or trim our hair to satisfy Eurocentric aesthetics, to which of us would braid the other's newly natural afro hair. Almost as soon as I arrived on campus, I was immersed in black student conversations about issues ranging from the small and declining number of black students admitted to the College, to the role of students in the emerging Black Power movement, relationships with Africa and African students, and the war in Vietnam. This activist spirit soon led us to create a formal organization, SASS.

My new friends were not like any friends I'd had before. At home, friends were confined to separate boxes, physically and culturally separate worlds of my Jewish school, Virgin Islands church and family, and Caribbean neighborhood. I never had friends with whom I lived, studied, organized, and struggled every day. Each of the Seven Sisters and our Brother was shaped by a particular environment and personal history, and a very specific black experience. We each brought a unique array of qualities to our group and to SASS. In varying degrees, we were writers, orators, leaders, and managers, and we were serious, funny, analytical, detail-oriented, and big picture folk. We complemented and educated each other. I savored and learned from our diversity. It was an unexpected, and no doubt unintended, gift that the College gave us—and itself.

There were four of us Sisters in the class of '70: Aundrea, Bridget, Myra, and me. Because we were in various majors, we shared few classes, and so our study sessions were more like support group sessions where we encouraged each other to stay awake, meet our deadlines, persevere, and excel. Our study breaks were filled with the far-ranging personal and political conversations that kept us sane and made us "sisters." When we needed to push past exhaustion, we often spilled out of the dorm and ran across campus to the athletic field. There in the bracing night air, we raced around the darkened track, laughing and shouting defiantly at the starlit sky. Although we never became great swimmers or excelled in the broad range of sports the College believed students should master, we had found our own way to subscribe to its philosophy of developing sane minds in sound bodies.

Of course, my friends were not the only black women students. In fact, there were almost twenty other "sisters" at Swarthmore in spring 1969. I remember a few as cherished younger sisters, friends, or at least fellow travelers, but many of the other women only flicker through my memory like pale ghosts. I see them as if from a great distance. I recall one solitary figure bundled up against the autumn afternoon breeze. She was the only student I knew of who lived off campus. I only ever saw her hurrying down McGill Walk, focused on catching the train that took her away each day back home to Philadelphia. I see another young black woman drifting across campus toward Sharples Dining Hall. She is alone and aloof, seemingly oblivious to my presence. But mostly the other black women are absent from my memories. I can't visualize them with me in any of my classes nor can I imagine them joining those of us who were uplifted by singing gospel songs together at our table in the dining hall. They did not congregate in any of the dorm rooms or brainstorming sessions that framed my campus life. But perhaps they spoke to me with concerns that I no longer recall. I realize that I never really knew them or truly understood how they negotiated their version of life at the College. Nevertheless, in the end, it turned out that we had enough in common so that almost all of them ultimately took a stand with us in the admissions office.

Finding Joy Off Campus

In the mid-1960s, Swarthmore was going through the motions of closely overseeing its incoming women students, perhaps trying to strike a balance between privilege and independence on the one hand, and paternalism on the other. Our parents were offered several options with respect to how much supervision we required. My parents chose a middle ground. I could leave campus at will, but I was supposed to sign out and indicate my destination and when I would return. It was a minor restriction. Nevertheless, it bothered me that some students might have more freedom than I did. After all, I had just won the battle to leave home. But in the end, my parents' choice made no difference at all. The dorm monitor knew nothing of my frequent comings and goings nor of the profound impact my time away from campus was having on my education and the direction of my life. If she had asked, I might have said, "I am 18 and I love African dance. I wear bold patterns and colorful fabrics. I love the music and the freedom of movement. I love feeling graceful and strong. I feel like a beautiful African woman. This is who I am."

North Philadelphia was only a few miles from Swarthmore, but a world apart. I had to take the suburban commuter train from campus into Philadelphia and then a city train or trolley up to a North Philadelphia dance studio to take classes with the Arthur Hall Afro-American Dance Company. I probably drafted Aundrea to go with me a few times, but most often I traveled alone. It was a long trip, but a welcome escape from the campus cultural void. In Arthur Hall's classes, I wasn't a token "exceptional minority." I was just a young woman from the community (albeit a distant one) who loved the African sensibility that was embodied in the fabric of our attire, the music, and the dance.

I had danced since I was a very young child. At first, it was the standard ballet and tap dance, but before long, my mother found Ismay Andrews at our Harlem Community Center. Although she had been a student of the great African dance pioneers and a teacher of celebrated dancers and drummers, she also brought African culture to young people in community centers like ours. In high school I studied with anthropologist Pearl Primus. Much later I learned that Arthur Hall had also been a student of Pearl Primus. These dance masters introduced young people like me to an African aesthetic we could celebrate as our own, a joyous cultural self-determination, and serious predisposition to activism. In 1963, Pearl Primus famously described the power of dance:

> Why do I dance? Dance is my medicine. It's the scream which eases for a while the terrible frustration common to all human beings who because of race, creed, or color are 'invisible.' Dance is the fist with which I fight the sickening ignorance of prejudice.[16]

I had gone off campus to hold on to this treasured part of my old life, but in North Philadelphia, I also explored the possibility of a new form of self-determination. Most of my weekends would be spent with a Namibian named Hidipo and other African students from Lincoln University.

I met Hidipo early in fall 1966, my first semester at Swarthmore. He was among a group of students from nearby Lincoln University who came to Swarthmore to meet with black students who were just beginning to organize. We had reserved a secluded private room in the College's elegant chalet-like dining hall for the meeting. I recall the event as if Olympians had come down from the mountain to speak to us. The Lincoln students were mostly Southern African and Kenyan, the first real Africans I had ever met. Many of them were significantly older than the typical college undergraduate. They were all men; we were mostly women.

From that meeting, I remember clearly only a handsome soft-spoken Kenyan named Henry who drove the Lincoln group to Swarthmore for that meeting. I was surprised and flattered when he sent me a letter afterwards. But I don't recall actually seeing Henry ever again. Years later, I learned that he had been shooed away by the inner circle of the group when, unbeknownst to me, Hidipo had staked a claim on me. Hidipo was the intellectual leader of the group. His comrades called him "Ho Chi" after Ho Chi Minh, the charismatic political strategist of the North Vietnamese revolution. Just as he had planned, well before the semester ended, Hidipo and I were a couple and I was spending much of my free time with him in Philadelphia.

Hidipo was a very serious, purposeful student, preparing to take his place in building his country. A voracious reader, always taking copious notes, he pored over his books searching for lessons that could be applied at home. His mission of liberation for South West Africa was consuming. But he was ever optimistic about friends and relationships and the possibility of finding common ground with political adversaries. He affirmed and modeled the optimism and sense of responsibility that we felt at Swarthmore, but on a larger stage. His example made me feel that my choices and my life could be significant beyond the small circle of my family and friends.

Academics

It took me longer to get excited about schoolwork. I was disappointed with my first semester grades. I hadn't gotten all As. My philosophy class notes featured meaningless squiggles made by a sleeping hand. While I had excelled in Spanish and math in high school, those classes progressed from too easy to too challenging without ever becoming engaging. Worst of all, although I had expected to major in psychology, I found the introductory course so tedious that I napped during the midterm. Introduction to Psychology was one of the few very large classes at Swarthmore, so large that it met in a tiered lecture hall rather than a regular classroom. I was immediately turned off by the size and anonymity of the class and the drone of the famous professor. He never learned our names and didn't really seem to care about teaching. I was even more disappointed by the focus on the anatomy of the brain. Was this really psychology? Clearly, I hadn't understood the scope of the discipline. By the time we finally progressed from brain functions to cognitive dissonance, I had effectively checked out as a psychology major. In my first semester, an aloof professor had derailed my youthful plans. I hadn't realized how little I actually knew about psychology. Now I understood that I was truly in uncharted territory. I would have to keep an open mind to find out what I really wanted to study.

And then, somehow, I found Bernard Saffran. He had just joined the Swarthmore faculty in fall 1967. Although he never became a mentor, he remains one of the few Swarthmore professors whose spirit stays with me. His economics course was a revelation. Here, unexpectedly, was a subject matter that was immediately relevant and engaging. Most importantly, it was being taught by a professor who actually saw me and valued my particular experience and unique contributions to the class. I can recall the thrill of realizing that I could see myself and my community in the urban markets that were being described. Now, finally, I was awakened. Economics would be an important part of the International Relations/Political Science major I designed for myself, but I never imagined that in a few years I would be the one teaching economics with Professor Saffran's class fresh in my mind.

African politics would also be an essential part of my major. It was taught by another new faculty member, Professor Hopkins. It was the only class in which I remember actually having fun. Before the substantive discussion, each session began with our own version of the *Jeopardy!* game. There were about a dozen students in the class, including a couple of the Sisters. As we faced off around the conference room table, we mercilessly grilled each other on major and minor features of contemporary and historical Africa. Each week, the questions grew more and more challenging. No one wanted to make the first mistake and have to pay penance by bringing increasingly imaginative and sophisticated refreshments for the following class meeting. Before long, we had graduated from pretzels and potato chips to such gourmet delicacies as the crab dip supplied by Myra.

We thought we knew just about every detail of African geopolitics, but we had actually paid little attention to developments in the Horn of Africa. So, it was ironic that, in addition to Professors Hopkins and Saffran, the fall 1967 cohort of new faculty members also included, Asmarom Legesse, an Eritrean from the Horn of Africa and the College's only full-time black faculty member. Just as ironically, although Professor Legesse would become well known for his scholarship on indigenous political systems, he was an anthropologist and so he did not teach the African-Politics course.

Like other Africans from the region that I would meet later in life, Professor Legesse's was yet another face of the diversity of the continent. With medium brown skin, wavy hair, an aquiline nose, and slightly hooded twinkling eyes, he was strikingly handsome in a different way from my Namibian friends or the Nigerian horsemen who had captured my imagination as a child. Although he was a bit formal in demeanor, he was also warm and welcoming. It was heartening to have a black faculty member who could relate to our concerns both in and outside of the classroom. Professor Legesse would play an important role in supporting our efforts to create a Black Studies concentration, serving as our liaison to the faculty during our occupation of the admissions office and continuing to advocate for us in the immediate aftermath of the Takeover.

A Parting Gift to the College

I always looked forward to Christmas vacation. It was long enough to touch base with my old life, be embraced by family and friends, and also to recharge and prepare for the flurry of activity that marked the end of the semester. Christmas vacation 1968 was all of that and more. Those of us who could be in New York had been entrusted by the other Sisters with planning the logistics of the Takeover. Marilyn A., Harold, Aundrea, and I met at Marilyn A.'s house in Harlem. I was back in the neighborhood, just blocks from the streets where I had spent my early childhood, to gear up for the coming confrontation that would be the climax of my third and final year at Swarthmore.

I was taking twice the normal number of courses so that I could graduate early. It could be done, just barely, but I couldn't afford to slack off on my coursework just because I was part of the occupation of the admissions office. I had my wedding and graduate school planned for that fall, so my textbooks and notebooks were among the essential items that I brought into the admissions office with me. In fact, everyone brought books and intended to continue their coursework.

My memories of the Takeover are not of the scenes that are depicted in the grainy black and white photographs that have survived, but rather, I still see vividly the office's carpeted floor, heavy wood furnishings, generously upholstered armchairs and sofas, and its large square coffee table. They were all designed for the comfort of visitors—not occupiers—especially prospective students and their parents. No doubt, the imposing portraits of the College's founders were also intended to impress, if not intimidate. During our occupation, all of this was dimly lit. The office windows were papered over to block prying eyes, so there was little natural sunlight and no distinction between nights and days.

We spent many long hours around the coffee table. It became the conference table where we debated our strategy for engaging the College community and pressuring the administration. We also labored over the exact wording of each statement that would be disseminated or delivered by our spokesmen. Our objectives were ambitious, but we believed them achievable. It felt really good to have taken action and to have been able to enlist most of the black students despite some dissonant personalities and a wide range of backgrounds, personal histories, and even political persuasions.

Chronologically, we were just barely adults—eighteen to twenty-one years old—but we had a mature sense of responsibility and an amazing optimism. Although some of us were considered to be weak, "at-risk" students, we believed that we had the capacity to challenge the trajectory of an institution with 100 years of history. We had been disappointed by the College's sins of omission and angered by actions that were at best thoughtless and at worst willful. But we believed—correctly, as it turned out—that we could use the College's sense of itself as a progressive and fundamentally moral place to ignite a dialogue about our critique and that the dialogue would ultimately require the College to accede to our demands.

Because we believed in ourselves and our vision of a more inclusive college, we also believed that we were responsible for doing everything we could to change the College. Those of us who were graduating had a particular sense of urgency. We wanted to make a lasting difference before we left. We felt especially responsible to those black students who would remain after the Takeover and those who would come when we were all gone. How could I have known, then, that there would be so many college conference tables in my future and that very similar goals and objectives would still be on those tables?

Cold Reality in Montreal, 1969–71

After the Takeover, we immediately plunged into the final exams and papers that had been postponed by the "Crisis." The spring semester that followed flew by in a blur of coursework and SASS activities. I raced to complete my overload of courses in order to graduate early and to be one of the first to earn the concentration in Black Studies that we had fought for. Instead of a fourth year of college, I would go out into the real world.

When I left Swarthmore, I was sure that I knew just what my future would look like. I was very wrong. McGill University in Montreal was supposed to be the first leg of my journey to the exciting new life I imagined. I could probably have gone almost anywhere I wanted to for graduate school, but as a political refugee and stateless person, Hidipo had fewer choices. His sponsor, the African American Institute, was sending him to McGill, a fine university in Montreal, so that's where we went. We arrived in mid-September, soon after our wedding. By October, it was snowing. Over the next seven months, each new storm added to the densely-packed accumulation covering every open space except the plowed streets and roads. There were very few hours of daylight, and it was bitterly cold. That first year we lived in Longueuil, a metro ride away from campus, so for several months it was dark when we left home for school in the mornings, and the sun had already set by mid-afternoon when our classes ended.

Fortunately, I was eager to begin my studies in economic development and public finance. With these skills, I could make a difference in Africa. But there were few Africans, Caribbean immigrants, black Canadians, or African Americans at McGill, so the perspective I brought to classes was often unique. The few African Americans we met around town were paradoxically apolitical, self-absorbed, draft dodgers. They were refugees trying to blend in with white Canadian girlfriends. The students of color were mostly across town at working-class Sir George Williams University, and I would not meet many of them until my second year. McGill was an elite English language outpost in a bilingual city in the francophone province of Québéc. Although the Caribbean presence in the city and at the more accessible Sir George Williams University had just begun to increase significantly, French Canadians, not black people, were the significant national minority. Québécois struggles for political and cultural self-determination dominated the activist discourse at McGill. I felt almost invisible there.

Worse yet, that first year at McGill was a "qualifying year" during which Hidipo and I had to prove ourselves academically in order to be formally admitted to our respective master's programs. My Swarthmore degree didn't impress McGill any more than Hidipo's degree from Lincoln. We were both deemed to be lacking in the fundamentals of the disciplines we had chosen. Having to qualify was an unprecedented academic rebuff and a mortifying way to begin. Hidipo was more resilient and seemed unfazed, but for me, it was devastating. Invisible and powerless, I soon realized that I was not going to make it as an exile in Canada. Unlike Hidipo, I was not prepared for the life I had chosen. Despite his best efforts to save our marriage, after two years in Canada, Hidipo and I went our separate ways. I was twenty-three years old.

An Unexpected Career

When I left Montreal, I began a doctoral program in Economics at Columbia University in New York. Although I had not anticipated an academic career, a year after completing my coursework, I began teaching Black Studies at the City College of New York. But the fact that I was still working toward the doctorate, the ultimate academic credential, made me feel like the proverbial imposter rather than a young professional embarking on a career. I had completed the structured component of the doctoral program expeditiously, but without gaining a foothold in Columbia's academic community. I had no faculty mentors to guide or encourage me to complete the dissertation and few relationships with classmates. Like my earlier experience at McGill, I was completely alienated from the University. This time, however, the rest of my life was very full. I was at home in my city. By 1974, I was teaching full-time in the African American Studies and Economics departments at John Jay College with a predominantly black and Latino student body. I was thoroughly engaged by a lively social and cultural life. It was an exciting time, enriched and connected to earlier visions of a life in Africa by the vibrant African immigrant and diplomatic communities in which I was immersed. It would take me years to refocus on completing the degree and to get serious about advancing the academic career into which I had fallen.

I had been teaching at John Jay for a year or two when a corporate recruiter approached me. AT&T was looking for staff economists. Although the Business School courses I had sampled at Columbia were incredibly alienating, I still thought it might be interesting to try the corporate world.

So, I agreed to an interview. I had very little invested in the process other than pride in performing well. When I was actually offered a position, I didn't hesitate to ask for a salary that was significantly higher than what I was making as a college instructor. After all, I already had a full-time job with benefits that included summers off, the freedom of a two-day-a-week teaching schedule, and a relatively diverse and liberal environment. The company would have to offer a lot more to be competitive.

The recruiter was furious. Didn't I realize that he was doing me a favor by getting me the job offer? How dare I ask for so much? As we shouted at each other over the phone, he insisted that I would never have such a great opportunity again. Perhaps he could have won me over if he had tried to entice me with prospects of personal growth and career advancement rather than trying to intimidate me with insults and scathing condescension. Fortunately, he was not that insightful, or I might have given the corporate world more serious consideration and missed my calling in academia.

Full Circle

While we at Swarthmore were demanding Black Studies, our contemporaries at colleges and universities across the country were doing the same. We assumed that the students who succeeded us would make sure that promises were kept and that the changes we had won were institutionalized. I hadn't expected to be a part of that process, but there I was, just five years after the Takeover, teaching in a newly created Black Studies Department (or African American Studies as we renamed it in the 1980s) at John Jay College of Criminal Justice in the City University of New York. I became a tenured faculty member; department chairperson; program founder and director; and finally, graduate studies dean. In these roles,

I was able to create opportunities for others and be the mentor and advocate for students and colleagues that I had lacked in my own education and career.

For me, founding and directing the College's first program to prepare first-generation—mostly of color—college students for doctoral study, and responding to the rash of police involved deaths of blacks in the 1990s with a program to educate a non-racist NYPD leadership were natural extensions of my position as chair of African American Studies. As chair, I was able to raise the profile of the African American Studies Department and use it to help develop a sense of community and optimism among black administrators, faculty and staff much like the camaraderie and inclusiveness of our Swarthmore group.

I did not know that I would stay at John Jay for 39 years. As a young person, I had a very simplistic notion of what it would mean "to see the world." At the time, it meant visiting as many countries as possible. Although I continue to travel, seeing the world became less about visiting places and more about being a part of an international network of friends and family. It also came to mean working with graduate and undergraduate students, colleagues, and guests from all over the world at a college not narrowly focused on criminal justice, but rather increasingly addressing social justice issues, from local to international, as I had always insisted it should.

Unlike the usual subdued formality of the retirement receptions the President of the College hosted for executive staff like myself and occasionally for senior faculty, my retirement reception was a crowded, boisterous affair. I was particularly touched by a faculty colleague's observation that I had not been so much concerned with "being" important as with "doing" important things for the students and for the College. I had stayed true to the values and leadership style that the Seven Sisters and a Brother had developed decades earlier and that had served us so well as students who were determined to make a meaningful and lasting difference at Swarthmore College.

THE TAKEOVER

Day Six

DAY SIX
Keeping Up Morale

By day six, the strains on our morale were beginning to show.

Smiles were harder to find on the faces of the nineteen- and twenty-year-old occupiers. Our notoriously loud bursts of laughter became rare. Worries that the unthinkable might happen leaked out more often in our conversations. What if they refused our demands? What if we didn't get amnesty? And, in our brainstorming to write public statements, one could detect a little more testiness and impatience with the foibles of one another.

Some of us who felt the weight of leadership may have fared better if we had given ourselves permission to take more breaks. But, at this point in the protest, there never seemed to be a lull in the activity. Having each brought perhaps only one change of clothing, most of us had not left to return to the dormitories to freshen up. Although we had decided ahead of time how to divide duties once inside, we felt responsible for everything that involved us.

Those outside would present our demands and arguments to the College administrators, faculty, and the media, and then meet with the group inside to ensure everyone agreed on the next course of action and on any public statements. Would we push for Black Studies to be a major or minor? A department on its own or a special concentration? Should black upperclassmen assist in admissions for next fall or should we hold out for hiring a black administrator immediately? An outside black expert had agreed to consult with Admissions, but they had rejected that idea before. Clinton and Don, SASS chairperson and vice chair respectively, met daily with faculty and administration representatives to explain our position, get faculty reaction, and bring the results back to those inside, as planned.

Inside, we did the crucial work of planning strategy in response to the issues and proposals brought back by the spokesmen and maintaining group cohesion and morale. Should we tone down the stridency in our language or in the immediacy of the changes we demanded? Or resume participating in joint committees to work on issues even if it took the rest of the school year to resolve them? Should we even consider partial amnesty as a compromise position? At the same time, the leaders inside distributed provisions and counsel. They empathized when a first-year student couldn't fight back tears of worry.

Additional students were deciding, almost daily, to join the group inside and had to be oriented to the routines. Some who had never attended a SASS meeting, or even publicly identified as black, unexpectedly felt compelled to take a stand with us. We remember that they were there only because they appear in photos we took during the sit-in. We still look at those images with some disbelief because it was so rare to see them in our midst.

Supporters from the community were showing up at the window and had to be received and updated. They often brought us clippings of articles in the press, committee minutes and recommendations, and copies of open letters written by faculty, students, and other commentators. Sitting around the large coffee table, we worked on drafts of written responses to those that were ill-informed, unworkable, or critical of us for the official spokespersons to use. No, we could not wait for the usual hiring process to search for a black dean. There was already too much resistance from the admissions dean, and we needed a professional to represent our concerns in administration meetings. People like Marilyn H., who was applying to law school and would become a civil rights lawyer in the future, were already honing their skills by carefully stating our positions. Life on the inside was calm, but with all the comings and goings of visitors to the window and students newly deciding to join, it was proving difficult to get much schoolwork done.

Several parents made telephone calls to the campus asking for their children or actually came to the campus to see them. Most likely, that happened when they heard the mostly negative news accounts of the Takeover. Myra's sister told her that her parents received a call from Swarthmore about her involvement in the Takeover. Marilyn A.'s mother got what seemed to be a form letter from SASS explaining why we had taken the action. Her mother and uncle showed up in person. Everyone had some explaining to do since informing parents ahead of time was not feasible. Most parents were satisfied to hear our voices saying that we were okay. Others were completely dismayed and surprised because their children had never been outspoken about the issues SASS raised. Sherry B.'s parents were among those. She describes how, living right in Philadelphia, they first discovered that she was part of the Takeover when they saw their daughter on the local evening news. A camera crew had caught her on film as she timidly climbed back into the admissions office window after returning from taking a shower in her dorm.

Years later we learned that one student, who was not a member of SASS and did not join the sit-in, wrote an open letter of support despite his father's threats to not pay tuition for his final undergraduate semester if he joined the protest. We recently read that Ruth W.'s parents came to the College and asked to speak to President Smith. Her memory is that when they introduced themselves, he turned his back and walked away. Ruth didn't return after her freshman year. She has become a renowned scholar of black history, completing her undergraduate work at a different institution.

Although we checked in with each other several times a day, it is likely that neither group—those primarily outside nor those primarily inside—ever fully understood exactly how the other group had experienced the turmoil. With no clear end in sight and the semester scheduled to end that week, the College faculty made an unprecedented agreement to allow all students to negotiate individual arrangements for completing course requirements, in light of their likely having been affected in some way by the "Crisis."

That concession by the faculty allowed us to exhale a little, although we were increasingly aware of the danger of reprisals and repercussions for those of us on scholarship, those with foreign visas, and those with parents who disapproved. Our demand for total amnesty was becoming more important to us; it was one demand that we could not relinquish.

Seeing the Unseen—Marilyn A's Story

MARILYN ALLMAN MAYE

Finding a Guardian Angel

I knew I was prepared for the academics. I had already won a competition for a freshman merit scholarship. Now, arriving the first day to live at college, I sensed how much I needed a different kind of help. I needed the unseen help my father described in his sermon, "Seeing the Unseen." God's aid is always right there, he'd explain, just beyond obvious obstacles and limitations. We miss it because "man looks at the outward appearance, but God looks at the heart." Use God's eyes and accomplish what you must.

You might have expected any other mother to seek out an influential professor or the Dean of Women or even an older female student, but Daisy Allman was about to entrust me, her last-born, to one of the least visible adults on the campus, a lady in a brown, cotton uniform with only a first name on her lapel pin.

"My name is Marion," the chocolate-hued, full-bosomed woman began. I would later learn that she was Mrs. Showell, "I'm the maid for this floor of Willets dormitory. You don't have to worry. I will look out for your daughter."

That's all she said. Then she and my mother exchanged knowing smiles and I could see the wave of relief come over both of them.

In the nearly seventeen years of my life, my mother had almost never left me overnight anywhere, and then only in the care of someone she trusted deeply. Yet on that September day, she committed me to a total stranger, surely an answer to her prayers. My mother had never forgotten her humble roots and bonded easily with others in service roles. She was sure I would need a guardian angel in this college where she knew no one and where she had agreed to let me stay against her better judgment.

I never uncovered the journey that Mrs. Marion Showell took to becoming a campus domestic worker in midlife. If she ever felt humiliated by young people who could be her grandchildren calling her by her first name, she never let it show. Helping the young women in the dormitory was more than an obligation to her employer. Her warm manner affirmed she understood her value, especially to the handful of black girls there.

I'm sure she recognized the panic in my eyes as I stopped midway along the dormitory stairwell, gripping the handrail, my eyes following the parade up and down of shoeboxes moving in for one student. Mrs. Sowell dusted the rooms of girls from all backgrounds, the girls in stockings and designer shoes and those just as wealthy who walked barefoot everywhere. She also understood my sinking fear that I didn't belong there, and she made it her project to check on me regularly until I realized I did.

My mother's confidence, both in her own child-rearing and in the black employees who maintained the campus, would prove well-founded. She returned home to take up the role of chronicler, keeping me informed weekly, by letter, about life back home.

An Affirming Eye

> The Millers christened their new baby on Sunday.
>
> The Olivers were home on furlough from India. You wouldn't recognize Beverly, she's as tall as her mother.
>
> Ms. Murray's blind choir performed Handel's "Messiah" yesterday afternoon.

> Tell the operator to reverse the charges if you don't have money to call home.
>
> Ms. Winters sent this dollar. Said for you to buy ice cream.

If I had kept every Monday morning letter lovingly handwritten by my mother to me at college, I'd have close to two hundred. These typified the devotion my mother displayed for each of her three children. It was fierce and undeniable.

There was little in those weekly letters I felt I could share with friends on campus. I knew no one else whose family's lifestyle was like mine. Also, there was never any bad news. My mother believed students away at school must be given no cause to worry about their family's well-being—nothing that might impact their studies or grades. So, I didn't get a letter informing me my father had had a massive heart attack and was hospitalized for the first time in his seventy-two years. That letter didn't come until a few days before graduation after all exams were safely completed. While reading my mother's letter as I rode the Media Local train, I learned he wouldn't be able to attend. Tear drops silently rolled down my face. No one else's attendance at graduation would have meant more than my father's, not even hers. Ma provided all the emotional support, but Daddy's elusive affirmation seemed to matter most. My disappointment ripped all the joy out of the coming graduation celebration.

I took for granted my mother's nurturing skills, but they were hard-won. As a teenager, Daisy's family's poverty and her own reputation for not being lazy prompted her second cousins, the Watsons, to legally adopt her. They brought her with them when they migrated to New York City from the American-ruled, segregated Canal Zone in Panama, where she was born. Daisy leapt at the chance for a new life and her gamble paid off handsomely. Once in Harlem, she absorbed the home-making skills of her second mom and built on the survival skills of her birth mom. Working her way through night school, she earned a high school diploma and the registered nurse certification at the historically black Lincoln School for Nurses. By the time she qualified to sponsor the immigration of her biological mother and siblings, she had married and had her own children and had developed into a force of nature.

In my head, I play videos of my mother's wizardry in managing the men in our lives. I see her getting access to and cooperation from the mostly white and male school administrators in the segregated elementary school in Harlem that her children attended. She organized fellow "baketivists," among the handful of active Parents Association members. They baked cakes and sold slices to the students and staff at lunch time, using the funds to provide small extras for the students and classrooms.

When my PS 68 classmate, Jenny "Jezebel" Saxby, stood outside our house wailing because her mother was wildly waving a 10-inch blade at Jenny's father in broad daylight, threatening to kill him, my mother came outside and put her body between Jenny's raging mother and her "lying, no-good" husband, and pre-empted a murder. She cajoled Mrs. Saxby into the Allman house to wipe the sweat from her face, regain her dignity, and eat some homemade cake while Mr. Saxby got taken away by the police to the relief of Jenny and Marilyn.

Peace-making and cake. Among feuding relatives or church members. To boost someone on the social margins. I didn't know then that I was being tutored in the arts of female leadership and activism.

It is not surprising that my first forays into activism featured those arts. When I was a teenager, my mother had apprenticed me to a neighborhood seamstress to make sure I acquired skills to sustain a wardrobe. My portable sewing machine accompanied me to college and stitched my outfits for social events and curtains for my different dorm room windows across the four years. Most significant was its use to make dashikis, West African-style shirts, for the black males on campus to celebrate our heritage, to resist Eurocentrism.

I witnessed how narrow constraints on social roles breed creativity, and creativity generates unconventional movers and shakers, even if they are invisible to those in the mainstream.

Taming the Dragons

Early in my freshman year, I discovered female students from more privileged backgrounds than mine often had very different role models for their activism.

My first roommate Laura and I both hailed from Northeastern states, but that is about where our similarities ended. Raised in a small town, she had early childhood memories of being wheeled in a stroller to peace movement demonstrations. Her mother regularly mailed her the latest edition of *I.F. Stone's Weekly*—a radical left journal I had never heard of before meeting her.

As a child, the closest I came to a personal connection to anyone in public life was my mother pointing with pride in actually knowing the celebrity in newspaper photos of the late US Congresswoman Bella Abzug. Bella was ten years old when my mother worked for her parents, cleaning their apartment. A teenager herself, my mother traveled by subway to Bella's neighborhood where white New Yorkers lived. After work, she went back to Harlem for classes at Wadleigh High School. Aside from a very few exceptionally privileged blacks,

Daisy and others like her who aspired to a public high school education had to do so at night in 1920s Harlem.

Laura's stridency in protesting the Vietnam War and the boldness of the honorable Mrs. Abzug reflected the lifestyles and options available to women of their race and social class. I had no more enrolled at this college to become an activist than my mother had thought of herself as one as she tamed the dragons around her family and community.

Although the gulf between Laura and me was as wide as that between our parents' experiences, eventually, her life as an anti-war protester would overlap with mine (although on different issues) before we graduated. But that first year, each morning, my rising an hour before class and my trips between our room and the shower disrupted Laura's sleep. She could go from bed to classroom within fifteen minutes, stopping only to brush her teeth. It seemed to me she bathed only on weekends, and, in between, wore the same jeans and T-shirts every day. It likely seemed to her that I washed my hair only once in a blue moon and was standoffish when I declined to wash my clothes with hers to save laundry expenses.

While my friends and I walked around with our hands clutching our purses, Laura and many from her background walked across campus with both hands in their pants pockets (like tomboys, my mother would have criticized) and were frequently barefooted in nice weather.

"Why in the world do you (and other city girls) get all dressed up, wearing stockings, shoes, skirts, or dresses like commuters just to go to class or to a meal?" she asked.

At the end of our freshman year, the annual process for bidding on new dormitory room assignments provided relief that the end was near of our poorly-planned experiment in cross-cultural living.

Coming of age in this understated context had a fairly permanent impact on me. I never fully returned to the fancy, colorful, obsessively matched style of dressing that was the norm among the working-class black folks with whom I grew up and worshipped on Sundays. My mother expressed her disappointment at the gradual change in my appearance as she muttered to herself, but loud enough for me to hear: "After all that money I spent to help her go away to college, now she walks around dressed like a bum."

Seeing the Cultures

Before college, I had had six years of boot camp in being different in fundamental ways from everyone else in my small private school. But, unlike a real boot camp, I went home every day and every weekend and was reaffirmed by my biological and church family. The residential setting of a college campus at that time was incredibly isolating. I detected unspoken critiques of the features that made me different, even more than I had in prep school.

The people I went to high school with had famous parents whose names sometimes appeared on marquees where the City's elite socialized. Almost nothing they recounted about their weekend activities was even remotely familiar to me. And when I ventured to share any tidbits about what I'd done, my truths were scorned, not with meanness, but with simple ignorance and indifference.

The people who populated my weekends had names no one in mainstream New York City would recognize. Yet they were singers and actors and gourmet cooks and hosts to international guests from nonwhite countries. If my life seemed tiny and cramped by comparison, it was very rich and very full to me—full of people, full of activity, never boring. Even the hours-long funerals in my community were lively and eventful, and they regularly brought together neighbors grieving the premature deaths of those crammed into unwelcoming Northern neighborhoods, the children of two great migrations—from the Jim Crow South and the colonized Caribbean. I was shocked to discover girls my age who had never attended a funeral for anyone.

I remember calling on my faith for validation during high school days—especially on Mondays. I would scribble in my notebook when I should have been taking lecture notes. I consoled myself with the lyrics of gospel songs I'd learned, listening to "America's first black radio announcer" Joe Bostic's *Gospel Train* daily radio show on WLIB. It was located at the end of the radio dial where my schoolmates never ventured. "I've got Jesus, and that's enough, O Lord, that's enough."

With dormitory living, areas of my private life were exposed to the scrutiny of people of a different race—how I did my hair, the extent of my wardrobe, how I spent my leisure time, and how I worshipped. To this day, I prefer not living in a majority-mainstream neighborhood. I bristle when even the well-meaning but entitled comment or make inquiries that show they don't understand that their lifestyles are not normative, that we may all live differently and still be okay.

At the time I arrived at college, I had just survived my first cross-cultural baptism. I had not yet developed a counter-narrative to the propaganda that I did not have a culture worth studying. I had not yet read the great writers whose glorious prose affirmed the people I knew.

I wanted to safeguard the future of society's standards as I had been taught and understood them. To overturn the system? I don't see a trace of that thought when I look back at my pre-college self. I had trouble even grasping that there was such a thing as a system—something that existed apart from the official rules. Although I was on track to be valedictorian, unlike the more socially savvy classmates in my high school, I remember my disbelief when the student who was number two in class rank told me the two of us couldn't get into trouble there because we were too important to the school's standings to be suspended.

"Who else would get into elite colleges and make the school look good?" she declared. She understood her political power. I naively believed the rules trumped individual prerogative. Her cynicism proved justified the one-time I ever inadvertently broke a serious rule against cutting classes. I found myself, with her, too late to report to a class after staying too long in the locker room chatting after a cliffhanger. After hours of worry about possible consequences, I was amazed and relieved that, as my rival predicted, no one in authority ever called us to account.

Seeing Our Value

By my sophomore year, I'd managed to win the trust of a generally untrusting mother. Despite her serious misgivings, she was there for me as I headed off on what was nearly the most dangerous trip of my life.

Ma bit her lip and fought back tears as she waved goodbye to our group of a few dozen American and Canadian college students who walked through the gate at the Air France terminal. It was 1967, and no airport security denied her and over a dozen other relatives and friends final hugs and what they feared might be their last glimpse of me in life. They were worried I would not survive three months doing construction in a work camp in French West Africa. There would be no telephone access, and a huge proportion of my luggage included medicines and survival tools.

In my mind, however, I was fully prepared for such rigors: two years of living away at college under my belt, seven years of French courses, and a year of dating Paul, an East African student enrolled at historically black Lincoln University. What more did I need? When we arrived, the first sights we observed in Dakar and Abidjan belied the stereotypes of wild, primitive, and starving Africa. These were modern cities which had multi-story retail spaces with escalators, taxicabs, and modern cars, and beautiful, urbane women in colorful fashions.

Only eighteen, I was experiencing increasingly powerful opportunities for self-discovery, one after another. Affluent white students with whom I'd gone to high school had spoken glowingly about their trips to "the Continent"—their Continent, Europe, didn't need to be named. Now I was walking on My Continent, and the excitement I felt was explosive.

The majority of my time in West Africa was spent not on the sophisticated streets of Dakar, Abidjan, or Accra, or at receptions at local USAID officers' homes. We were there for cultural immersion and to challenge assumptions about Africa. An African American pioneer Rev. James Robinson had created Operation Crossroads Africa, the program on which the Kennedy administration had modeled the Peace Corps. College students and graduates would perform service activities "to promote the dignity of physical labor among educated individuals."[17] Most days we hauled rocks along with Peace Corps volunteers and local young adults, called our "counterparts." We passed the rocks uphill from one person to another and onto a truck. The job culminated in creating cinderblocks and building a one-room schoolhouse.

That summer before my junior year was a life-altering one in which I experienced 1960s West African health and sanitation conditions. For several months after my return, I was uncomfortable, fighting traces of malaria and dysentery I contracted during the trip. But the thrill did not wear off of having explored my African roots firsthand.

I pondered the gap between the positions occupied by the people of African descent, with whom I'd been living and learning, and the ones occupied by those of European descent. Who in West Africa was really helping whom? Beyond there, in American black communities? On US college campuses? Whose contributions mattered most? Who determined the value of each group's contribution? I returned to campus in my junior year with a burning desire to learn more about African history and the contributions of my ancestors there and in the "New World."

Prior to my African experience, I thought individuals had almost limitless power, with God's help, to change themselves, their families, groups and local situations. I didn't see much that needed changing beyond that. I believed the smooth running of institutions was the ultimate achievement. What was needed were competent, moral people in authority.

Transforming the institutions themselves was not yet on my radar.

Seeing What's Inside

Perhaps my father had had enough of the humiliations he'd endured as the invisible restaurant busboy, the dock worker helping but not a member of the unionized force, and eventually as the postal employee after the postal service integrated its ranks. He felt compelled to quit a job he really needed rather than obey orders to put picked-over food from a customer's plate back into the kitchen to be served to other unsuspecting diners. It also highly annoyed him when he'd been questioned by another subway passenger about whether he understood the copy of Homer's *Iliad* he was reading. He'd borrowed it from the public library and was reading it on his way from his Harlem apartment to work downtown.

It had been a difficult decision for Luther to quit his secure government job to pastor, full-time, a small congregation in Harlem. He knew it would be hard to feed his family on the subsistence-level salary they offered. With no written contract, he couldn't be certain on any Sunday that the donations would stretch to pay his salary, especially during wintertime when the church's lighting and heating bills were priority.

Most of his parishioners worked as laborers, nannies, and custodians for wealthy whites in Manhattan and Westchester County. They relied on him to go to court to speak on behalf of their children when they got into trouble. He also made sure the elderly had roofs over their heads and offered counseling to spouses to help them maintain their marriages despite their social and economic pressures. His construction skills saved the church hundreds of dollars in repair costs.

In return, he no longer had to face the daily microaggressions his siblings and other congregants endured as they went to work and school in mainstream institutions. He could spend hours each day studying to prepare highly educational sermons for the parishioners. He also learned all the vocal and instrumental parts of music scores for choir and orchestra rehearsals.

Without fail, in spite of the workweek challenges, the members came for Sunday worship, Tuesday testimony meeting, and Thursday Bible studies. On Friday nights, they came with scores in hand to rehearse cantatas and other sacred music for recitals and concerts to be performed on Sunday afternoons. On rare occasions, one of their employers and his family would show up at a performance amid much fanfare and praise for visiting their helper's neighborhood. Most knew virtually nothing about the personal lives of the people who daily worked for their families and businesses.

My mother provided the soundtrack, but my father was my muse. His seamless blend of spiritual and intellectual absorption while enjoying ordinary labor was, to me, the gold standard. He was my model of servant leadership.

Luther had been the bookish one among the six surviving siblings of thirteen born to Charles and Clara Allman on a plantation in colonial Barbados. Like other rural children of his day, he regularly drank milk directly from the cows, without the then-unknown benefit of pasteurization. This practice most likely was responsible for his nearly fatal case of typhoid fever in an era before antibiotics were discovered. The illness left him weakened and housebound for months, and his mother thought him too sickly for active play. This forced time inside was his family's explanation for how he developed his love of words, written and spoken. His formal schooling amounted to little more than rote learning, reading, and memorizing the works of Englishmen like Rudyard Kipling. Lower-class families like his could not hope to send even their most promising child to high school. His post-primary school trade of bricklaying provided few opportunities for livable employment for black "subjects of the Queen" like him. So, at age twenty, he set out in disgust, walking the twenty miles to Bridgetown, the capital city, to board a ship for America. His older siblings had emigrated there already. He left behind his parents whom he would never see again.

Once in New York City, Luther survived at first as a day laborer. Evenings found him in the public library, teaching himself to master English language and culture. Before long, his church recognized his self-taught mastery of standard English and asked him to teach it in classes for fellow immigrants after work. He had also learned to play the cornet and formed an orchestra he conducted with other musicians from the community.

Like my father, most of the orchestra musicians were self-taught or had teachers who lacked formal training. Even in the poorest villages, people valued the ability to play instruments and to sing European choral music. In the legacy of colonialism was the idea of "high culture," as compared to popular and worship music rooted in African rhythms in which they were likely more proficient. To ensure our access to the former, Daddy made the sacrifice of paying $3 per child, which totaled more than one-third of his weekly salary, so that my siblings and I had piano lessons every week.

I trace my appreciation for the music I would perform at college to these influences. By the time I got to campus, I could already read musical scores and learn vocal parts quickly. Fifty years later, I can sing the opening lines of the opera, *Boris Gudonov.* We performed it entirely in the Russian language at Philadelphia's Town Hall, "Akh na ko-vo ty nas po-ki-da-jesh', otec nash!" We studied the music of a people across the planet while never, in my four years in the College chorus, performing the work of an African American composer. Ironically, the Russian composer Alexander Pushkin, their favorite poet, was of African heritage, a fact likely unknown to everyone involved in the performance.

Although immersed in cultures not our own, my warmest memories of my father are of my grade school self clinging onto his neck as he worked through the word puzzles in the monthly edition of *Reader's Digest.* I perched precariously on the available space on his unpadded "office" chair. With no private space in the house or church to support daily studying, his reading and studying seemed a seamless part of his presence in the home. His makeshift office was a corner of the large room that tripled as my parents' bedroom, my dad's study, and the space where their two young daughters had their beds.

When I try to get in touch with the feelings that underlie my dedication to education, I revisit the closeness I felt to my father which was rare and widely held as off-limits for men of his generation. I bask in his unarticulated approval of my success at school. I share his pleasure in a pastime, a rare indulgence, talking about words and stories far removed from the practical demands of our lives on the margins of the great city in which we lived.

Epiphanies

I remember the professor, the class, the semester in my sophomore year when everything changed about schooling for me. My entire freshman year, I remained the model student my scholarship had helped to fund. Not unlike my father's colonial schooling, my education through that year never critically examined the realities underlying the social systems where we lived. If I had not had the good fortune of finding a seat in an American history course with a young, little-known Professor George McCully, I might have exited the College the same way I had entered.

I had known that primary sources expressed their author's views, but it was an epiphany that seemingly anonymous and impartial textbooks were written by human beings with distinct and often conflicting worldviews. I was so liberated by this insight; I have never been the same as a learner and consumer of the written word.

Before that class, my teachers referred to textbooks by title more than authors' names. The "facts" of history seemed immutable, not subject to scrutiny. I recall being ill-equipped to form my own opinions about world affairs when, in the summer of 1966, I was challenged about my views of America's role in the war in Vietnam among a group of peers from different colleges. I am still chagrined at my clichéd rationale for supporting the war: "It's my country, right or wrong." Even I realized it was pathetic I had such an unexamined perspective.

Professor McCully had an immaculate, clean-cut look in stark contrast to my other professors, most of whom dressed down. Brilliant, articulate, radical, and fashionable, he did not fit in. Later, I heard rumors that he questioned the "facts" around the John F. Kennedy assassination, but he had never revealed his political views in class or attempted to radicalize students. I learned from him to notice the names of authors and to interrogate their backgrounds, schooling, professional associations, and other writings. He pointed out in texts examples of opinions disguised as facts, obvious omissions, and where questions should be raised.

At a crucial point in my life, he changed my study habits. Eventually, my writing, my research, and my teaching followed. My father gifted me with the curiosity and love for learning, but formal schooling seemed too precious to critique. Thanks to Professor McCully, critical thinking in matters of academics had arrived for me at last.

Where I had experienced critical thinking at home was in matters of faith. My family read scripture, discussed our spiritual lives and prayed together every Sunday morning before going to church. Personal piety was a big deal and an open struggle. We children challenged the sacrifices we were called on to make, including giving up our beds to strangers whom my parents took in when they wandered by with stories of financial crisis.

But as college years approached, I remember praying often that going away to school would not change me into someone I didn't want to become, arrogant and denying that God exists. I had met persons like that. Once educated, they abandoned the faith that got them there.

Among the reasons why my family thought Swarthmore was a better choice than some other well-known Ivy League colleges were its Quaker roots and reputation for having a moral core and spiritual enlightenment. What a surprise it was to discover how much more secular the campus was than I had imagined!

One of the first things I did when I arrived on campus was look for students who practiced faith in the Wesleyan Reformation tradition to which I was accustomed. I expected to find them sitting with Bibles in small groups at least once a week, praying openly, sharing personal challenges. I didn't anticipate that they would all be white. A married couple who had just left the College in the passion of newfound faith hosted Bible studies in their apartment in the "Ville," as the tiny college village was called. On Sundays, I joined a classmate's family, the Elgins, for dinner after attending church with them. On Friday evenings, monthly, I got rides to meetings sponsored by nationally-funded campus outreach ministries. Speakers led cerebral discussions on supposedly cutting edge Christianity. It didn't begin to bother me until later, but nothing was ever said at these gatherings about the struggle for Civil Rights, and no speaker was ever nonwhite.

As the Seven Sisters and a Brother began to bond, there was an easy acceptance of each other's faith orientation. All had church backgrounds, Joyce, for example, attending services in the Ville in a more liturgical tradition than mine. Others, I realized later, were open to, but somewhat skeptical, of people who seemed to wear religion on their sleeves. They looked more to the actions of those professing faith rather than their words. Aundrea, with her African Methodist Episcopal background, was comfortable casually singing gospel songs and talking about her faith in unscripted ways. We both attended black denominations that grew out of being excluded from equal worship with whites and were used to black leadership in our churches.

Looking back at how conservative politics held sway over American evangelicals, I don't know that I could have found the spiritual resources to respond to my growing awareness of the need for change if I had remained close to those with whom I had connected in freshman year. Early Protestant reformers had courageously fought against slavery, child labor, and unhealthy workplaces. But by the 1960s, that history seemed to fade from the prophetic teaching among whites as black Christian leaders drew on it for inspiration as never before. The Quakers on campus were good on some social justice issues—anti-war, anti-poverty. However, I could not draw the inspiration I sought in their subdued worship services, and they seemed oblivious to the unequal experiences of the black students there.

With Aundrea traveling back home most weekends, I took solitary Sunday trips to Philadelphia and Chester to find black churches where I could experience more of what I needed. Those weekly times off-campus connected me to my spiritual roots and strengthened me for the major struggle that would climax in our senior year. It is ironic I matured spiritually as I embraced my call to activism, a sense of urgency to right a wrong.

Although most people probably never thought of the Takeover as a spiritual struggle, it was always primarily that to me. My scriptures taught that our struggle is not with flesh and blood, but with spiritual forces of evil in the unseen world. Taking over a building would be a metaphor for taking control of false narratives, for taking spaces that unfairly excluded us, for taking the College to a future that better reflected its own ideals.

Seeing a People

Even before our student protest would target the building in whose entryways they presided, those awful, huge, commissioned portraits that featured almost exclusively old white men were off-putting to me. Their dominating presence seemed to say that people who looked like me had no heritage there. What a mistaken idea! I didn't find out until gathering recollections for this memoir that several of those old leaders of the College made their money in neighboring communities like Chester and Media. They relied on the labor of black people to acquire the wealth they could then contribute to the College's growth.

I knew nothing about Chester until I observed Joyce tutoring two Chester high school students in mathematics. She introduced me to the fun of spending time with these skinny, teenaged girls, just a few years, but seemingly a generation, younger than we. Being around them provided a link to the ever-evolving black music culture, hair and clothing fashions, and dance and hip sayings. These high schoolers joined us to our younger, happier selves. They "fell out laughing" at all kinds of things, whether funny or painful, in just that familiar way we did in our own families.

Eventually I was assigned my own "tutee," as they were called, bussed to the campus for afterschool academic support. Sometimes, I visited my tutee at her home for mathematics tutoring when she couldn't get to campus. I rode a commuter bus the twenty or thirty minutes it took to get from our suburban campus to the black part of Chester and made my way on foot to her house. People there looked like people in Harlem, and I grew comfortable walking alone on those streets.

On the afternoons when I visited, my tutee's mother treated me like a special member of the family and prepared delicious, Southern-style meals for me. I have forgotten their names and the street on which they lived, but I recall the juiciest pork chops I ever ate at that home. Her mom seemed young to be the parent of a high schooler. Her hair was always immaculately pressed and highly-styled. She guided me to places where I could get my hair done and to churches like Shiloh Baptist with good choirs that worshipped with the fervency and style with which I was comfortable.

Over time, my contacts extended beyond my tutee's family. When SASS hosted parties on weekends, Chester high school students who knew us through programs like Upward Bound attended and became part of the campus black community. As we got to know each other better, I attended church in Chester some Sundays, and the city began to feel like home to me in many important ways. A close friendship with a black Swarthmore alum from there taught me so much about love for one's people, but was cut short by an untimely death.

Covert Leaders

A child in my family could get scolded for being idle. "Get up and find something to do!" Any little snatches of time I stole would not be used for introspection or rumination. My reflections were about the world around me and the people near me rather than on myself. Third-born in a boisterous household that included both nuclear and large extended family, there was always something that needed attention or fixing, someone who needed assistance. My gaze was fastened outward.

Perhaps that's why I missed recognizing a lot of my own impulses and why my militancy took even me by surprise. But neither I nor my parents should have been shocked that they'd nurtured a rebel.

Both of my parents had walked away from their parents and from their cultures of origin. They often defied societal norms in their lifestyle choices. They didn't speak about their lives in terms of breaking ranks or challenging authority, and I was not inclined to do so either. However, there was always in me a quiet stubbornness, if made indignant by some rule. There was no one else to blame for having undue influence on me. It sprang from the same well of idealism and affirmation as does patriotism or nationalism. In a different context, it may have been seen as admirable. But for people who are on the margins of society, it is called rebellion.

Soon, the compliant overachiever was writing notes like this on my stationery to Dr. Bramson, Chair of the Department of Anthropology and Sociology:

> I appreciate the A grade; but I don't agree that my paper is a "polemic." I spent weeks in New York City at the Schomburg Library researching my sources. The readings you assign by people like Irving Kristol, now those are polemics. He opines about people of African descent without input from any of them, and you consider his works scholarly?
>
> Marilyn Allman '69

Dr. Bramson's department was new and needed to recruit good students as majors to build the program's credibility. What a surprise to find out later that none of my black classmates had an advisor who engaged with them as he did with me! I figured, incorrectly, that at a small college, every student had at least one caring adult with whom to wrestle and test ideas.

The dissonance came on imperceptibly at first. When my Department Chair offered to recommend me to the University of Chicago for a "cushy" life as an academic, I declined. I believed I should not risk the loss of my identity building my career in the Ivory Tower. Youth in my community were suffering in substandard schools. Gaining a good education was their only way out. I had to get back home to serve as a public schoolteacher. He warned me that I'd be bored to death and my spirit would be crushed by the system.

The more socially conscious I became, the wider the range of concerns that triggered my activism. Moving from one SASS student activity and program to another, I hoped to save the black race in Africa and in America while I could. I tended toward hyperactivity, but masked anxiety with laughter and camaraderie.

Among the family we built, I found kindred spirits who shared my urgency for change. We collaborated continuously and debated issues even during social events. My social dancing taboo yielded to comfort in the joyful rhythms and movement introduced to me by the music of our African friends.

Although the Seven Sisters had no leader, I was viewed as an elder by some, possibly because I was already a sophomore when four others enrolled, and possibly because of some confidence I exuded. Despite several years' experience in organizing, leadership, and public speaking, I shied away from formal leadership. A coed college with more diverse students seemed too complex and without the dedicated faculty guidance provided in prep school.

Among our fledgling black student group, there was a strong feeling not to self-aggrandize. We all had potential to lead, had done so in high school, and would do so later on in our professional lives. But we had seen in our history as a people how leaders had often been targeted to be co-opted, so in SASS, we believed a collective model would make it harder for detractors to strike. Though we elected officers, they were shielded by not knowing all the plans in detail. Chair Clinton and Vice Chair Don would become the iconic images of our takeover as spokespersons for the press, but the role of our group of eight has been untold until now.

As Black Studies provided so many new intellectual outlets, I embraced my regular studying and sought more knowledge. Six years in prep school equipped me to manage a college workload, even when tedious and narrowly Eurocentric. Now, I had a real use for study and research. My extracurricular activities did not prevent me from completing two majors and graduating with induction into the Phi Beta Kappa honor society.

Many of my friends today see me as one who is spiritual or connected to God—the friend they can call in crisis and depend on to pray. Before college, I worried I might lose my faith. Instead it was deepened by my college experience. I see harsh political realities in the ancient scriptures, and I understand faith as source of courage and thankfulness. Building community where it's hard. Being bold to express black perspectives in inconvenient settings. More appreciation for my African roots. Challenging myths that divide black couples. It guides me to wholeness, aligning my identities as a black person in America and a black Christian in a nation with white supremacist instincts. To be true to myself and my calling.

Perhaps reading our stories will facilitate more honest conversation with the white students on campus with whom I had been friendly upon arrival. Evangelical Christians and Jewish New Yorkers were the subcultures I knew best. But we lacked the skills to speak truthfully about our increasingly divergent consciousness. I felt I had to suppress too much of myself to thrive in their social circles, and they likely had to do the same to feel comfortable with my black college family. Perhaps there are still productive alliances we can forge in the current period of fragmentation.

In exchange, at that time, I sought out and developed lasting relationships with people on my side of the racial and political divide. These relationships enriched my life enormously. I trusted the other six sisters and Harold; trustworthiness was key to our familial relationship. And they did not disappoint. With them, I found lots to celebrate and laugh about, even when we held each other accountable during disagreements. We arranged interventions when one of us seemed to be about to make a mistake. Joyce can't forget how we traveled to Boston when we worried that she might be rushing into marriage too soon after graduating. I remember more than once when a guy was challenged by the sisters, and a brother or two, if it was discovered that he was cheating on one of us. I was probably saved from heartbreak by Joyce making sure I found out that Paul had a relationship with another woman on his campus. After college, we would be bridesmaids and helpers in each other's weddings, godmothers for each other's children, and unofficial marriage counselors for each other.

Their egos were in check. They didn't need others' approval so much that they would be tempted to grandstand or to divulge our plot to force a confrontation and spark a revolution. Trusting my new family, I said nothing to my original family as we plotted and planned the Takeover right in their dining room during Christmas break in 1968. My family had no idea what we were organizing. No idea whatsoever.

When it came to public light what we had done, my mother came 100 miles to dissuade me and turned back after the briefest exchange.

"Ma, I can't come out of the building. I'm one of the leaders."

Then she put my uncle on the case—a much more worldly-wise Christian soul and well-traveled in the African Diaspora.

He questioned me to make sure I had neither lost my mind nor my faith. And they left, satisfied. No one in my family tried to convince me to abandon the cause again. I will never know exactly what they went through as they followed newspaper reports and propaganda in the national press from a distance. However, I was affirmed in my confidence that my family understood I was doing what was right, and they had to trust God to defend me.

Remaining Vigilant

I didn't realize the extent of it then, but my four years at Swarthmore College were like special forces training for the life I lead and my multiple careers and avocations since college.

When I am drained after a meeting at one of several organizations I serve in leadership, I continue to draw on the stamina I developed in my college years. Like the faculty committee meetings on introducing Black Studies at Swarthmore where I served with other SASS representatives, the power differential between me and many others in these settings is still daunting today. Often, I am the only black person in the room who asserts herself and challenges the majority, usually male, white, and wealthier than I.

I have been on the faculty for decades at two public universities, a mathematics education consultant for public school systems, an IT consultant and appointed official for local government, and a volunteer member of school and church boards. Whatever the forum, I am often a gadfly–espousing non-traditional ideas about teaching and learning, challenging mandates that have an inequitable impact on people of color, and finding ways to incorporate the work of black subject matter experts, to the delight of minority participants and the amazement of others.

To my first major in sociology-anthropology I added mathematics, which helped prepare me to dabble for a decade in information technology systems as a contractor for local government. Bidders' conferences tested my mettle as the only gender- and race-minority vendor, and my ability to withstand the psych-out-the-competition tactics was probably birthed in those faculty and administration confrontations I experienced when I was nineteen and twenty-years-old in college.

Early on, my future husband saw me in action and saw how his many skills in the arts could round out my repertoire as a social justice warrior. We collaborated for a while on a community-based publication, and thereafter on marriage and a family. Our family mission statement has the well-being of people of African descent as a lifetime commitment.

To that end, I co-founded a community-based public charter school and helped win over skeptical elected officials. One by one, defenders of the status quo were disarmed, and often, our petitions prevailed, in like manner as did the SASS student demands in my earlier life.

The lessons I've carried forward as one of the Seven Sisters with our brother continue to serve me well. Leading from the floor instead of from the dais can be just as effective.

From my first forays into spaces of privilege until now, I look back on the limitations I face daily and see that they have developed me much more than have my privileges. At college, we black students on scholarship realized we would have to push against our limitations if we were to be strong enough to take on those who felt entitled by their family wealth.

For us, that resistance training meant many hours of studying our history, collaborating with black people of diverse backgrounds, critiquing what was presented to us as inevitable, and developing skills in communication and service. We helped build a movement that continues to matter today. We offer our stories to encourage another generation and our presence as guardian angels wherever they find us.

Looking back, actually, we soared. Disadvantaged? At-risk? Underprivileged? Not so.

THE TAKEOVER

Day Seven

DAY SEVEN
Standoff

As our occupation continued into the seventh day, the editorials and articles in the *New York Times, Washington Post, UPI,* and other mainstream media were becoming more and more strident and overheated. The coverage in general showed little interest in reporting the voices of the SASS students who had put their educational goals at-risk to fight for a cause they believed in. This would continue into the next month. Six weeks later, nationally syndicated columnist Drew Pearson, who happened to be the brother of the College's Dean of Women, promoted a maliciously distorted view of us.

> Almost every case of student unrest this winter has originated with a black extremist minority making almost identical demands for more admission of black students, regardless of their scholastic ability.[18]

How wrong the national media campaign to discredit us proved to be when all of us managed to graduate in good standing!

> The great majority of students at these colleges has been out of sympathy with the militant black minority; likewise, the majority of the faculties. Clinton E, Black Power leader at Swarthmore, is certain to flunk, and certain to claim he's being discriminated against. Real reason he is certain to flunk is that he has devoted so little time to his studies.[19]

When FBI files were reviewed years later, rumors that the FBI was tracking us and had informants on campus were proven true. J. Edgar Hoover viewed us as a national security threat. Fortunately, Hoover's views did not prevail or prevent

Clinton from representing the United States after college by serving in Africa in the Peace Corps and modeling good citizenship throughout a successful career as a businessman.

Tensions among the faculty and administration were taking their toll as the protest approached an unprecedented weeklong duration. Professor Asmarom Legesse was the only black faculty member during this period. Perhaps because of concerns raised by SASS, he was hired for a temporary position for the 1967–68 year and later received tenure. As an African, he had not grown up with American racism, yet he was expected to be the voice of the African American students. He was a friend to many of the black students and did an admirable job as liaison to our organization during the College's "Crisis." As a non-tenured faculty member, he took considerable risk in his public support of our organization. Like some white professors who had publicly expressed admiration for how we had conducted ourselves, he did not endorse our tactics, but he urged the faculty and administration to rise above their personal indignation and listen to our well-presented positions.

Through letters to the administration, public statements at meetings, and articles we submitted to the College paper, the entire campus understood that we wanted the College to enroll more black students, hire black faculty and administrators, launch a Black Studies Program, remove the offending Dean of Admissions (if he refused to change), and institutionalize supports for black students such as a black cultural center and a minority dean. The Takeover negotiations, and the many open letters that students, faculty, and administration had published in response, sharpened our vision of what we needed to realize change for black students on campus. We added a few more demands, the most dramatic perhaps being the aforementioned demand for amnesty, something we had not considered at the start. The possibility of granting us amnesty raised the stakes for the hard-liners who became more concerned about setting a bad precedent with each additional day.

Leading up to the Takeover, the Student Council quickly passed resolutions in support of our objectives. During the sit-in, many students and even faculty were outspoken in their sympathy for our demands, and they even raised money for food. But other students and faculty criticized leaders of the Student Council for their enthusiastic support for these radicals.

Outside of the admissions office, this historic event consumed everyone's attention. The absence of nearly all black students from the cafeteria and dormitories was probably very noticeable. Our actions had brought normal campus life to a standstill, while the faculty met around the clock and various student committees met to provide advice, welcome or not.

Black students were not just sitting in, we were standing up. We had gained the full attention of this liberal institution and, by Day 7, nobody knew how this would end. But the very next day, our world would come to a complete standstill.

From Down South to Up North—Marilyn H's Story

MARILYN HOLIFIELD

Roses from My Father, My Mother's Dreams

My inspiration to open doors to unfamiliar racial terrains flows from several generations of my family's resistance to second-class racial status dictated by Jim Crow laws and American traditions. I do not know how my grandparents, son and daughter of slaves, acquired a five hundred-acre farm in Scott County, Mississippi. Family stories tell of my grandfather, my father, and his nine brothers successfully defending their farm from the Ku Klux Klan. My father left central Mississippi when he was fourteen and traveled to Tuskegee, Alabama for high school and college to study agronomy under Dr. George Washington Carver. Later in life, he shared his love of farming with his family. We spent many Saturdays at my father's farm on the outskirts of Tallahassee planting pine trees, fishing, and feeding cows. With my father's tutoring, the farm girl in me planted lilies and tomatoes in the yard of our home in Tallahassee. My father planted roses underneath my bedroom window, and I loved my mother's beautiful smile when he surprised her with bouquets of red roses from his garden. Spring daffodils in Swarthmore's Crum Meadow reminded me of my father's beautiful roses and my mother's joy.

While growing up in Tallahassee, I often looked outside my bedroom window and tried to imagine my father, his nine brothers, and three sisters growing vegetable crops and cotton on their farm in Mississippi. Sometimes my heart pounded with fear from thinking of my father's courage to leave Mississippi and travel alone more than two hundred miles to Alabama to work his way through the racially segregated high school and college at Tuskegee Institute, now Tuskegee University.

When my teenage father left the family farm to attend Tuskegee Institute, Scott County did not permit education of blacks beyond the eighth grade. Tuskegee was located near Montgomery, Alabama, which was the first capital of the Confederate States. Montgomery prided itself on being the Cradle of the Confederacy. Black publications back then like *Crisis Magazine*, published by the NAACP, reported intimidation and cruelty of white racist terror, torture, and lynching of blacks in Mississippi and Alabama. I will never know the sacrifices my father made to leave Mississippi for his education, but I will always hear his voice telling me how his Tuskegee education transformed his life.

My father's determination and tenacity made him stand tall in my eyes. It took many years for me to see that he did not reach six feet. He walked with a limp, but I saw strength. His permanent limp from a childhood injury that did not receive proper medical treatment in staunchly segregated Mississippi did not diminish his determination to seek a better life. He became the first black soil conservation agent for the US Department of Agriculture in the State of Florida. By day, my father taught North Florida farmers about soil conservation and federal farm programs.

By night and on weekends, my father bought and developed land. I probably got in the way, but I loved tagging along and watching him transform empty lots into crisp brick apartment buildings that provided housing for students at nearby Florida A&M University. It was my thrill to hold tools while he hammered, painted, cleaned, or supervised. My father and mother shared a belief that developing land could forge a path to a better life. Over the years, they worked as a team to acquire land, develop apartment rentals, raise livestock, and grow and sell timber.

My father's quiet determination accentuated my mother's brisk Boston, Massachusetts pace and her impatience with racial suppression. His southern-flavored strength contrasted with the fire and rapid pace of my mother's spirit. My mother's father from Barbados and my dad's father from Mississippi passed away too early for me to know them.

Mississippi's reputation of racist terror against blacks limited our visits with my dad's family, and I did not get to spend much time with my Mississippi grandmother. Our family regularly traveled to Boston for summer vacations and holidays. My mother filled our Boston visits with fun at museums and parks that were free of racial slights.

My grandmother was the main reason I loved "Up North" in Boston. A native of Suriname, a former Dutch colony in South America where blacks escaped to the interior and resisted enslavement, Nana knew what to do to bring me joy. She would put on her 1950s island-styled dress, hat, gloves, and her big eyeglasses and take me by the hand to board the trolley to Jordan Marsh's Bakery. During the trolley ride to Jordan Marsh's, my head swirled with anticipation of the sole purpose of the trip—to get hot blueberry muffins smothered in butter that tasted like paradise. Up North in Boston, no racially segregated seating on the trolley and no racially separate lines at the Jordan Marsh's counter interfered with my joy. Even today, my love for blueberry muffins sparks anticipation of joy when they are in sight.

At times when I looked at my father's rose garden through my bedroom window, I wondered whether my mother, her three sisters, and brother, first generation children of Caribbean immigrants, liked Boston's snowy winters and its big city mysteries. My mother was one of two blacks in a class of about fifty in the nursing program at Boston City Hospital. After earning her registered nursing license, Mom and two of her white classmates applied for jobs with the federal government. The lure of a federal job outpaced fear of the Deep South and tapped her adventurous spirit when she accepted a job as a registered nurse at the Veterans Hospital in Tuskegee, Alabama. She courageously left family, friends and all things familiar to enter a rural culture and a world of Southern traditions far removed from Boston's Up North urban lights. I did not question, and she did not suggest, why the federal government assigned her two white classmates to a Veterans Hospital in Maine and my mother to the Veterans Hospital in Tuskegee, Alabama, where Mom met and eventually married Dad. Annual family trips to Dad's beloved Tuskegee Institute showed me that the black college world of Tuskegee and the black medical community at the nearby Veterans Hospital carved out a protective sanctuary from Jim Crow harshness and fostered a vibrant black educational, cultural, and social enclave.

My father showed me the beauty of roses and courage to face Jim Crow. My mother's smile showed me the joy that beauty and love bring, and she taught me courage to dream. After she obtained a Bachelor of Science degree from historically black Florida A&M College, now a university (FAMU), she saw exclusion of blacks from licensed practical nursing education as blocking blacks from a better life. Refusing to accept Tallahassee's status quo, she pursued a dream to establish a licensed practical nursing program where blacks could be trained. She faced immense obstacles.

Mom's strength in meeting multiple rejections with persistent determination inspired me at a young age. Our family celebrated victory when the Leon County School Board finally approved her petition and appointed her founding director, charging her with creating a licensed practical nursing program at the then all-black Lincoln Vocational High School. Her tenacious spirit showed me that doors closed by racism could be pried open. Her creation of a nursing education program for poor black people in Tallahassee in the 1950s against formidable opposition taught me lifelong lessons in courage, the power of believing in dreams, and the importance of service to others. She had high expectations of her students. In fact, one hundred per cent of her students passed the state licensing examination during the nearly 11-year life of her program. Mom's successful nursing program instilled confidence in me to knock on traditionally closed doors.

My mother's love of the arts inspired me to play the piano. From my beginning piano lessons at an early age when I missed many notes to when I practiced a Bach fugue, Mozart sonata, or Rachmaninoff prelude, she listened and encouraged. Even when I played monotonous scales, she made me feel as if I were creating beautiful music. My two brothers abandoned the piano early, but I loved practicing for hours nearly every day, knowing that my mother's encouraging support was near. She and I listened to recordings of professional orchestras performing and dreamed about seeing them in-person. Listening to my mother play the piano was a special treat.

My parents inspired my embrace of civic engagement and service. The courage of my parents made it natural for them to reject fear and register to vote in Tallahassee's elections long before Congress passed voting rights laws. They supported FAMU student protests against segregation and were active members in the community, from holding offices in our church and black civic organizations to leading Boy and Girl Scouts and 4-H Clubs. Our family conversations never strayed far from challenging suppression of blacks. Their unrelenting spirit to serve others and build their business taught me to press forward and seek the promise of freedom from intimidating Jim Crow laws and traditions. In their fifty-seven years of love, marriage, and faith, they created a legacy of breaking down barriers and defying staggering odds to help build a new day for our family and community.

Looking Back When Segregation Ruled

My two years of enduring racial hatred up close at Tallahassee's formerly all-white Leon High School made going to college Up North my grand escape. From the first day I entered Leon High with two other black students, until graduation night two years later, white students called me the "n" word as if it were my name.

I am not sure if I will ever know how to fully share my Leon High School experience. Piercing hatred can be numbing. For decades, I did not mention that every day at Leon High, white student haters had fun hurling the "n" word at me. They "greeted" me with the "n" word when I arrived in the morning, when I walked the halls to change classes, when I entered the lunchroom to eat in isolation by myself, and when diplomas were awarded at the ceremony on graduation night. The classroom functioned as a safe haven. In class, under watchful teachers, verbal abuse sneaked into silent corners and temporarily hid.

Virtually all of the abuse was verbal, but the day my hateful Leon High schoolmates splattered me with raw eggs as I got off the school bus was the day I resolved they would not chase me away. The splash of yolks and messy wetness somehow made me feel weak and strong at the same time. Weak, because that was the only time white hatred made tears rush down my face. Strong, because their hatred fired up my inner spirit and kicked away any notion of surrender.

Every day that I attended Leon High, my father drove me to a black elementary school where I boarded the school bus, which filled up with students going to the black high school. On the way to school, the bus stopped at the black high school first, then took the three of us to the bus drop-off at the back door of Leon High. The day hate and raw eggs collided with me, a black school janitor drove me home where my father was the first to meet me. His subdued strength let me know that he was proud of my courage, but worried. My mother's job was more distant from our home, but she soon joined us with distress on her face. The three of us hugged, and they comforted me. After changing clothes, I insisted on returning to school that same day because I did not want the haters to feel victorious. I do not know what my mother and father said to the school principal, but my teachers became more watchful and encouraging. I became more determined.

The nearly two thousand white students at Leon High blurred into a sea of hate and hostility that strangely fueled my desire to tough it out and work hard to graduate at the top of my class. The haters overshadowed the one or two white students who expressed support. The haters resented my stellar academic performance and nicknamed me the "Brainy n." It took many decades for me not to cringe on hearing the "n" word. I doubt I will ever understand racial hate.

I wanted to go Up North to Swarthmore, a college I had never visited, because I thought it would open a new world to me, free of racial hostilities. As I was growing up, summer and holiday travels took our family to Boston to visit my grandmother, aunts, and cousins. In Boston, we did not encounter racial restrictions against eating in restaurants, drinking in water fountains, going to movies, or sitting in trolley cars.

During the drive to Boston, our family would stop in Washington, DC to tour monuments and museums. We stayed at the all black Dunbar Hotel. DC represented a North/South racial dividing line. Across that line, further north in New York City, my mother's cousin from Suriname, who was an immigration lawyer, directed us to hotels that accepted blacks and whites where I did not feel racial stress. In Boston, racial restrictions did not intrude when we played in Franklin or Monroe Parks or visited the Children's Museum and Planetarium. During our family visits to Boston, Up North did not feel heavy with hate. Years later, I discovered that our Boston visits had been carefully orchestrated to avoid overt racial hostilities associated with various Boston communities and institutions.

In Tallahassee, our racially segregated college community shielded me as much as it could from racial hatred. I lived several blocks from FAMU and attended its demonstration schools from kindergarten through tenth grade. Our cultural life revolved around FAMU's theater performances, symphonic and marching bands, national speakers' series, on campus movies, and a multitude of sporting events. I knew I would never be good enough to be a professional dancer, artist, or actress, but along with my friends, I attended dance, art, and children's theater classes offered by FAMU. The wife of a vice president of FAMU, who had studied at the Boston Conservatory of Music, taught my piano lessons. The "First Lady" of FAMU sponsored a social club for teenagers, and we enjoyed her kind hospitality in the president's mansion. Back when we lived under racial segregation by law, FAMU created our warm protective cocoon.

One of FAMU's legendary coaches taught me the discipline and technique required to swim competitively and the skills to become a certified lifeguard. At morning and afternoon swimming practices, I would swim for hours to increase speed and endurance. Poolside parties after practice added to summer fun.

When I was in elementary school, FAMU students interrupted the status quo and refused to accept state-enforced racial segregation on public buses. FAMU students started Tallahassee's bus boycott against racially segregated seating and white-only bus drivers. Reports of mass arrests and harsh treatment of students flooded into black homes and ignited peaceful support of the boycott. As I walked through the FAMU campus to and from school with my classmates, we wondered what was happening to the College students who had become our heroes. At home, voices outraged by cross burnings and other intimidation tactics filled the air without a hint of fear. I overheard neighbors and my parents make plans to support the students. The black community came together while white Tallahassee stubbornly resisted. Ultimately, the courts prodded the slow process of rescuing our humanity and dismantling Jim Crow laws.

By the time I graduated from Leon High School, civil rights laws of the mid-1960s permitted blacks in Tallahassee to ride the bus, eat in restaurants, and drink from water fountains, free from racial restrictions enforced by law. Changes in laws granted rights, but entrenched racist traditions and practices continued long afterwards. My experience at Leon High showed me an in-your-face slice of white resistance to acknowledging the humanity of blacks and intensified my excitement to escape Tallahassee's Confederate flag and Dixie. I blocked Leon High from my thoughts for dozens of years and did not know how to say to anyone that I was one of three black students among nearly two thousand whites who was the daily target of unrelenting racial slurs.

Escaping to Up North

The day I read the letter admitting me to the Swarthmore class of 1969, I had not thought of bringing change to the College. I met a Swarthmore alumna living in Tallahassee who had graduated from my segregated high school years before me.

She shared my excitement without mentioning whether she had met a black student at Swarthmore. It did not occur to me to ask. No one informed me that the class of 1969 represented an effort to overturn Swarthmore's nearly on hundred-year history of intentionally restricting admission of black students.

Tallahassee's hot summer sun could not melt my anticipation of escaping to Up North to enter Swarthmore College. I had turned seventeen during the summer and could not wait to get away from the stifling tradition of white supremacy in my segregated southern hometown. Shortly before leaving for Swarthmore, I attended an Episcopal Church camp near Tallahassee for a week. The camp and other integrated church youth activities created a racial oasis reflecting the new day. The integrated staff and campers fostered an environment of inclusion that helped me to look forward and push thoughts of Leon High's hostilities far away. The camp assigned black and white campers as roommates to the same sleek, modern cabins that looked like a movie set on the waterfront. As we learned and laughed together, the week at camp allowed me to envision Swarthmore as a similar oasis.

The day finally came when my parents, my brother Eddie, who attended nearby Franklin & Marshall College, and I piled into our family station wagon to drive to Swarthmore. With safety in mind, we bypassed places in the South that served only whites even though they were obligated by law to serve blacks. We avoided the racial hostilities and white bitterness the new laws fueled. Our food and juice were packed. Our single-focus mission was to get to Swarthmore safely.

When our Ford station wagon approached Willets Dorm, anticipation of a new beginning danced in my head that mild September day. No thought surfaced that fewer than one hundred black persons had ever graduated from Swarthmore in its one hundred years of history. No thought suggested that underneath the surface, lush landscapes quietly covered Swarthmore's legacy of excluding blacks and its Eurocentric complicity in omitting black history and culture from academic canons. No voice murmured any need to question the comfortable status quo at Swarthmore in the September sun of 1965.

Soon, Swarthmore introduced me to my "Big Sister" Joyce through its orientation program that matched a more senior student with a first-year student. I did not know what big sisters were supposed to do. I was seventeen, undecided, uncertain, unsure, and insecure about the adventure of an uncharted environment. Her wise voice reassured. Her determination instilled confidence. Her kindness inspired a cherished bond. One holiday, Joyce invited me to Baltimore to visit her relatives. Her family took me to see Diana Ross and the Supremes, my first live show of Motown glamour and glitz on a huge stage. Joyce's Big Sister warmth created an unforgettable evening and an unending friendship.

I greeted Swarthmore with excitement coupled with fear of the unknown and insecurity about the uncertainty. Like many first-year students, I did not know whether or how I would fit in the strange land of Swarthmore. I assumed Swarthmore matched roommates based on common interests or potential synergies, but later discovered that I was assigned to my white roommate because she responded on a questionnaire that a black roommate would be acceptable. What a surprise to discover that, unbeknownst to me, my race mattered when assigning my roommate. The decision to give my white roommate an option based on race without informing me told me that the College cared more about my white roommate than me.

My roommate tried to be friendly. We had no classes together, our interests were not similar, and our paths went in different directions. After my first year, I lived in Parrish Hall without a roommate, except for senior year when I was assigned to a two-room double with Marilyn A., which meant we each had our own bedroom and shared a bathroom.

Quaker influences at Swarthmore reinforced Dr. King's message calling for peace and inspired me to make friends with campus "Peaceniks" soon after I arrived. We marched and fasted in protests for peace. We boarded buses to New York City to march in front of the United Nations building and brought messages of peace to protest the Vietnam War. Police on horses met peaceful demonstrators, swinging heavy clubs causing confusion, chaos, and bloody heads. Although the police beat and scattered demonstrators, Dr. King's enduring teachings about the power of peaceful protest continued to guide my thoughts about bringing change.

Dr. King's influence during my pre-Swarthmore days made it easy for me to be open to friendships with students from different backgrounds who protested the Vietnam War. Somerville was Swarthmore's Student Center, a casual place to gather and get snacks. I met Vin in Somerville over apple cider, sticky buns, and conversations about the peace movement. Little did I know that our meeting would start a friendship that blossomed over several years into much more. Our conversations covered music, politics, protests for peace, sports, and seemingly everything under the sun. He and his family were welcoming and warm. That he was white did not create barriers in our eyes as we evolved into a couple. Our friendship bonds were strong, but ultimately, we parted ways.

Swimming at Swarthmore, Protesting to Swim at Home

An early exclusion whispered clues of racial tension hovering beneath Swarthmore's surface. Soon after my arrival,

I tried out for the swim team and tied with a competitor when we raced freestyle. The coach kept the team all-white, saying my competitor was chosen because she could also dive. She never discovered that my motivation for swimming arose from a tragic drowning of five black children attending a picnic in Tallahassee, one of whom was the sister I never met. My sister's drowning when she was less than four years old led to a family tradition that required my brothers and me to learn to swim and participate on a swim team. Nearly every Sunday after church, my family visited my sister's grave where we placed flowers. Somehow, those visits ignited a burning desire in me to swim the fastest.

Unlike my FAMU coaches, the Swarthmore coach did not try to see a personal dimension in me. If she had, she may have uncovered the source of my intensity and determination to swim, which may have benefitted the team.

Looking back, I wondered whether the coach could "see" beyond my skin color to see my potential. I wondered why she was not curious to learn how a black student from the South had learned to swim fast enough to match, stroke for stroke, the speed of the white student she accepted on the team and why she nor the team members made any effort to invite me to practice. I will never know the difference it would have made if the coach had reached out to include me at practice or if I had questioned or challenged this exclusion. In rejecting me without seeing my humanity or seeking to discover it, Swarthmore lost. So did I.

Under Jim Crow, Tallahassee excluded blacks from swimming in public pools until the city built a separate swimming pool for blacks. Its water sparkled in high noon sun against the light blue painted walls and floor of the pool. I was one of three girls on the black swim team, and I fired up fans when I finished races ahead of boys. To this day, I laugh with my brothers about how they and other boys trailed me in races.

Tallahassee's pride in being the only capital of a Confederate state not captured by the Union Army proved consistent with its decision nearly a century later to close all public pools to avoid complying with the Civil Rights Act of 1964. Before Swarthmore, my closest in-person experience to picket lines and protests were from news reports on television and in print media. I first participated in protest marches when I joined Swarthmore schoolmates and heeded Dr. King's call to peacefully protest the Vietnam War. Swarthmore's spirit supporting peaceful protest slipped into Tallahassee when we fought the city's pool closings.

During a summer break, fresh from anti-war protests at Swarthmore, I joined my two brothers and local activists to picket and protest Tallahassee's closed pools. My poster, containing words provided by my brother Eddie, said, "My bathtub isn't big enough." In spite of white resistance, the power of our peaceful protest and engagement of community support achieved change that caused the City of Tallahassee to reopen public pools on a desegregated basis. Mean-spirited whites who controlled Tallahassee's City Hall reopened pools in white neighborhoods, but kept the only pool in a black neighborhood closed when they succumbed to community pressure and protest to allow blacks and whites to swim where they chose. This meanness deprived black citizens of easy access to a public pool, making our victory against City Hall bittersweet.

Finding a Velvet Voice in Philadelphia

Before Billy Paul won a Grammy for his hit, "Me and Mrs. Jones" and the student government granted SASS official status, our Seven Sisters and Brother had fun exploring life beyond

Swarthmore. Usually Harold would drive the van provided by the College for student use. One evening, we drove to Philadelphia's Sahara jazz club to see Billy Paul, whose velvet voice was magical. When he sang, his smooth voice seemed to be singing directly to us. After the performance, we delighted in talking with him, and we kept in touch. Billy Paul later performed at Swarthmore during one of our annual Black History Week events.

Our excursions to Philly and other places to socialize and attend cultural events fostered our trust and friendship and laid the foundation for the creation of SASS. At the beginning, I saw SASS as a home away from home. I did not know that we were creating an infrastructure which several years later would become instrumental in transforming Swarthmore's admission of black students, courses in Black Studies, employment of black faculty and administrators, and respect for black workers.

All the SASS issues were important to me, but black studies resonated in a special way. One holiday break, Marilyn A. introduced me to the Schomburg Library (now known as the Schomburg Center for Research in Black Culture) in Harlem. While the building looked ordinary, its extraordinary collection of books, research, and art focusing on people of African descent worldwide opened my eyes wide. I felt as if I had discovered the "New World"—a world where black history, art, and culture were important. The Schomburg's embrace of the African Diaspora convinced me that academia's exclusion and even denigration of black history and culture deprived me and every student at Swarthmore of a full education. The Eurocentric focus within academic canons denied us opportunities to acquire knowledge about the role of black people in the development of the Western world and the joy of discovering the creative genius reflected in black culture and art.

SASS petitioned the College to offer a Black Studies Program. I, Marilyn A., and other SASS members participated with faculty on a Black Studies Curriculum Committee. We submitted proposals and discussed Black Studies for countless hours. We were not able to persuade the College to offer a major or even a minor in Black Studies. Instead, the College created a "concentration in Black Studies," something less than our request, but an important starting point in a marathon journey which has not yet ended. In May 1969, Marilyn A., Harold, Jannette, Michael Graves, and I were the first students to complete the requirements for Swarthmore's "concentration in Black Studies." Students today continue to raise questions and petition the College to establish a Black Studies Department that offers Black Studies as a major.

Bringing Change to Swarthmore

In offering me an excellent education, the College assumed I was grateful. Indeed, I was, and I remain thankful. The College saw its closed doors cracking open. I walked through those doors seeing edges of their white world while encountering exclusion and inequality.

No one in the faculty or administration ever became my advisor or provided insights on a course of study or path after Swarthmore. As the time approached to select a major, I remained undecided, uncertain, and insecure. I had not found a course of study that sparked passionate interest or a department that I felt welcomed me. Feeling that Swarthmore did not care about me, thoughts of transferring to another college entered my mind from time to time. My brother Eddie, who was a year ahead of me at Franklin & Marshall College, had suggested Swarthmore to me in the first place and became my advisor. He had majored in economics and "advised" that I could do the same. Given my family's strong commitment to education, I knew I did not have the luxury of finding a major that sparked passion. I accepted his advice without regard to professors, courses, or my level of interest.

The total absence of black administrators and tenured faculty at Swarthmore allowed the College to stumble into waters that showered black students and our families with what we perceived as fundamental disrespect. The reasons Swarthmore's administrators and faculty persisted in giving public access to private information about its tiny population of black students, even after SASS repeatedly objected, remain unexplained, unresolved, and unexcused.

When I provided the College with personal information, I trusted the College to protect it as private. They could not see the dehumanizing inequality in singling out black students to disclose personal information. I will never know what made administrators and faculty at Swarthmore blind to the fact that their conduct offended vulnerable students, or why they turned a deaf ear to black voices seeking respect, or why the College never admitted that it was wrong. To this day, I do not know why my privacy and humanity were invisible to the College.

Unwittingly, the public disclosure of my private, personal information taught me painful lessons. I learned that Up North, my humanity could be invisible, ignored, and violated by white administrators and educators at a College with a history that included support for the movement to abolish slavery. Swarthmore's proud history of creating Underground Railroad safe havens was insufficient to enable the College to see the full humanity of its black students 100 years later.

By the fall of my senior year, graduation for several of us was less than six months away. When I took my first steps on Magill Walk to Parrish Hall in 1965, I could not have imagined that our diverse group of black students would encounter disrespect and inequality at Swarthmore. The lack of meaningful movement by the College confirmed that they did not hear our voices. I saw indifference and felt our invisibility. We had grown to trust each other's courage and united in feeling the urgency of the moment, which deepened our commitment to bring change.

During Christmas break of senior year, I returned to Tallahassee, as I had done every year, and missed the planning meeting for the Takeover. I returned to campus in January 1969, in full support of our peaceful efforts to bring change to Swarthmore. My support of the Takeover stemmed not only from the need to capture the attention of the College to see our humanity and hear our voices, but to change Swarthmore's direction.

Years later, Russell, then a freshman and now a lawyer, reminded me of how I persuaded him to come through the Parrish Hall window and join us in the admissions office to take a stand on the right side of history. When Russell's parents drove from Baltimore to campus, I asked Michael ("Mike") S. who monitored one of the Parrish windows to go outside with Russell and explain the reasons for the occupation. Most persuasive was Mike's report to Russell's parents about the refusal of the College to withdraw its public display of family incomes and other private information. When Mike climbed back through the window to join us, Russell returned, too. During the occupation, I occasionally served as an emissary who brought food and supporters inside.

Our sense of urgency did not override our deep commitment to non-violent, peaceful protest. Our quest for respect and recognition of our humanity reinforced our commitment to show respect to others—including College administrators who did not respect or fully acknowledge our humanity. Principles of respect and peaceful action prevailed. Even though few of us had ever met or had a conversation with the President of the College Courtney Smith or other administrators, we never lost sight of the importance of showing respect.

None of us could have anticipated the health condition of President Courtney Smith during our occupation of the admissions office, and we were shocked and saddened by his passing. When the president passed away in January 1969, I was twenty and six months away from my twenty-first birthday. Cruel, unfounded accusations blaming us for his untimely death deepened the shock of the tragedy and reinforced the chasm many of us felt in our relationship with the College. Somehow, I completed the semester, exhilarated and relieved.

During my senior year, my brother Eddie entered a doctoral program in economics at University of Pennsylvania, but I was not interested in pursuing a similar path. Our family joke was that my brother, Bishop, wanted to be a lawyer before he entered kindergarten. Bishop entered his final year at Harvard Law School the same year I entered my senior year at Swarthmore. He had co-founded the Harvard Black Law Students Association and knew that he wanted to be a civil rights lawyer. I had given little consideration to becoming a lawyer, but Bishop advised me to apply to Harvard Law School. His encouragement and work as a summer intern at the US Commission on Civil Rights inspired me to believe that I could become a lawyer who could bring change. After graduation, I entered Harvard Law School.

Continuing on the Road to Change

Swarthmore's lessons on race made it easy for me to have minimal contact with the College after graduation. Surprisingly, I was elected to the Swarthmore Alumni Council in the '80s. As Swarthmore reached out to me, I looked past disappointments and difficulties of my student days.

The College appointed me as an alumni member to its Board of Managers in the '90s and re-appointed me to the Board of Managers nearly two decades later for a lengthy term. I began to pay more attention to Swarthmore and realized that my contact with black alumni beyond my two friends, Joyce and Marilyn A., was nominal. Seeing a vacuum, I sent an email asking a number of black alumni for their thoughts on coming together as an alumni network. The responses led to the creation of the Swarthmore Black Alumni Network (SBAN) to connect black alumni to each other, students, and the College. Originating in 2013, soon after my appointment to the Board, SBAN garnered participation of black alumni from every decade since the '60s, annually raised funds to support summer student internships, institutionalized annual Garnet Weekend homecoming programs, sponsored regional alumni gatherings, and started an SBAN fund to permanently endow an internship. Our brother Harold, a co-founder, has participated with me in the leadership of SBAN from its beginning.

My service on the Board of Managers brought an unanticipated surprise. In my second year, a trip I was planning conflicted with a board meeting. Looking for solutions to minimize the schedule conflict, I studied the Swarthmore calendar. To my astonishment, I saw that the College did not cancel classes for the national holiday honoring Dr. Martin Luther King, Jr. even though President Ronald Reagan had signed legislation authorizing the holiday in 1983. I posed the question to the Chair of the Board in December, 2014: "Is Swarthmore's tradition of refusing to suspend classes on the national holiday for Dr. Martin Luther King, Jr. a source of pride?" The response proved that more than three decades of entrenched tradition concerning the holiday could change. For the first time, in January 2016, Swarthmore cancelled classes in honor of the national Dr. Martin Luther King, Jr. holiday.

Returning South to Florida

After Harvard Law School, I joined the NAACP Legal Defense & Educational Fund in New York City and worked to change our country by enforcing the civil rights laws. In my first case, we sued the Georgia State Prison. No blacks worked as officers, and black inmates claimed white officers used ax handles to beat them. We invoked laws to end brutality and racial discrimination. The federal court listened. After years of litigation and prodding by the court, the State of Georgia agreed to change. We brought a new day to the Georgia State Prison—the same prison where Georgia had jailed Dr. Martin Luther King, Jr. in 1960.

When I decided to leave New York and return to Florida, a former schoolmate who had grown up with me told me there was no place in Florida for a Swarthmore/Harvard-educated black woman like me. His comments ignited the spirit of my parents in me, which fired up my efforts to knock on traditionally-closed doors in Florida's corporate legal community. Holland & Knight LLP, a law firm that traces its origins in Florida to the 1890s, cracked opened its door. In 1981, I became its first black attorney and surmounted steep hurdles to become the first black female partner in a major Florida law firm on January 1, 1986.

I started in Holland & Knight's Tampa office and later moved to its Miami office, which offered national client development opportunities and international flair. In Miami, I met my husband. Our marriage ended in divorce, but not before we shared nearly twenty-five years.

Harvard surprised me when it nominated me for election to the Board of Directors of the Harvard Alumni Association

(HAA). While serving on the HAA's Executive Committee, I co-chaired the HAA's Global Month of Service, which emphasized connecting alumni to each other and their communities through volunteering. At the start of my journey Up North from Jim Crow-segregated Tallahassee, no one, including me, my family, or Swarthmore, could have predicted that I would be appointed to the Swarthmore College Board of Managers or that I would get nominated and then elected to one of Harvard University's governing boards, the Harvard Board of Overseers, in 2018.

When I advocated for Black Studies at Swarthmore, no one could have predicted that I would become a co-founder of the planned Miami Museum of Contemporary Art of the African Diaspora, Miami MoCAAD, which seeks to build a global museum that blends art and technology to inspire curiosity about contemporary African Diaspora art and modernize museum experiences.

When I entered Swarthmore, I did not know whether "the experience" would change me. The experience unceasingly challenged whether I belonged, but produced friendships lasting fifty years. My father's red roses underneath my bedroom window in Jim Crow Tallahassee and the courageous spirit of my parents to pursue their dreams against overwhelming odds continue to inspire my journey for change.

THE TAKEOVER

Day Eight

DAY EIGHT
Change of Course

On the morning of the eighth day of our occupation, one of the maintenance workers quietly but frantically banged on the chained doors of the admissions office. The student on guard duty at the door loosened the chain to hear the news, "President Smith just died!" Before we could grasp fully what we were hearing, a student who was returning to the office from outside confirmed the news, adding to the rumors that angry fraternity brothers were planning to evict us with baseball bats. The atmosphere inside the admissions office changed abruptly with this news that the College's president was dead.

Although he had announced his intention to retire, he maintained a relatively youthful appearance and appeared to be in excellent health. None of us was aware of his severe heart condition. Everyone was sad that this had happened. None of us had felt personal animosity toward him. We seemed at a loss as to what to do. The president's fatal heart attack, shortly before the faculty would have taken a critical vote on our demands, stunned everyone and, upon reflection, pressured us to change course. Although we had been keenly aware that our protest might not go exactly as we planned, no one could have imagined this. The death of the College president tragically changed the dynamics of the situation. We were no longer just protesters. To some on campus and in the national media, we were murderers. It was reassuring to later hear that the president's family did not hold us responsible for his death.

It did not take much discussion for us to agree that a strategic retreat and public statement were necessary. We knew we wouldn't have much time to agonize over the wording of our statement for the College and the press, but this might be our most important press release. We struggled. We went back and forth trying to find just the right words and tone. We meant it when we said:

> In deference to the untimely death of the President, the Swarthmore Afro-American Students' Society is vacating the admissions office.
>
> We sincerely believe that the death of any human being...is a tragedy...

"This wasn't our fault, but we are going to be blamed."

"Yes, but don't let them forget that black people die in the struggle. We can't let this derail our struggle."

> Whether he be the good president of a college or a black person trapped in our country's ghettoes, the death of any human being is a tragedy.
>
> At this time, we are calling for a moratorium of dialogue, in order that this unfortunate event be given the College's complete attention.

We knew we had to change course out of respect for President Smith and his family. In addition, our safety was very likely even more at-risk now. Police had been involved in black student actions at other colleges. Many faculty, students, and administrators were already opposed to what they considered the use of forcible tactics to get our way. The fact of the matter is that a strong wind could probably have broken through the flimsy chains that separated us from a possible attack by angry white students or locals. President Smith's death dramatically increased the level of emotion on both sides and greatly increased the risk of retaliation. Rumors ran wild, including that the Klan was sending a group to storm the campus. While that rumor was never substantiated, there were more credible stories about a group of fifty or so white fraternity brothers who planned to organize their own vigilante justice.

Our mission had not been accomplished, and many of us did not like the idea of just abandoning our action. So, we made certain to end our statement with:

> However, we remain strong in our conviction that the legitimate grievances we have voiced to the College remain unresolved and we are dedicated to attaining a satisfactory resolution in the future.

People from the community organized our retreat from the campus just hours after the president had died in his office upstairs from where we were in the admissions office. Years later, a community organizer from Media told us some of the older black adults in the area with ties to the College and who cared deeply about our well-being, got him involved with helping to secure a place for us to stay.[20] By the time we finished wordsmithing our public statement and packing up to leave, being careful to leave the office as tidy as possible, there was a caravan of black station wagons and vans lined up outside the window, doors open, waiting for all of us to pile in. The ministers who provided transportation and lodging for us were strangers to us until we met them that day.

Greeted by taunts of "murderer," Don read our prepared statement to the media and did a fifty-yard dash to the other end of Parrish Hall to escape with us in the caravan. By leaving, we could continue our protest in exile from the campus while showing respect for the Smith family. When the College held a memorial service for President Smith the following Sunday, most of us did not attend. It was a difficult decision, but we felt that our presence would be a distraction.

On the afternoon of day eight, a Thursday, we were whisked away to a church in Media that we had never visited before. We were driven through winding, suburban roads to a small town with few people on its streets. The days of self-exile were a blur of setting up camp in an unfamiliar place not normally used for housing people and constantly debating the events that had gotten us there. The bare wooden pews made for very uncomfortable sleeping. Some of us had to figure out how to use what the church provided—large pots and large bags of rice for us to prepare for our group of twenty-five or thirty hungry students—another unforgettable experience of the Takeover. Again, the division of labor made it work.

> I've seen the mothers at my church cook rice in these giant pots for Sunday dinners. But I never had to figure out the proportions myself.

That would have been Marilyn A. She, Harold, and Joyce were math majors, always studying together, calculating things.

> Now I really miss Joyce. Her dad worked in catering and she would know exactly how much we need. I hope she feels proud that she did her part for SASS and to see us carrying on the struggle after she graduated last year.

> We should just wash the rice and add enough water to rise about an inch above the rice.

That was likely Aundrea, or maybe Jannette. They were familiar with the ways of cooking for large family gatherings.

Years later, we visited several churches in Media trying to locate and thank the church and the minister who rescued us. We spoke to several elders at each church. They consistently told us:

> It could have been any one of us. We were watching you and we knew what you were going through. It could have been any one of us.

They embraced us as their own children.

During those visits, we saw artifacts on display in a church in Media recalling the history of the community providing safe haven in their attics for runaway slaves from the South along the Underground Railroad. Putting us up was part of a tradition we didn't know about at the time, but on reflection, we see parallels.

Supporters on campus worked on renewing negotiations with the College for our return with amnesty. Professor Legesse was an important early voice in maintaining the momentum we had initiated. Weeks later, he would be quoted in the campus newspaper as saying:

> It would be a grave error to attribute the President's death to the student protest as if the students had control over the lives of their fellow human beings. Even the most oblique reference to this idea is deeply offensive to our sense of morality.
>
> It is not SASS but individuals outside the College community who resorted, on at least three occasions, to violent threats. If SASS did jeopardize anybody's life, it now appears that they jeopardized their own.[21]

Word soon reached us that the shocked College administrators were ready to put the "Crisis" behind them. Classes for spring were scheduled to begin soon. The College would grant our demands and we would be able to return without penalty, as long as we agreed to act in "good faith." The few days and nights in that unfamiliar and uncomfortable environment made us also willing to accept the College's good faith proposals—as long as amnesty was included. We will never know what the outcome would have been if the president had not died.

Tao: Finding My Way— Harold's Story

HAROLD S. BUCHANAN

Elephant in the Room

People may wonder what circumstances led to my being the only brother associated with this group of Seven Sisters. When it came time to plan and execute things like the organization of SASS and the Takeover, I was included because we had similar objectives. We often did things together based on common interests. We were primarily the ones who went to other campuses to take courses in Black Studies and attend black cultural events. I was the only black male student who was passionate enough, or perhaps foolish enough, about the black liberation movement to put activism ahead of academic success. As SASS developed, most of the black males eventually supported its goals. The difference is that their priority was graduating and mine was "the struggle."

I became friends with the sisters before they were labeled as a group. Marilyn A., Joyce, and I were math majors, so we had shared the associated pain and often studied together. Because Marilyn A. and I were in the same class year and major field of study, I had more classes with her than any other person. I got to know Marilyn H. because we were both activists against the Vietnam War. Bridget's US home was also my birthplace of Brooklyn, so it was convenient to drop her off on my way to my home on Long Island. Being one of the few students on campus who had a car put me always in demand. My car helped me to spend time with Marilyn A. as I attempted to teach her to drive. Joyce was not as familiar with auto maintenance, so I helped her out when she showed up on campus with her wood-paneled station wagon. Myra, Bridget, and Aundrea were all a year behind me, but I got to know them well when we spent a summer working together. I knew

Jannette the least, but well enough to be the photographer at her wedding after we graduated.

A major reason that I became associated with these ladies is that I was comfortable with women as friends. I never played organized sports and I didn't grow up with a gang of boys around my age, so I never learned "locker room talk" and never viewed women as inferior. My parents had different roles in the household, but they worked together and respected each other. Our backyard was the neighborhood playground where boys and girls played games like "hide-and-go-seek" and "kick the can" together. We also played team sports like kickball and softball. The teams were mostly comprised of the four children in my family and our twelve cousins who lived next door, so it was a family affair.

The high school orchestra was the nucleus for my closest circle of friends in high school. Practicing with the orchestra allowed more time for social interaction. In my inner circle of friends, we had a string quartet with Josiah on violin, Pat on viola, Margo on cello, and me on upright bass. Culturally, we had a Jew, a Catholic, a Protestant, and an African Methodist. It seems that we were always practicing after school or performing. The high school music room was our hangout. Thinking back, learning to make beautiful music was a good way to bring us together.

I never had a girlfriend in high school or college, so it was nice to have beautiful, intelligent women around to talk to. When I became an upperclassman, a fair amount of my time was spent visiting in the women's dormitories. My photographer's eye found the women much more photogenic than the men. They sometimes served as models for my photography. There were only a few times when I was uncomfortable being the only guy in the group. The Sisters can certainly speak for themselves, but my guess as to why they put up with my being around all the time has something to do with my uncommon habit of being reliable and doing exactly what I say I will do.

When the Sisters and I were deciding who would be the best chairperson for SASS, we agreed that it would be politically wise to have a male in that position. I then had to explain why I was not a good fit. My childhood experience was not one of confrontation or leadership of any kind. Despite being considered intelligent, I have never been good at thinking on my feet. My style is more contemplative. When you added in my tendency to avoid conflict, I was not a good candidate to be the chairperson, so we selected another male.

There have been many other times in my life when I was the odd man in a group. I have always been the "elephant" in one-room or another. This started in early childhood, when I was one of the few left-handers in class. I had to learn to do many things backwards. I was also usually only one of two black children in the classroom. In junior and senior high, the school grouped students by "academic ability," and there were even fewer blacks with me in the advanced classes. Over the years, I have become comfortable standing out from the crowd. As an adult, I have segregated myself by my unorthodox lifestyle. I was a vegan and a natural food junkie before most people knew what those terms meant.

I Made It Myself

I wrote my first book in first grade. Mrs. Bedell directed the class in writing and illustrating our own books. Although mostly a picture book, I was proud when the single copy was distributed to my parents. The book, entitled *I Made It Myself,* was the story of me as a young scientist who had built his first rocket ship. It consisted of several watercolor pictures of me and my rocket, ending with a blast off and the caption "I Made

It Myself." At that early age, I had big dreams and saw no limit to what I could accomplish on this earth. I signed the book as Harold Buchanan, PhD.

I was destined to life as a *doer*, someone who gets things done. I have since rescinded my goal of achieving a PhD but have spent my life *doing* many things. One of my high school heroes was the ultimate Renaissance man, Leonardo Da Vinci. I was inspired by his exploration of so many diverse fields. I chose mathematics as my college major because it is involved in so many disciplines. If I were to write a complete resume, it would include pizza deliveryman, newspaper boy, draftsperson, custodian/janitor, camp counselor, taxi driver, printer/typesetter, clothing salesperson, business proprietor, computer programmer, database designer, systems analyst, network manager, short order cook, academic advisor, project leader, research interviewer, elementary school teacher, and college instructor as vocations. My list of avocations is just as deep.

Made from Scratch

Of all the things I have done, cooking has been one of the most rewarding. I was a chubby child and always loved to eat. I recall a picture of me in about the third grade, displaying a tin of cookies I had made and chomping down on one. I spent many years assisting my mother and sisters in preparing all types of dishes, and by high school, I had advanced to making ravioli from scratch.

It should be no surprise that I enjoy food and cooking since I literally grew up in the kitchen. The kitchen was the center of our small bungalow home on Long Island and the kitchen table was where everything happened. It greeted extended family and guests as they entered our house. There was almost always someone sitting at that table; either preparing food, talking, or playing a game. The kitchen was very important in our family, and that table was the centerpiece.

My fondest memories of growing up were of family meals, and Thanksgiving was the ultimate one. Everyone helped with the preparation or cooking, depending on their ability. Back then, everything was made fresh, so there was plenty to do in washing vegetables, chopping onions and celery, or making fresh cranberry sauce. One Christmas, I worked with my parents around the table to make candy for gift trays. I remember the care that went into making marzipan acorns that were the centerpiece of our cookie tray. We had never worked with chocolate before and were all learning the process together. The events around our kitchen table were instrumental in forming my sense of family.

I say that I grew up in the kitchen partly because it was the family center, but also because my brother and I shared a small bedroom adjacent to the kitchen. The room was originally designed to be a dining room. There was only a ceiling-to-floor-length green curtain to separate us from the action in the kitchen. Day or night, everyone had to walk through our bedroom to get to the only bathroom and my parents' bedroom. Our dresser was right next to the doorway to the kitchen, so I could get my socks with one hand and open the refrigerator with the other. There was no door to close if we wanted privacy. On the other hand, that thin curtain didn't afford much privacy to the adults playing cards in the kitchen as we lay in bed.

Our attic was converted into two tiny bedrooms where my sisters shared one room and my grandmother had the other. My parents' bedroom was the only one with an actual door. My most private moments were lying outside under the big oak tree, gazing up at the clouds in wonder. That is one reason that I grew up with a love for nature and the outdoors.

The kitchen was even more central to family life because everyone, except my brother, cooked. In my parents' generation, there were no boxed cake mixes. Everything was made from scratch. They were slow to adapt to the "instant" gratification afforded by Pillsbury and Duncan Hines, so I was able to learn the basics of cooking sitting around the kitchen table.

My college classmates never knew that I was accomplished in the kitchen. People generally assumed that men didn't know much about cooking, and I never let on that I often knew more than they did. When I entered college in 1965, l left my apron at home. The only exception to this was when I had a work-study job cooking steaks in the cafeteria.

Freshman Year

During my freshman year at college, I was what Black Nationalists described as an Oreo: dark on the outside, but pure white on the inside. My small black community in Bellport, New York was an ocean of whiteness. Our small church and a barbershop in a nearby town were the only black institutions that I knew of. It was not until I was in high school that blacks began to make regular appearances on TV. As a freshman, I began to awaken to the painful reality that this world did not live up to the utopian images portrayed on TV. The seeds of transformation had been planted, but it would take time for the blackness within me to come to full bloom.

My freshman year was full of typically "white" activities. I tried spelunking, but one trip to a hidden underground cave was enough for me. I could think of much better ways to die than starving to death, wedged into a dark, damp crevasse that was just big enough to squeeze into and barely big enough to get out of. Folk dance club was infinitely better. I enjoy many types of music, so it was something that I found pleasant, if not truly enjoyable. I went back several times. In the end, though, my lifelong aversion to dancing won out and there would be no more square dancing. I lasted an entire semester as a DJ on the campus radio station. I played mostly classical music at a time of day when hardly anyone was listening. Come to think of it, I don't recall anyone ever even talking about anything that they heard on the campus radio.

My real joy in extracurricular activities was the College chorus. I had been in the high school chorus and discovered that I truly loved to sing. I was really pleased when I was accepted into the chorus as a tenor. This was the first time that I ever had to audition for a spot. That was almost enough to scare me away, but I figured that I had nothing to lose but pride. I remember our being coached by the Russian professor, so that our pronunciation of the opera *Boris Godunov* would be accurate. It was a very rewarding experience. My singing skills were pushed to the absolute limit. I know that because my voice gave out to laryngitis two days before our major performance in Philadelphia. It was not fun to sit in the audience, listening to the show that I had trained so hard for.

By the end of the freshman year, that Oreo cookie had begun to crumble. I had met most of the black students on campus and had, for the first time, discovered a community of peers. My musical preference had morphed from classical to folk and black soul music.

NOT Business as Usual

The soundtrack for the sixties was so much more than a playlist to sit and listen to. Many songs were a reality check for those who were not paying attention to current events. Nina Simone revived Billy Holiday's groundbreaking "Strange Fruit" to remind us that the days of lynchings were not just historical events. Her "Mississippi Goddam" talked candidly about the injustices of the South, and how it was time for a change. Roberta Flack's "Business Goes On As Usual" let us know that, while we were listening to music and studying the Philosophy of Language, our brothers were being killed in Vietnam.

> Business goes on as usual
>
> Except that my brother is dead
>
> He was twenty-five and very much alive
>
> But the dreams have all been blasted from his head

My own brother was fighting with the US Army in Vietnam as I listened to this song. Fortunately, he was not dead, but the star pitcher of our high school baseball team was not so lucky. Having grown up playing softball with "Skippy," I am sure he did not understand why he was fighting in Vietnam. That song captured what I had been feeling, as I learned the extent of injustices and inequalities that blacks faced in this country, as we questioned the Warren Commission Report on the murder of our president, and as we tried to understand why our country was sending its young men to die.

Like many college students of that era, I took these songs as marching orders: words to live by. One of my favorite protest songs was Buffy Sainte-Marie's "My Country 'Tis of Thy People You're Dying." The title tells the story. It is about how the genocide committed on Native Americans was a basic building block for America. It told me that there was something inherently wrong with America. American institutions were founded on the principle of white supremacy. In addition to the many specific points made in the SASS position paper, "Why We Can't Wait," we expressed a strong motivation to act. As Nina Simone had warned, white people keep on telling us to "go slow." In 1964, there were riots in Harlem, riots in Newark in 1967, and Baltimore in 1968. Dr. Martin Luther King, Jr. had been assassinated, and we were busy studying non-Euclidean Geometry. These events were shaping our young minds and hearts. Our future at Swarthmore and beyond was changing in ways that we had never imagined.

In addition to protest songs, we were regularly exposed to speakers and events that helped to shape our world view. One person that made a lasting impression on me was a former student who returned to campus. Delmer was one of the few black students who preceded us at Swarthmore. Since there was no black community on campus during his time there in the mid-sixties, it was not surprising to hear that he had dropped out. He was a relatively short person with a small frame. He always wore a car-length brown leather jacket that portrayed an air of toughness. His wire-framed spectacles transformed his image to that of a classic nerd. None of us checked to see if he really had been a Swarthmore student. He was not a very impressive person until he opened his mouth. When he spoke, it was clear that he was Swarthmore material. A virtuoso of the spoken word, he was soft-spoken, but extremely eloquent and very intense. He spoke of the black struggle and our need to be involved in a way that made it obvious that he had given this topic quite a bit of thought. His intensity was flavored with a note of arrogance that turned off many of the black students. If you dared to ask, he had all the answers. Delmer was not a business as usual type of person.

Except for his previous Swarthmore affiliation, he did not say anything about why he suddenly appeared on campus or what he was currently doing. Some suspected that he might be an undercover FBI agent. If he was an agent, there was not much to investigate at that time. By the time that SASS became politically active, Delmer had just about disappeared. As a person who was eager to learn more about black history and its impact on my life, I was not turned off by his arrogance. As an itinerant, he needed someplace free to sleep when he was on campus, and my floor was available. With so few black upperclassmen at Swarthmore, it was not easy to find someone to look up to. Delmer filled that void for me.

I had spent two summers working as a custodian at "The Lab" near my home on Long Island. The Lab is Brookhaven National Laboratory, a government atomic research site. I had mastered the art of "looking busy" early in that career. When Delmer suggested that I work with him in Philadelphia the next summer, it offered an opportunity to do something more productive and, perhaps, make a difference in the community. Delmer proposed working for Gray Printing, an activist black print shop in the heart of North Philadelphia. We would be helping recently widowed Mrs. Gray get her business back on track. The summer of 1967 would not be business as usual. In addition to the obvious need to learn about printing, I would have to learn how to live with no income. Mrs. Gray was not able to pay us for any work we did. As a scholarship student from a lower income family, I relied on summer jobs to provide spending money for the school year. Fortunately, my scholarship included a work-study job during the school year.

Latifah Gray was an elderly black Muslim woman who ran the printing business alone after the death of her husband. She was a pleasant person who could go from a sweet soft voice to a no-nonsense business manner in an instant. Based on my limited experience, I believed that it was unusual for someone of her age to be active in the "black struggle." She did not dress differently, cover her face, or always cover her hair, so I did not think she was affiliated with Elijah Muhammad's group.

Mrs. Gray didn't completely trust us at first, but she was overwhelmed with work and needed help badly. Hers was a small "job shop" that printed business stationery, booklets, and flyers. The willingness to print political flyers or a controversial booklet was what made it an activist print shop. After a few weeks, I was doing most of the printing, freeing Mrs. Gray to catch up on the management of the business. Working side by side with me helped to overcome her initial distrust. Unlike me, Delmer was a visionary and a thinker. His contribution to Mrs. Gray's business was finding new customers. To his credit, he also correctly figured out that I was a good fit for this job. Mrs. Gray never did trust him and his mysterious life.

In high school, I was often called a Renaissance man because of my versatility of talents. Learning the craft of printing in the Gutenberg tradition reinforced that image of me. The equipment that we used was mechanically advanced, but was otherwise not very different from what Gutenberg had invented. Unlike Gutenberg's machine, the letterpress that I used was automated. The speed of the motor could vary according to the skill of the operator. His job was to carefully place a card or piece of paper onto the bed of the machine in exactly the right position, before the press automatically closed to make an impression. If you were too slow, the powerful steel jaws could crush your hand and arm. If you were too quick, you would save your hand, but the card might be a little off center. How long would it take before I could do it as well as a seventy-or-so-year-old woman?

The primary benefit of my summer adventure was living amidst the action in North Philadelphia at the peak of the Black Power movement. Our compensation for helping Mrs. Gray was "free" rooms in her large brownstone near Columbia Avenue, a commercial district lined with small storefront businesses. It was the scene of the 1964 race riot over police brutality in Philadelphia. From this location, I could walk a few blocks to the Church of the Advocate on Diamond Street. Reverend Paul Washington was the progressive rector of this

Episcopal Church that was a key feature in the Philadelphia Black Power movement. Many community meetings were held at the church with black thought leaders such as Walt Palmer, Playthell Benjamin, and Cecil B. Moore. It was a wonderful opportunity to live amongst people who were helping to shape the future of blacks in this country. This was particularly true for a young boy from the white suburbs.

When I was not working or attending black political and cultural events, I was usually at my home for the summer. There, I was introduced to urban nature in the form of pigeons, cockroaches, and mice. Once, I even came face to face with a rat in the hall. He was at one end of the hall and I was at the other. We each stood our ground and stared at each other until I chased him away with a broom. He quickly disappeared, but for the next few nights, I didn't sleep quite as soundly. I had never lived in a row house before. The experience of walking out the front door and having your neighbors right in your face was an adjustment for me. My days of solitude with drifting cloud formations had been replaced with a street full of children playing, music blaring, and adults fussing against a backdrop of asphalt, bricks, and concrete.

At the end of June, things got more exciting as we embarked on a trip to attend the second Black Arts Convention in Detroit. Delmer was from a small town near Detroit, so he took advantage of this opportunity to go home for few days. We had made a few friends in the black community and ended up with a carload of people in colorful African garb making the trip in a rented station wagon. We loaded it up with people and luggage until nothing else would fit. I don't know about the others, but the twelve-hour ride to Detroit was the longest road trip I had ever taken. Judging from the way they handled the overloaded car, I suspect that some of the other drivers were also inexperienced with driving on a superhighway.

We handled the excursion like a bunch of adolescents, not thinking to rest up beforehand. At one point, I was alarmed to see that the person driving had completely fallen asleep. Halfway through Ohio, we discovered that they used radar to enforce the speed limit. This was apparently a speed trap to help the local economy. We had to follow the officer's patrol car back to town where a justice of the peace was conveniently waiting to impose a fine. We had little money to spare. One of us had the brilliant idea to pretend that we were visiting dignitaries from Africa. When we arrived at the courthouse, our "translator" explained the situation to the judge and asked for mercy. I am certain that the judge had never encountered African dignitaries before. I don't really know whether he believed our story or not, but he did not put us in jail. We were allowed to pay a smaller fine and continue on our journey.

Detroit, the home of Motown, was a natural location for the convention. One of the key speakers that year was SNCC chairman H. Rap Brown, one of the more militant leaders of the movement. He made headlines that year by saying:

> Let white America know that the name of the game is tit-for-tat, an eye for an eye, a tooth for a tooth, and a life for a life. Motown, if you don't come around, we are going to burn you down![22]

Right after we left town, Detroit was the scene of some of the worst riots of that era with 43 dead, 1,189 injured, and nearly 700 buildings burned to the ground.[23]

A few brothers decided to make a second trip to Detroit immediately after we got home. Days later, Andrew returned, badly injured. On the way home, the car had overturned, and a brother named Acel had been killed. That week, I learned a valuable lesson about taking risks. It could easily have been any one of us who was killed in that car.

I could not have imagined all of what I experienced during that summer in Philadelphia. I learned a lot about myself, my capabilities, and my limitations. I got to live closely with people who were not my family. The methodical process of printing helped me to develop a patience that has been my foundation as I make my way through life. I made it to Detroit and back safely, avoiding the riots and a fatal automobile accident. Our failure to plan and prepare ourselves for the trip made it an unacceptable risk that I learned to avoid in the future.

That summer, I took a major step toward breaking out of my cocoon and seeing the world for what it was. When I returned to Swarthmore, I had to figure out how my academic pursuits fit into that world. Far removed from my childhood dream of a PhD, it would be a struggle to continue down this Eurocentric path. Even as we had been motivated to act by protest songs, we were also inspired by songs of hope that we could also have an impact on the world. My favorite singer from those years was Nina Simone. She wrote so many songs that had an impression on me and inspired my life. Perhaps the most important, "To Be Young, Gifted and Black" was released as we graduated in 1969. I view it as Nina's gift to our generation:

> To be young, gifted, and black,
>
> Oh what a lovely precious dream...

Blactivity

My sophomore year was the year of awakening to the political reality of the '60s, but the junior year was the year of *blac*tivity. SASS became a fully functioning and active campus organization. Social, cultural, and political activities were happening at a fast pace. Blacks on campus were the center of attention. Many because they congregated in groups that threatened the establishment by their very existence. Others because they were not a part of those groups. Most white students also took sides: either in support of our right to pick our own friends or in reaction to the perceived threat to their own dreams. My physical appearance had changed from a pudgy, clean-shaven, oft-smiling kid to a lanky black man with a jet-black, bushy afro and beard that masked the friendly smile. Many said that my persona was frightening. Even my one-time black roommate said he was scared when he first saw me. My red-headed, freshman year roommate once pulled me aside and offered to help me buy guns, should the need arise.

Toward the end of that school year, there was an opportunity for summer jobs with an Upward Bound program in Boston. After working for free during the summer of '67, I needed the extra money. A few of us were hired for that program and Aundrea's parents hosted us at their large brownstone house for the summer. Myra, Bridget, and I bonded closely in our first official experience as the adults in the room. I remember the weekend that we took a busload of our young tutees on an overnight trip to the White Mountains. None of us got much sleep as we dashed inside and outside, from room to room, counting teenage heads in a futile attempt to keep boys and girls from getting too close. I will never forget watching Myra fix fried corn for breakfast as dawn finally arrived. We had survived the night!

Lost

The summer of '68 began with a letter from the College explaining that I had flunked out of school. In my enthusiasm for learning about all things black, I had lost interest in Western education. I finished my junior year with three Fs, including two in my chemistry major. Although my overall grade point average was passing, the year was so bad that something had to change. Clearly, a career in chemistry was not in my future. Notably, the Chemistry Department didn't seem to notice that a prospective major was failing tests and not showing up at labs. As always, my parents were supportive of me. They never mentioned any disappointment that I might not fulfill their dream of having a child graduate from college. When faced with problems, their response was to look for solutions, like suggesting that I could complete my studies at the local university.

I hastily enrolled in what I hoped was an easy math course at Boston University. I had accumulated extra credits, so that one course would put me back on track for graduation with a new major in mathematics. My grade of B convinced the College that I was ready to work again, and I was readmitted for the fall semester with no time lost. In the best of Swarthmore tradition, my financial aid package also survived intact. That setback gave me the motivation I needed to get through the senior year. I was permitted to rejoin my classmates for what would be one of the most significant events of our lives. Only my closest friends were aware of my precarious status.

That fall semester featured a showdown with the College over their half-hearted commitment to diversity. It also cemented the bonds of trust that had been developing between my activist Sisters and me. Having just flunked out of school and then readmitted, I had a lot to lose as our discussions with the College escalated into demands. Instead of finishing my coursework, I was on the frontline in our struggle with the College. I joined a few of the Sisters in Harlem to plan our action. As we transitioned from negotiations to aggressive action, we knew that our futures were on the line. Over the past few weeks, I had studied the blueprints and visited the admissions office to get familiar with the layout. Instead of the guns my former roommate had offered, I entered the building armed with chains and padlocks. I quickly secured the back doors as my sister-friends convinced the office personnel to leave.

As with the other students, my survival equipment included a stack of textbooks, but when the dust settled, my fall semester grade report featured another course failure. Ironically, it was in Computer Science, a nascent field of study that would end up becoming my career for thirty-plus years. That left me one course short of the minimum graduation requirement. I got permission to take a course at the University of Pennsylvania. Unfortunately, that class finished two weeks after graduation, so I was not able to walk in the ceremony. I have always tried to live my life without regrets, but I do wish I had had the foresight to realize that my actions meant that my parents would not have the honor of watching their son walk at graduation. I am forever indebted to my parents for the unselfish trust they put in me.

My Number Is Up!

My number had been called for the draft into the army and I was scheduled for a pre-admission physical. I fasted for a few days and stayed up all night to meet this challenge. The only thing standing between the Vietnam War and me was the mercy of God. I had deferred this moment for four years as a student at Swarthmore and another two years at Temple University. I declined to seek out doctors who could fabricate a medical excuse for me. I summoned what remaining strength I had and reported for the army physical. To my relief and amazement, the doctor said I was not eligible. My blood test showed protein in my urine, an indication of a possibly serious disease. I was classified as 4F: medically unfit. That blood condition never appeared on future tests.

Joining the Teacher Corps program at Temple University had given me a desperately needed path forward after my tumultuous senior year. Equally as important, it provided that two-year extension of my student deferral from the draft. During the Vietnam War years, decisions on how to handle the draft were foremost in the minds of most young American men. My relatively low draft number meant that I would almost certainly be called to serve in the army. I wish I could say that my use of the College deferral was based solely on the unjustness of the war, but it was also a matter of survival. Life and death decisions like this paved the path to adulthood. Many of us who took advantage of this privilege also felt the need to speak out for an end to the war.

The Teachers Corps was a federal program that sought to attract more and better teachers to low-income areas. It gave participants an opportunity to earn a master's degree in education while providing community service. Since the climate of the sixties and my exposure to Black Nationalism had derailed my childhood expectation of earning a PhD, a career in teaching was a reasonable next step. I had long been a "teacher" in the informal sense; having helped siblings with homework, taught Sunday School, and even done some tutoring in high school. I enjoyed helping others to learn. In the Teacher Corps program, I co-taught fourth grade at the East Falls Elementary School with an experienced teacher and did volunteer work in that Philadelphia community for two years.

East Falls was what was known as a "project." It was a planned community entirely of subsidized housing with a mixture of tall (high-rise) apartment buildings and small individual homes. "The projects" created an unnatural environment in which the entire population was low-income. The high-rise units greatly increased the density of low-income residents and contributed to a high crime rate. One day, toward the end of my first year, my star student failed to show up for class. She was a beautiful, intelligent fourth grader who was well liked by her classmates. She had a wonderful personality and excelled in her studies. Students like her made the teaching experience more enjoyable. I discovered that her father had murdered her mother. She had been uprooted to live with a relative in another part of town and would not return. I felt completely helpless. This experience was a major factor in my decision against a career in public education. It seemed to me that public school teachers were fighting a losing battle.

Tao: Finding My Way

As I neared graduation from Swarthmore, my friend Delmer reappeared and introduced me to one of his friends, Jerry, who was teaching a series of classes on black history and culture in Philadelphia. While attending Temple University and teaching, I started the next session of his class. The curriculum organized and summarized many of the things I had learned in my college years, going even further with an emphasis on living a healthy and principled lifestyle, similar to the teachings of the Black Muslim organization. After the historical context had been established, the core of the teaching was on the Seven Principles and how to apply them to daily life.

As defined by the founder of Kwanzaa, Dr. Maulana Ron Karenga, the Principle of Nia (Purpose) means:

> To make our collective vocation the building and developing of our community in order to restore our people to their traditional greatness.

To live this principle requires that a person focus his life on abandoning negative personal habits and cultivating positive traits. Black Nationalism was about discovering the lost learning and traditions of our African ancestors and using that knowledge to rebuild our families and communities. Who would argue with the goal of making our people great again?

As part of that class, we also studied the ancient Eastern philosophies and the quest for spiritual Enlightenment as taught by Confucius, Lao Tzu, and Buddha. Few followers of these religions ever achieve Enlightenment, but they can improve their lives by moving along the path of Tao, or The Way. We also learned about traditional African civilizations and the Songhai Empire, about Timbuktu and the fourteenth century University of Sankore. We read about eating low on the food chain in *Diet for a Small Planet* and learned *How to Eat to Live* from Elijah Muhammad. We read Linda Goodman's *Sun Signs* and learned how astrology affects personality and relationships.

As the class neared completion, it was revealed to us that The Way being recommended here was to join a new cultural organization that was being formed. The group was called the Sankore Society after that North African Center of Learning. It was a small group of blacks whose goal was to develop a community based on an adaptation of the Seven Principles of Kwanzaa. Sometime during my Temple studies, I was initiated into the Sankore Society. None of us who completed the class fully understood what we were signing up for. We had a general idea of the goal of building a quasi-traditional Afro-American community, but how that would happen was yet to be revealed. It was clear to me that whatever I might do within this organization, it would NOT be business as usual. Having grown up in a strong family and maturing with an extended family at Swarthmore, I was attracted to the communal aspect of the organization. Having lived with Delmer for a summer, I trusted that he, and by association, his cohorts, had good intentions. Hopefully, it would not be the good intentions that paved the way to Hell.

The most dramatic consequence of joining this group was a change in diet. Members were expected to adapt as closely as possible to a vegan diet and to eat one meal a day. The foods chosen should be as wholesome as possible. Whole grains and fresh vegetables were better than white flour, white sugar, canned vegetables, and chemical additives. Many of these dietary practices that I learned fifty years ago are now popular. I was dismayed to learn that even the food I had been eating had been corrupted by Western society.

The transition to a vegan diet required both a high level of commitment and creativity. The willpower necessary to never eat another cheeseburger, bacon and eggs, or even a milkshake can be understood on an intellectual level, but the average American could not fully appreciate how severely this diet limits one's choices in eating. In the seventies, there were few commercial food establishments that offered vegetarian options, and even fewer with vegan fare. It was pretty much a requirement that most of your meals were prepared at home. The "fast" in fast food had become a "four-letter word." If you wanted a sandwich, you might have to make your own mayonnaise and bread.

It was said by the Hindu god Krishna that there are many paths to Enlightenment. Everyone who seeks spiritual growth must find their own path. Consequently, there was no Sankore police force to make sure that everyone practiced vegetarianism or ate one meal a day. This was your personal quest for self-improvement and could go as far as you would take it. Your inner voice guided you on your path. Some people reached the one meal a day goal more easily than others. Many people gave up and left the group. I eventually settled into a practice of a daily vegan meal, with a weekly fast and a light afternoon snack on more difficult days.

My attraction to this lifestyle was that I no longer fit into mainstream American society. In truth, I had never quite fit in. My relationship to television is one of the best examples of that. Television was newly introduced in our generation, so I had started life without it. I recall the arrival of the first television in our home on Long Island when I was in the second or third grade. Back then, everyone would sit around in the living room, watch a show together, then engage in conversation about it. By high school, the novelty was wearing off for me as the number of TV hours was increasing and gradually squeezing out other family activities. By the time I entered college, I had completely abandoned TV.

Two People Walking in the Same Direction

The first time I met my future wife, Camille, was on a trip to pick up a few single women and take them to their first meeting of Jerry's class. My penchant toward punctuality was confronted with her prerogative to be not quite ready when I arrived. I remember waiting in the dimly lit living room of her mother's row house while she gathered her things as if time didn't matter. She was smiling and seemed very outgoing and confident. I have retained an image of her being so graceful that she appeared to almost float across the room. I later learned that she actually had training in how to behave at a "finishing school." I did not recognize it as "love at first sight," but she definitely made an impression on me.

I was attracted to Camille and enjoyed her company, but she was not my first choice for a mate. That was partly driven by the fact that she had a two-year-old daughter. I very much wanted to start a family, but knew nothing about parenting. I knew intuitively that it would be much more difficult to build a relationship with three people than with just two. As it turned out, the decision was not mine to make. It is said that the Lord works in mysterious ways.

Camille and I had an arranged marriage. Just like her untimely death after forty-two years of marriage, our union was preordained by a higher power. To an objective observer, we were an obvious match. Camille was accomplished in the "feminine" skills and wanted to have a family of twelve. I was likewise accomplished in the "masculine" skills and had a family as my primary objective. We never told others in the group, but Camille had been a tomboy growing up and was familiar with some masculine skills like electrical wiring. That was why her father sent her to a finishing school. Likewise, I was secretly very competent in the kitchen and knew a little about sewing from maintaining my mother's sewing machine. Jerry suggested to me that Camille and I would be a good match. He had spoken to her, and I knew that she believed in this pairing. I had not realized the obvious, but it was certainly a reasonable conclusion, so I set out on that path. Camille and I met privately and discussed our feelings for each other and the possibility of marriage. We were not "in love" at the time, but decided to spend more time together over the next few months to see if this was the right path for us. We did just that, sharing our views on life and love and family, and falling *in love* along the way. In the end, we developed a bond of complete love and trust in each other that even death could not break.

The ultimate test in our relationship came after about seven years of marriage and four children. We had become disillusioned with the leadership of Sankore Society. Our belief in this path had brought us together. Dare I suggest that we leave the group and the friendships we had built? Would our love be strong enough for us to continue on our own? We had built a relationship strong enough to discuss our deep feelings with the assurance that we both had the same vision for our future. We decided that Krishna was right in saying that everyone must find his or her own path: we must be true to ourselves. We had learned what we could from the Society. It was in the best interest of our family for us to move on, and we knew that our love was strong enough to survive the test.

Families are the building blocks of most societies, but our "modern" style of living has fostered the disintegration of the family. Following the lead of my parents and the lessons I learned from studying non-Western cultures, my life has been devoted to family. My white high school friends and I were quite close, and I learned from them that real friends can be like family. Although the Sankore Society was not perfect, it provided me with an extended family and a supportive environment in which to raise children. I survived the rigors of Swarthmore with the support of my adopted family of Seven Sisters. One of the things that has bonded our group together was the importance of family to each of us. We were all raised by parents who loved us, but had enough love to share with others in their communities.

Together in our extended family, we changed the narrative at Swarthmore College. We refused to let blacks be viewed and treated as just objects of their Quaker charity. The Takeover of the admissions office lasted eight days, but the change in direction of the College has been enduring.

Epilogue

JANNETTE O. DOMINGO
MARILYN ALLMAN MAYE

A Sankofa Moment

In 2009, forty years after the Takeover, the current SASS members used the Ghanaian Sankofa bird as the symbol for the celebration of the founding events. By bringing the SASS founders back to campus to tell and record our stories, they demonstrated that they were inspired by the spirit of a bird whose feet are firmly planted forward, even as its head looks backwards. It encourages us to remember and learn from the past in order to plan for and protect the future.

When we arrived that day, the campus was resplendent with colorful fall foliage, just as it had been on those chilly autumn afternoons so many years ago. Black students and alumni from around the country packed the Lang Hall auditorium, warmly welcoming us for a panel discussion on the founding of SASS and the 1969 Takeover. Most of us Seven Sisters and a Brother had seldom spoken publicly of our Swarthmore experiences, and only a few had returned to campus or maintained a connection to the College after graduation, so the audience was astonished by the revelations of our previously untold stories. We dispelled myths and misconceptions about ourselves and SASS, and about the seminal events in which we had participated. We spoke of the power of collaborative leadership and of the community and camaraderie, energy and purposefulness, and courage that characterized the early days of SASS and made the Takeover and its lasting impacts possible. The audience gave us a standing ovation. Some held back tears. Forty years earlier, the activism of black students at Swarthmore and many other colleges across the country had led to greater opportunities for black students, black faculty and administrators, and the establishment of black studies programs and black cultural centers. It was important to remind them—and they seemed most surprised to realize—that we had been regular students, not unlike themselves. Their responses ranged from "Most of you were first generation college students?" to "We thought you were students who came from money. You risked your scholarships and disappointing your parents." And the important conclusion reached by some: "We probably would never have been here if you hadn't done what you did."

Later during that fortieth anniversary weekend, SASS members videotaped interviews with us and other SASS founders with the intention of preserving our stories. The interviews took place in the Black Cultural Center (BCC), a large three-story house that had served as a women's dormitory when we were students in the 1960s. How moving it was to see the words *Black Cultural Center* inscribed on the sign in front of the house. We had always believed that having an organization wasn't enough. Black students needed a sanctuary where they could develop together, away from the campus microaggressions and stresses. Even while doing the initial organizational work for SASS to become officially chartered in 1967, it was obvious that SASS students would need meeting and performance space for the many educational, cultural, and social events we were always initiating at the College. Fraternities and other student organizations had dedicated spaces for activities that were often much less inclusive and beneficial to the College as a whole. We had dreamed of it, but it would take another year of activism by our SASS successors, including a brief sit-in in the new president's office, before the College designated a building for use as the BCC and provided professional staff to support it. As we had expected, the BCC has helped promote and sustain the development of Black cultural expression among students of all backgrounds.

Inside the BCC, the walls were lined with framed black and white portraits of pioneering black faculty members and artifacts of decades of SASS struggles. The front parlor featured a portrait of Dr. Kathryn Morgan. Salt and pepper braids had replaced the afro haircut she had worn in the 1960s, well before most professional black women. But, in the intense eyes that peered out at us, we could still see the striking and charismatic University of Pennsylvania doctoral candidate who had so impressed us when we met and interviewed her in spring 1969, soon after the Takeover. In fall 1970, after we had graduated, she was hired in the History Department and became the first African American woman tenured at the College. She went on to win many academic awards as a pioneering African American folklorist and historian and as a renowned champion of the legitimacy of storytelling and the power of telling one's own story. Just as importantly, she became a dynamic member of the Swarthmore community, a legendary and revered presence on campus, the kind of mentor that many of us had craved in the 1960s.

After the Takeover

Seeing Professor Morgan in person decades later at the Sankofa celebration, reminded us of the whirlwind of activities in which we were engaged in the weeks and months immediately after the Takeover. With most of us graduating that spring, we had redoubled our efforts to safeguard the progress made toward institutionalizing our goals as much as we could before we left. None of those goals was more important to us than ensuring that high-quality Black Studies would continue to be available to future students. Building a faculty and establishing a curriculum would be essential to achieving that goal. We had previously taken the initiative to broaden and enrich our education ourselves. That spring, in addition to searching for and interviewing prospective full-time black professors, we served on the College curriculum committee. Although unremunerated and untrained in curriculum development, SASS leaders worked hard with college faculty, meeting often to draft the curriculum for the first Black Studies concentration.

We were racing to complete our degrees, but we made time to enroll in the first courses in the new Black Studies concentration despite the fact that they were often more intensive than the already rigorous courses in our traditional programs. Because we had taken on the responsibility for this critical component of our education, it meant so much to us to be the first students to have a *concentration in Black Studies* noted on our Swarthmore diplomas.

Since SASS's 1969 demands for more black faculty and Kathryn Morgan's breaking of the tenure glass ceiling in the 1970s, generations of black faculty, administrators, and counselors have had outstanding careers at the College. Dean Janet Smith Dickerson was among them. As Associate Dean and Director of Academic Support Services from 1976 to 1981, she spearheaded the development of those services and brought legitimacy to academic support. As Dean of the College from 1981 to 1991, she brought greater attention to the quality and inclusiveness of campus life. Black alumnus Maurice Eldridge, '61, joined the College development office in 1989. By 1998 he had become an indispensable member of the administrative team and risen to the position in which he would serve for almost two decades, Executive Assistant to the President and Vice President for Community Relations. The College has also been enriched by the scholarly contributions and social justice initiatives of black alumnus Keith Reeves '88, Professor of Political Science and Department Chair as well as Director of the Urban Inequality and Incarceration program at the College's Lang Center for Civic and Social Responsibility. Because of black professionals like Dickerson, Eldridge, and Reeves, black students no longer have to regularly take the lead in developing and sustaining significant institutional services and curriculum while at the same time completing rigorous academic studies as the SASS founders did. Black Studies has become an established discipline at the College. Although not a department, a Black Studies Program with associated faculty and scholars, including the current Provost Sarah Susan Willie-LeBreton and President Valerie Smith, both African American, provides students with a faculty-led curriculum and an opportunity to be mentored in their pursuit of a Black Studies minor or major.

Black Alumni Thrive and Give Back

Black student enrollment grew in response to the increased recruitment efforts that SASS had helped inspire. By 1971, there were already enough black students to transform the impromptu gospel singing in Sharples Dining Hall that had helped strengthen our bonds of friendship and create a sense of community into an actual gospel choir. When those students graduated, the choir became the Alumni Gospel Choir, a first-rate musical force performing on campus, nationally, and internationally. The Alumni Gospel Choir has been the most enduring connection among black alumni and between black alumni and the College, and, for many years, the most visible way in which black alumni as a group have given back to the College.

There were only about fifty black students enrolled at the College at the time of the 1969 Takeover. Now, the College admits that many black freshmen each year, and the ranks of black Swarthmore alumni have grown. They spread their influence in diverse fields. We Seven Sisters and a Brother have continued our love of learning and served in leadership roles with the pioneering spirit of our years in SASS. Included among us are a Phi Beta Kappa graduate and four graduates who were among the first to add a Black Studies concentration to their diplomas at Swarthmore College. All eight of us completed advanced degrees at prestigious universities, earning eleven masters and six doctoral degrees from Columbia, Harvard, McGill, Temple, Tufts, and University of Massachusetts Boston. We represent an array of fields: a medical doctor, a lawyer, a biologist, four educational leaders, and a computer scientist.

Reminiscent of our experiences at Swarthmore, some of us became the first African Americans in high-level positions in our workplaces. Others created innovative programs and policies and pushed them forward despite resistance. The Seven Sisters and a Brother were not without passions outside of our careers. Our interests include photography, art, animal care, and genealogy. We are proud Swarthmore graduates, grateful for a liberal arts education that fortunately has become more inclusive since the 1960s.

Black alumni have also become increasingly engaged in college governance and alumni affairs. Marilyn H. and others have served on the Board of Managers, charged with fiduciary and policy-making responsibility for the College. Harold, Marilyn H., and alumni from more recent classes have also organized the Swarthmore Black Alumni Network (SBAN). SBAN's organized activism and material support of current students have made black alumni more visible and given us a significant voice and a means of building on the legacies of five decades of SASS activism.

Sesquicentennial: Another Sankofa Moment

The College's commemoration of its sesquicentennial, or 150th anniversary, in 2014, was another Sankofa moment. Although the campus was abuzz with celebratory events, it was also a time for looking back critically at the College's history in order to better understand how and why it had grown over time and what its future could be. A documentary film, *Minding Swarthmore*, was commissioned as part of the College's reflection and celebration. Several members of our group as well as other SASS leaders were interviewed for the film. In it, SASS activism, the Takeover, and its aftermath emerge as a watershed moment for the College's recognition of its historical strengths, acknowledgement of its shortcomings, and the beginnings of important changes.

That sesquicentennial fall, several of us also participated in History Professor Allison Dorsey's *Black Liberation 1969* project. The project's goal was to archive the record of black student activism at Swarthmore from 1968 to 1972 lest, as Dorsey admonished, the College lose or forget that critical part of its history. Student researchers interviewed us and other early SASS members, probing our individual and group recollections of SASS and the Takeover. Their interest, but also their unasked questions and unspoken assumptions, as well as the fact that our own semi-centennials—fiftieth anniversaries—of SASS and the Takeover were only a few years away, awakened us to the need to take ownership of our own story and the importance of sharing its lessons and insights with current students and younger alumni.

As our memoir project progressed, our interactions with other black alumni, especially some who were part of the influx of black students in the years immediately following our protests, also revealed lingering wounds from their Swarthmore experiences. For those black alumni, telling their own painful stories of rejection and alienation might well be healing. For the College, a truth and reconciliation process in which injuries are acknowledged and sincere apologies offered might help ensure the longevity of the substantial progress that has been made.

In fall of the year following the introspective sesquicentennial, the College celebrated a historic change in leadership, appointing its first black President, Valerie Smith. This second President Smith took office as the fifteenth President of Swarthmore College in fall 2015, only a few months after we began collaborating on this memoir. Early on, she made it clear that she intended to "bring [her] full humanity to [the] role" of President.[24] The College would have a president for whom the black experience is not a marginalized abstraction. Rather, for this president, it is both a lived experience and a scholarly passion at the heart of her academic career as a professor of African American literature and culture and many years as a director and developer of African American Studies programs at UCLA and Princeton.

Now President Smith strides comfortably across the Swarthmore campus, perhaps on the move from an Open House at the president's residence, to Board of Managers meetings, or to an SBAN event. A crown of short natural hair frames her deep brown face. A signature swirl of vibrant color, a bright shawl that suggests an African wrap, is draped across her shoulders. In 1969, few of us could have visualized a person who looked like Valerie Smith as President of the College, nor did a Black Studies career path such as hers exist. Her presidency encourages optimism that the College can continue to act upon its values of openness, collaboration, and inclusiveness in the spirit of those long-ago SASS demands.

Acknowledgments

We thank SASS students for their Sankofa celebration which underscored the importance of telling our own story; Professor Allison Dorsey who invoked her historian's skills to look back and bring us together; President Rebecca Chopp who supported the historical inquiry launched by Professor Dorsey and graciously thanked the Seven Sisters; Professor Keith Reeves whose brotherly love and belief in us inspired beyond measure; documentary filmmaker Shayne Lightner for gathering stories from our contemporaries that supplemented our own memories and for portraying them with care; every SASS member who participated in the Takeover; and all the supporters who took up our cause.

We are indebted to New Jersey City University Professor Edvidge Giunta who encouraged us to write and helped us learn the art of memoir; Annie Lanzillotto who kindly coached us to keep on writing when we were discouraged; Swarthmore alumna Sharon Brown, who, though she did not know any of us involved in the Takeover, listened to our stories during early planning sessions and affirmed that our memoir would have meaning to students who followed us; Melody Guy whose developmental editing helped weave eight individual stories into one; Robert J. Labate and Madelaine J. Harrington of Holland & Knight LLP who provided insightful counsel; Mango Publishing and Books & Books Press who believed that our story would encourage many; and Yaddyra Peralta who patiently guided us through the many complexities of the publishing process.

In honor of Swarthmore's black communities, the authors' share of the book proceeds will be donated to funds established at the College to support study, research, and celebration of black history and culture and to support the Swarthmore Black Alumni Network Endowment Fund. The SBAN Endowment—which requires that its funds be invested in non-fossil fuel accounts—will support student internships in collaboration with the Eugene Lang Center for Civic and Social Responsibility.

As always, we thank our families whose love and support throughout the peaks and valleys ease our journeys and help us reach our goals.

About the Authors

Marilyn Allman Maye graduated from Swarthmore College with a B.A. in Mathematics and Sociology-Anthropology and a Concentration in Black Studies. She earned her M.A.T. in Mathematics from Harvard University, and her M.A. in Mathematical Statistics and Ed.D. in Mathematics Education from Columbia University. She is an educator, leader, and advocate for high-quality teaching and learning for children and adults, especially in mathematics and in communities of color. A tenured professor in educational leadership at New Jersey City University, she has also consulted regionally and nationally for school districts, departments of education, and professional development organizations. For a decade in the 90s, she led diverse teams in New York City's technology agency, and, since then, in her Bronx community, Dr. Maye has served as a founding trustee of two charter schools and as a trustee in her church. She is author of three books, one co-authored with her husband, Warren Maye.

Harold S. Buchanan is a retired computer technology professional from New Jersey. He is also an accomplished photographer with a passion for nature and travel photography. He has traveled extensively to observe and photograph wildlife. Harold earned a BA in Mathematics from Swarthmore College and was one of the first to earn a concentration in Black Studies. He also earned a MEd degree from Temple University before marrying and raising a family of four. Harold is a co-founder of the Swarthmore Black Alumni Network (SBAN). He serves on the Board of Trustees for the Rancocas Nature Center and Helping Other People Evolve, Inc.

Jannette O. Domingo earned a BA in Political Science/ International Relations and a concentration in Black Studies at

Swarthmore. She earned a MA in Economic Development and Public Finance at McGill University and a M.Phil. and PhD in Economics at Columbia University. She is Professor Emerita and retired Dean of Graduate Studies at John Jay College of Criminal Justice of the City University of New York where she also chaired the Department of African American Studies, directed the Ronald McNair Post-Baccalaureate Achievement Program, and co-founded the Police Studies Certificate Program to educate socially responsible police leaders. Her mentorship and advocacy for students and colleagues helped create a more inclusive college community. In retirement, Dr. Domingo continues to pursue her passion for travel—especially with her husband Clifford Charles—and for researching the genealogy and migration stories of Virgin Islands families.

Joyce Frisby Baynes graduated from Swarthmore College with a BA in Mathematics. She earned her MAT in Mathematics from Harvard University, a MEd in Administration, and an EdD in Mathematics Education from Columbia University. After eighteen years teaching mathematics, she progressed to top administrative posts of three school districts in New Jersey, including serving as superintendent of schools. Dr. Baynes' great love of mathematics and her tireless work as a change agent helped underserved young people excel. In her retirement, she co-founded the non-profit Future Forward for Haiti, Inc., has served on the Board of Trustees of the Community Scholarship Fund of Teaneck, and is involved in other educational and religious affairs. Dr. Baynes resides in Teaneck, New Jersey. She has three married sons and six grandchildren who bring her much joy.

Marilyn Holifield is a partner in Holland & Knight, an international law firm whose history dates to the 1890s. She earned a BA in Economics and a concentration in Black Studies from Swarthmore and a Juris Doctor from Harvard. She and two other black students desegregated Leon High School in Tallahassee, Florida. After Harvard, she joined the NAACP Legal Defense and Educational Fund. Later, she became General Counsel to Peter Edelman at the New York State Division for Youth and law clerk to Paul Roney, Judge, US (former) Fifth Circuit Court of Appeals. At Holland & Knight, she became the first black woman partner of a major law firm in Florida. She serves on the Swarthmore Board of Managers, Harvard Board of Overseers, and University of Miami Board of Trustees. She has received numerous awards and is co-founder of Miami Museum of Contemporary Art of the African Diaspora.

Myra E. Rose earned BS degrees in Chemistry and Biology at Swarthmore College and an MD from Tufts University School of Medicine. Postgraduate training included internal medicine residency at Washington Hospital Center and fellowship training in hematology and oncology at Emory University. She entered private practice for a few years, but eventually joined the Department of Medicine at Morehouse School of Medicine as a member of the clinical faculty. Following a series of teaching and leadership assignments at Morehouse, she became Department Chair and has served as program director for the residency program, hospice medical director, and chief of medical oncology. The School established and named in her honor an annual lectureship on "Humanism in Medicine." Although Dr. Rose has retired as chair, she continues to see patients and teach. She resides in Atlanta with her husband, Clifford, their children and grandchildren.

Bridget Van Gronigen Warren was born in Guyana, South America. She obtained a BS in Biology at Swarthmore College, and studied for her MS and PhD in Medical Microbiology and Immunology at Temple University. Most of her professional life was spent as a professor of Microbiology and Immunology at the University of Panama's Faculty of Medicine, and as a microbiologist in the Panama Canal Authority. Since retiring in 2012, she has worked as a volunteer member of the Smithsonian Tropical Research Institute's Animal Care and Use Committee. Dr. Van Gronigen Warren, her husband, fellow Swarthmore alum Ferdinand, and their daughter, Nyasha, are active members of the Society of Friends of the West Indian Museum of Panama.

Aundrea White Kelley earned her BA in Sociology and Anthropology from Swarthmore. After working in the corporate and non-profit sectors, she returned to school and obtained an MS in Public Policy and an MBA, both from the University of Massachusetts Boston. She focused her public service career on advancing boundary-crossing initiatives to resolve tough education policy challenges. Starting as a graduate intern at the Massachusetts Board of Higher Education, she held a succession of impactful positions, including Commissioner of Higher Education (Acting). She was recruited by Quincy College, and after successfully leading the effort to secure its institutional and programmatic accreditations, retired as the College's chief academic officer. She remains passionate about civic engagement and the use of public policy to effect justice. She and her husband Robert, a retired law firm partner, take great delight in their sons Tyrone and Jeremy, daughters-in-law, Regina and Akosua, and granddaughter Lauren.

References

1 Personal communication from Rebecca Chopp to Marilyn Allman Maye, February 17, 2014.

2 Jeffrey Lott, et al, *A Community of Purpose,* (Swarthmore College, 2014), 46.

3 Martha Biondi, "How New York Changes the Story of the Civil Right Movement," online.

4 Bill Dorsey, "Hard Realities of the Civil Rights Movement Lead to Move to Organize Negro Students," *Phoenix,* December 6, 1966.

5 C. Gerald Fraser, "Ella Baker, Organizer for Groups in Civil-Rights Movement in South", *New York Times,* December 17, 1986. https://www.nytimes.com/1986/12/17/obituaries/ella-baker-organizer-for-groups-in-civil-rights-movement-in-south.html.

6 Sam Shepherd, "SASS Fetes History Week With 'Black Rationalism,'" *Phoenix,* February 13, 1968.

7 *New York Times,* Jan 9, 1969.

8 The Segregation of Black Students at Oberlin College after Reconstruction, Cally L. Waite

9 Oberlin College (1833), www.blackpast.org/african-american-history/oberlin-college-1833

10 Fred Hargadon, "Admissions Report No. 1," September 1968, 22–23.

11 "Why We Can't Wait," Swarthmore Afro-American Students Society, Swarthmore College, 1968. Chester, Pennsylvania is one of the oldest and poorest cities in Pennsylvania.

12 "New Faculty Announcements: African Included In List of 22," *Phoenix,* May 5, 1967.

13 Pearson and Anderson, *Washington Post,* January 13, 1969.

14 William and Eileen Cline et al, "Open Letter to the Parents of Black Students of Swarthmore College," *Black Liberation 1969 Archive,* accessed September 12, 2019, https://blacklib1969.swarthmore.edu/items/show/556.

15 William P. Cline was appointed to the position of Assistant Dean of Admissions in September 1969.

16 "Pearl Primus," Ric Estrada, *Dance Magazine,* November 1963, http://www.mamboso.net/primus/summary.html.

17 Fenner-Dorrity, Evelyn. "Operation Crossroads Africa," BlackPast. December 31, 2008. http://www.blackpast.org/gah/operation-crossroads-africa-1958.

18 Drew Pearson, Uprisings, *The Washington Post,* 2-23–69.

19 Drew Pearson, Ibid.

20 Robert Woodson, Executive Director of Media Fellowship house was interviewed for the Black Liberation 1969 project. This part of his account may be true, but he also mentions being involved in planning the Takeover. He may be confused with a separate incident that occurred a year later. No outside parties were involved in the planning or execution of the 1969 Takeover.

21 "An Open Letter to the Faculty of Swarthmore College," January 23, 1969, Asmarom Legesse.

22 Detroit—The Blood That Never Dried. "The Great Rebellion." detroits-great-rebellion.com.

23 McGraw, Bill. "Detroit '67 by the Numbers." *Detroit Free Press.* www.freep.com/storynews/michigan/detroit/2017/07/23/detroit-67-numbers/493523001.

24 Redden, Elizabeth, "Fostering Openness and Collaboration: Valerie Smith Steps into her Role as the 15th President of Swarthmore," Swarthmore College Bulletin, 63, no.1 (Fall 2015): 18.